DEATH ROW *Diaries:*

CRIMINAL JUSTICE

TOPER THORNE

www.deathrowdiaries.ca

Printed in Canada

ISBN 978-09809141-0-8

FIN 04 04 08

Library and Archives Canada Cataloguing in Publication

Thorne, Toper, 1958-
    Criminal justice / Toper Thorne.

(Death row diaries)
ISBN 978-0-9809141-0-8

    I. Title. II. Series: Thorne, Toper, 1958- Death row diaries.

PS8639.H658C75 2008   C813'.6   C2008-901098-1

This book is dedicated to my wife Beth.

My dream of reaching the top can only become achieved when the woman I love is always there to push me higher.

A special thanks to Lisa Sinclair who in the beginning kept me writing.

Thanks to Sarah, Matt and Trish for your editing thoughts.

CHAPTER 1

The lights for the TV cameras are bright. They intensify every nook and cranny of Death Row, making this an almost serene setting and removing the cold eerie feeling that clings to these walls. *Death Row Diaries*, a new Internet series, is about to air for the first time: an Internet Docudrama that lets Death Row inmates tell their story, no matter how gruesome it might be, and follows them through their final day, up to and including their live execution. The show is my brainchild and it has taken some time to convince the right people that this type of program needs to be done.

"Okay Emily, we're on in ten seconds," signals the director who is sitting in the next room behind the glass.

Father Joe sits out of camera range behind Seth, the guard that stands behind me. The TV camera is a remote, controlled from behind the glass in the next room. The show is about to make its debut. It will be done tastefully and safely, after all, this is about Death Row inmates. *Death Row Diaries* will air on the Internet, on a pay per view system. I will make almost three quarters of a billion dollars with an estimated seventy million viewers worldwide at a profit of $10 per connection. Since this is the first of its kind, people are curious and vengeful. Others have tried but the courts blocked their motion. The best part is they have all paid up front and the money is already in the bank. All I have to do is hope that the ISP doesn't go down. The Son of Sam law inhibits me from making a profit so I am using the money to start a youth ranch.

"Roll camera, cue Emily, intro music on, and ready to intro in three, two, one." The director announces as he points at Emily.

"Hello, and welcome to the most controversial show ever. My name is Emily Dickson. Today, we will question a Death Row inmate about how and why he killed. We will follow him on a journey of his life from start to finish. It will culminate with his live execution in the electric chair. Whether or not you support the death penalty, you will be intrigued by his story. You may feel sorry for him, or you may just want to see him meet his maker. Our convicted killer has had a rough life, but that's no excuse for murder. He says he did it for love. His mother died of cancer at a young age. His younger brother has Down's syndrome and his sister was murdered. He became one of the richest men in America by winning the lottery. But before he could decide what to do with $229,000,000 his life took another tragic turn. His wife was killed in a single car accident and his father, a veteran of the Pinellas County Police Force, committed suicide, after suffering from depression. Whatever your reasons, stay tuned. We will be back with his story in a moment."

"Cut," the director yells.

Emily grabs a huge breath and sighs. As she reaches to get a drink of water, I can see her hand tremble.

"Are you okay Emily?"

"Yeah, it's just that this show is making history as we speak."

"It's exciting, isn't it?" I didn't think I could get it to fly. All the TV networks turned it down, but because the Internet has different legislation I am able to broadcast it. "Emily, I want to thank you for being here today. It means a lot."

"Thank you, but you did hire me."

"Jack, how are you doing?" Adam, the director asks.

"I am a bit nervous. After all, the way in which I killed four people is going to be depicted worldwide. Seth, can I have a drink of water, please?" I ask.

With my hands and feet tied in shackles it is hard for me to fend for myself. It is hard to lift a glass to drink. The guard is a tall man, about 6'2", somewhat overweight, not muscular, but still strong enough. I have come to know him well. His name is Seth McPherson. He transferred here from a prison somewhere in upstate New York. Emily is over in the corner talking through a headset to Adam. They are making sure they have all the videos set up. As I am telling my life story and how I wound up on Death Row, video reenactments will cut in and out of the Webcast. I am at liberty to discuss anything I want because I own Intelenet, the Internet Company, and I've already been tried and convicted of murder and sentenced to death. I have no appeals for which to apply. My only hope is the Governor. Like in the movies there is a red phone on the wall in the room that houses the electric chair. The phone is linked directly to the Governor's office. If this were a movie, it would be sure to ring at 11:58 p.m. and save me from being executed.

"Okay, Jack. We're on in two," Adam blurts over the loudspeaker.

Everyone in the room looks warm, while out behind the glass it must be air-conditioned. Adam is pulling on a sweatshirt. Wes and Rocco are also there, they are the other two guards assigned to Block 53, and Mark is at the computer controlling all the video feeds, making damn sure the computer stays connected to the Net to feed the Webcast live. Even though this is my live execution, I am sure there will be more of its kind. I have assembled a good staff. I've developed the series so Death Row inmates can tell their side of the story live and uncut. Hell, unlike my case, there might even be inmates that are innocent.

"Welcome back to *Death Row Diaries*," Emily says into the camera. "For those of you that have been following the story in the media you must know by now that the prisoner we are speaking to is Jack Stevenson. Hello, Jack."

"Hello."

"Why don't you narrate the book from the beginning?"

I was born in South Dakota, as a matter of fact today is my birthday. I said I wanted a BBQ for my last meal, and what a BBQ it will be!

I still have my sense of humor. Otherwise, I will lose my sanity and the show will not go on. This is my baby and I am determined to see it through, not for myself, but for all the others that will follow me, telling their stories. The media has always flirted with the idea of a live execution, and so twisting some laws and using the Internet and its regulations, not to mention some bribe money, I will be the first.

I was the first of three children. My mom was a schoolteacher. She was a stern woman, but she was also my best friend when I needed one. She was always there for us, for

Jimmy and me. Ramona was quite young when Mom died.

While I am talking to the cameras, Mark, out in the control room will cut in with images, both still and video that I can see on the monitor to Father Joe's right. These are the same images that the public will view.

I can feel my brow begin to bead and my eyes begin to water.

Jimmy was delayed with all his life skills. Jimmy is almost five years younger than me. Mom never went back to work after having him. Her hands were full raising two boys. Even though I was in school part-time, it was tough. Two years after Jimmy was born, Mom had another child, a little girl.

I can feel a tear on my cheek as the monitor is showing a picture of her.

She was a cute girl, a good girl. Jimmy loved her to death. He always wanted to play with Moany. After Ramona was born Mom became ill, she had developed lung cancer. Mom never smoked, but my grandfather did. He was never without a cigarette in his mouth. I guess years of second hand smoke just took its toll on her. This left Dad to raise three kids on his own and juggle his job at the same time.

"In a moment we will be back with more," Emily says. With that, the cameras go off, and I am able to get another drink of water from the guard.

"Is everyone okay?" Adam asks. "Do you need anything? The camera angles look great, and Mark's doing an excellent job with the video feeds."

I have supplied several hours of video for the show. I want people to know who I am and why I did what I did. Even after my execution I want the show to go on. You may not agree with everything everyone says, but I truly believe everyone has a right to say it.

"I'm okay," Emily replies.

"I need some air," states Father Joe.

His presence won't be missed anyway. He is just going to be a silent bystander until it is time for my final confession. That will take place later, after the history of my crimes and my last meal. Father Joe excuses himself past Seth who has to have Wes open the door from the outside.

Ramona was only two years old when Mom passed away.

The one thing I remember most about my mom was her eyes. Even when she would use her strict schoolteacher voice to discipline me, I could see the love in her eyes, but the real reason I remember them is the look in them as she lay dying. It was if they could talk to me even though she couldn't. I remember hearing them, as she lay there motionless, staring at me. 'Listen Jacky,' they said. Mom was the only person I would allow to call me that. 'You need to be strong. Your father needs your support. Jimmy and Ramona will look to you for guidance, be there for them. I don't want to burden you, you're still young yourself, but I see in you the strength and determination that will help you succeed, take care of yourself Jacky.' Her eyes stopped talking as she closed them. She took a deep breath. Again they opened and screamed at me. 'I love you,' and then they closed forever. Dad was left to try to manage his career and take care of the three of us. I had no grandparents, my Dad's parents were killed in a car accident before I was born and my mom's mother died of a heart attack when I was three, my Papa died a year later of cancer.

My dad was a cop, you know, a Sergeant. He loved his job. He was a tall man, about six-foot-two. He had it tough with us three kids, especially with Jimmy having Downs. He had to take a lot of night shifts so he could be there during the afternoon and evening for us. He usually came home around 7:00 a.m. and sent me off to school. Jimmy and Ramona went with the sitter, Mrs. O'Malley, an old Irish lady that lived around the corner. She wasn't very old, maybe thirty-five, but when you're a kid everyone is old. She was fantastic with the kids. She never had children of her own. Her husband left her a year earlier for a younger woman. Mrs. O'Malley stopped trusting men and lived the rest of her life single. She thought of Jimmy and Ramona as her own. She had a bedroom for each of them. Ramona's had puppies on the wallpaper, because Moany loved 'woof-woofs'. Jimmy's room was papered with pictures of fire trucks. Jimmy loved the loud wail of a siren. No matter where we were, if Jimmy heard a siren he would race toward it. Maybe Dad being a cop had something to do with it. Dad often brought the cruiser home and he would let Jimmy turn on the sirens and the lights. Dad was always there when I got home from school. We would usually go for a walk to the park so we could, as Dad would say, let out some of the foolishness. After about an hour or so we would head home. On rainy days, he would drive us to McDonalds and buy us fries and milk so we could play in the indoor playground to release our energy. In the evening, we would usually just hang around the house watching T.V. or playing games until bedtime. Around 8:30 p.m. Mrs. O'Malley would come and spend the night. Dad had made a small room adjacent to the rec room where she would sleep. In the morning she would take the kids to her house so Dad could sleep. She was a great lady. This was the routine until we moved to Florida. Dad met Chief Howard at a police convention and he offered Dad a job in the Indian Rocks area of Pinellas County. Dad was assigned to the beaches, a very low key job, hardly any stress.

"Commercial break," Adam directs through the microphone.

The door of the room opens and Father Joe returns. After my last meal, confession and Last Rites, the priest, along with Emily, Jimmy and Warden Howard, will board my jet and head to the Vatican. Father Joe is going to become a Cardinal and Emily is going to cover the story for one of the networks. She is a freelance reporter. I hired her to cover the *Death Row Diaries* series. After my execution, Jimmy will be left with no family in the area. My in-laws, who live in Italy, have agreed to watch him, and why wouldn't they? He will be worth millions after my death and he can't live alone. It won't be that hard for Jimmy to adjust to Italy. He doesn't speak very much anyway and what little he does know can be easily translated to Italian. My in-laws have become fluent in Italian since living there and have been studying sign language.

Warden Howard comes in with the priest. He is as tough as nails. That's the persona he carries around the prison anyway. The only prisoners he isn't tough on are the 'fryers'. This is the nickname given to the inmates on Death Row. Warden Howard is a black man, not too tall, about my size. His hair is bushy, kind of like an Afro. He took the job as warden after leaving the police force due to an injury. He was walking home one night from the movies with Mrs. Howard. A gang of guys, Cuban I think, jumped them. They stole Mrs. Howard's purse, and when Mr. Howard went after them, they knocked him down and beat him up bad. He received several kicks to the face and head. One of the kicks crushed his voice box. He had to undergo a couple of operations but the Doctors were unable to repair it. He now uses one of those hand held microphones that he presses against his neck to talk. I think it's similar to a guitar synthesizer, making a twangy sound, not the kind of voice you would expect from a man in his position.

"How's it going in here, guys?" Warden Howard questions.

"Fine," Seth replies.

"Jack, how's your venture going? I haven't been able to watch. Business as usual among the general population you know. Inmates are always whining about something. They should try being in your shoes, right?"

"Yeah, I'd change places. I don't really want to end up like a fried chicken. By the way, Warden..."

"Now I told you, Jack, call me Bob."

"I was wondering if I could have the chains loosened a bit. I can't even drink myself. You know, I'm not going anywhere."

"Seth, remove the waist chains and chain his arms to the floor pins. Allow a ten-inch reach. That will give him some mobility, but it still gives us the restraint we need."

The Warden headed toward the door and stopped. "See you at supper Jack."

The door opens and he is gone.

Seth readjusts my chains and I grab my glass of water and take a large gulp.

"Why is he so nice to the fryers?" Emily asks Father Joe.

"Bob's been a friend of Jack's family for a long time," he replies.

"Back in five, four, three, two, one!" Adam yells from the other room.

"Hi, and welcome back," Emily announces. "We're here with Jack Stevenson. Jack is to be executed tonight for the murders of four people."

"Excuse me," I cut in. "I was only convicted of one of the murders."

"I'm sorry. Jack is being executed for the murder of Detective Jamie Winthorpe, but more on that later. Okay Jack, we've gone from your childhood up to when you, your brother, sister, and father moved to Florida. Please continue."

We moved to Florida so Dad could take it easy. Ramona was in school fulltime, I was a senior in high school, and Jimmy was in an integrated classroom at a school in the Tampa Bay area. Dad worked four 10-hour days, Monday 'til Thursday so he could have the weekends off with us. I was heavily involved in my schoolwork and football, trying to get a scholarship to Florida State. I wanted to be a Gator. When Ramona finished school for the day she would walk to the Howards. Warden Howard was the Police Chief when we first moved beside him. I had not known any black people before meeting them.

Jimmy was bussed from the city right to the Howard's door. Mrs. Howard watched them until either Dad or I got home. Moany was no problem, but Jimmy was becoming more of a handful, not only was he a big boy, fatter than most 12-year-olds, he was also coming into puberty. His hormones would sometimes get the best of him and he would constantly touch his privates. He was even doing this in public at times. Dad had the department's shrink talk to him, but because of Jimmy's learning disabilities, I don't think it sunk in. When Dad took the job, he did so because it was more of a relaxed pace. The house next to Warden Howard's was for sale and Mrs. Howard had offered her services to watch the kids after school. It was a great set up. Jimmy and Moany could play in our backyard and Mrs. Howard was able to keep an eye on them. The summers were tougher. Both Jimmy and Moany were out of school and I had a part-time job at one of the local wax museums. I enjoyed it a lot and got to meet a lot of people. I also got to go behind the scenes and learn a little bit about makeup and costume making. I had always been interested in Hollywood. I wanted to get involved in special effects for the movies if I didn't make it as a football player. I experimented a bit with it.

Then on July 26th my sister went missing. Jimmy was at the Howard's. He was in and out all day between their house and the tree fort we had in our backyard. It was a huge fort with a sand pit all around the tree, three feet wide. Jimmy spent a lot of time there. It was his little retreat. He could go out there and no one would bother him. Dad and I, along with the Howards had always respected that. We had a bell, a long handled brass bell that we would ring when it was time for him to come in. The bell was much like that of a Town Crier's bell. Jimmy reacted to it like Pavlov's dogs. He knew that food wasn't far off after the bell rang. It didn't take him long to come inside. Ramona had gone to the beach with the neighbours from the next street. They were there all day and arrived home around 4:00 p.m. Ramona was going to stay for supper, but we later found out that the Smyth's son had called from the airport and had a two-hour layover in Tampa so the Smyths went to the airport to have supper with him, asking Moany to go along with them. Ramona said she didn't want to and headed for the Howard's around five, but she never arrived.

It wasn't until Dad got home that it was even discovered that she was missing. It was when Julie Smyth called to tell Moany that they were back, and asked if Moany wanted to sleep over. Dad was confused, because she was supposed to still be with them. He asked to speak to Julie's dad and that's when he discovered Ramona went home in the afternoon. Dad immediately hung up and called the station to report her missing. Within minutes I think the whole Pinellas County Sheriff's Office was at our house. There were even some of Dad's co-workers who were off duty at the time. They immediately sealed off the neighbourhood for twelve blocks and started a grid search. By the time I arrived home from work, it was an all out effort. The search went on well into the night. We went door to door in pairs, armed with pictures of Moany. We checked the school, the parks, even the dumpsters behind the stores, but found nothing. The search was widened day after day for a couple of weeks. The whole time Jimmy stayed with Mrs. Howard. He started to become withdrawn. With each passing night, hope of finding her alive grew dim. There weren't even any clues. She had just vanished. This was extremely frustrating for Dad. She was not only his daughter, and the only female left in the family after Mom's death, but this was what he did for a living. Solving crimes was his specialty. He was one of Pinellas County's best cops. The search team was enormous. People from hundreds of miles away came. There were lots of police officers that volunteered their time to help after their regular shift. Several officers came from other counties, even as far north as Georgia.

Then one day, eight weeks after her disappearance, her body was found. The Howard's dog, Max, was playing with Jimmy in the backyard of our house. He started digging frantically in the sandbox under Jimmy's tree fort. Max uncovered an arm in the sand exposing one of Ramona's favourite shirts. Jimmy ran to Mrs. Howard, shouting, "Moany, Moany." He grabbed Mrs. Howard by the arm and raced her to our backyard. Mrs. Howard called Dad at work. For three days they took samples from the sand, the yard, and even the tree that housed the fort. Jimmy was devastated. Here was his little Moany, his best friend, lying silent in his favourite spot. Jimmy never went back to his tree fort or even in the backyard. He just followed me around, not letting me out of his sight.

For six months, the forensic team worked on the case. Dad seemed to live at the station. I had returned to school, Jimmy spent a lot more time at the Howard's. There weren't very many clues, the best one they had was some semen on Moany's underwear and a tissue with the same semen on it. This was strange. It was like the killer wiped himself clean after trying to rape Moany. I say tried, because she had not been penetrated. Her pants were down around her ankles, but there were no signs of trauma to her genitals. The only sign of trauma was a hit to the head. The forensic team figured she hit her head on something hard. That was the cause of death. There were a couple of fragments of hard wood pulled from her scalp. As for the semen, it was sterile. There were no signs of sperm. They concluded that the killer must have had a vasectomy.

It wasn't until a year later that the case was solved. I was now working full time at the university in the computer lab and building computers on the side. Dad took a leave of absence from work after Moany's funeral. After Ramona's death Jimmy became reclusive, he also didn't want anyone to touch him. Jimmy, who would try to hug the mailman for giving him the mail, became very distant. He would freak out if you tried to help him get dressed or have a bath. His behavior became so erratic that Dad attended a conference on Down's syndrome in Atlanta. While at the conference on Behavior and Sexual Management of the Developmentally Disabled, Dad learned that Jimmy's behavior was also congruent to that of someone with Down's syndrome going through puberty, but the most startling news Dad learned was that males with Down's syndrome are sterile. He left immediately, putting his red police light that he keeps in the glove compartment on the dash and sped home down the I-75 from Atlanta. I was watching Jimmy that weekend. Dad came in, looking very pale.

"Where's Jimmy?" he demanded.

"Upstairs," I said.

Dad marched upstairs, scissors in hand. A couple of minutes later he returned holding a lock of Jimmy's hair and out he went. The sample of Jimmy's hair matched the DNA sample of the semen. Nobody in their wildest dreams suspected Jimmy of killing Ramona. He was a gentle giant, easy going, fun loving and worshipped Moany. It didn't make sense. There was no indication that Ramona made it home that day from the Smyth house. Mr. Howard, who was watching Jimmy that day because Mrs. Howard was at her sisters, stated he never saw Ramona.

Dad kept this information to himself though. He was torn between doing what was right and protecting Jimmy. He had the semen sample re-tested to try to date the semen. Although it was a long shot maybe the body and the semen sample would be dated months apart, indicating that the tissue with the semen was dropped in the sand after the killer buried Ramona. Jimmy could have masturbated and hid the tissue there. Dad double-checked the tissue sample and the sample from her underwear. The test concluded that both samples were from around the same time, consistent with the established time of death of Ramona. It was conclusive. Jimmy was the murderer.

"Commercial!" Adam shouts.

I begin to weep as the recounting of the events is weighing heavily on my emotions. Emily hands me a tissue and helps me dry my eyes. I lift a glass of water, take a drink and swallow.

"Jack, I know this is hard, but what a story. From all indications this pilot project is a huge success," Adam encourages. "The chat room is just buzzing with excitement."

This is what I wanted. I knew it wasn't going to be easy, but I want the show to be a success. I want others to know about the criminals that are being executed. I figure that all prisoners about to be executed aren't the ruthless killers that the media has portrayed them to be. Some are normal people caught up in a moment at the wrong place at the wrong time.

"Emily, this is tough. The hardest part is that since we are live, I only have a couple of minutes rest while the Webmercials play to regain my composure and my thoughts."

"I know. That's why I'm here, to keep you on track."

"Back in three, two, one," Adam's voice interrupts.

"Welcome back to *Death Row Diaries*. Jack, continue with your story. What happened next to Jimmy and how did your father handle the situation?"

Dad struggled with the idea of right and wrong for a couple of days. Though he never said anything about it in those few days, I knew what was up when he rushed out with Jimmy's hair. The look of devastation and determination on his face said everything. He called Mr. Bartholomew Hibbs, our lawyer, and confessed his findings. Dad knew that Mr. Hibbs would steer him in the right direction. After the call, Dad spilled his guts to me. He told me about the DNA results. Jimmy wasn't able to comprehend too much of the conversation. Dad said that he was calling Mr. Howard and turning Jimmy in. Mr. Hibbs was going to handle it all. Bart figured that he could get Jimmy off on a mental instability clause and Jimmy would wind up in the sheltered prison down in the Keys. For Jimmy, this meant moving to a locked down facility that was more like a cottage setting. We would be able to visit with Jimmy daily if we needed to.

Like Dad expected, Jimmy was found not guilty, because of mental instability and was sent to Keycoast, a small facility in the Florida Keys. It had a few cottages that housed six boys each. There was two staff per cottage on at all times. Dad took an early retirement from the force and moved south, ten minutes from Jimmy. I got an apartment in Largo and remained in school. Dad visited Jimmy daily and I went on the weekends. Jimmy did well there and was oblivious to the lock down situation. They taught life skills and had a small recreational program.

My visitations with Jimmy brought me close to the staff and that is where I met Lynn, or "Ly-Ly," as Jimmy called her. She was an instructor at the cottage and we became good friends. We started dating on Saturday evenings when I would go to visit Jimmy. It started to get serious. When I finished school I quit my job and moved in with Dad to be close to Lynn and Jimmy. I took a job at a local bar as a bartender. I also set up a computer consulting business online. My expertise was always computers, that and mask making. I loved horror flicks and would make masks out of plaster of Paris. Once Dad moved down south, I started to get into latex masks. I only did a few, because the chemicals were expensive.

Lynn and I eloped after three months of dating. She continued to work at Keycoast, I worked online. We got a small one-bedroom apartment close to Keycoast. Dad still lived in the bungalow he bought when he retired. Jimmy had only us to visit him. The Howards came down a couple of times after he was first incarcerated. The drive was long and Mr. Howard was to take his new job soon as Warden of the Florida State Prison. The prison we're in now. It's ironic how he has been involved with our family. First he hired my Dad, then his wife helping with Ramona and Jimmy, and now being here in my final hours. Life was starting to turn around for Dad and I. Jimmy was content. I was married and Dad, well he just took life one day at a time.

Lynn and I never took a honeymoon, so on our six-month anniversary we took a flight to Atlantic City. We had managed to save up some money and my computer consulting was starting to take off. It didn't generate a lot of cash, but we were able to save for the trip. We stayed on the boardwalk and spent most of our time sightseeing. The slot machines called our names a few times, but we had pre-set a limit of thirty dollars a day each, so we wound up mostly playing nickel slots. At the end of the week we were up a mere $7.50.

We had a three-hour layover at the Airport. I stopped at the airport gift shop and bought Jimmy a small computerized slot machine. I knew he would love to watch the dials spin. I also bought three Powerball lottery tickets for the next draw. On the way back, I had arranged a different flight. Instead of going to Miami we went to Tampa. It was only a short drive to the Howard's. The next day was Mrs. Howard's birthday and I wanted to surprise her. Mr. Howard was in Alabama for a couple of days representing the force at a cop's funeral. Lynn and I visited for a bit, we spoke for a while, mostly small talk. We avoided talking about Jimmy or Moany, it was just too hard on her, on all of us. Mrs. Howard asked my advice on computers. She wanted to surprise Mr. Howard with a new one for his birthday, which was a couple of days after hers. In the morning, I went out and picked up a new computer, I grabbed a couple of his CD's to make sure it worked. He had a lot of files on CD. I transferred a couple of them, everything worked properly. I told her if Mr. Howard needed any more help to have him call me. He must have figured it out because I never did receive a call. Like any vacation it was too short and nothing had changed when we arrived home. Back to the same old grind, work and more work.

Dad seemed quite down when we arrived home. Without Lynn and I there, he visited Jimmy more and you could tell it was taxing his emotions. He was also getting consumed with worries about finances. Having retired early he didn't receive his full pension and he was afraid he was going to run out of money. I assured him that there was always a place for him with us, although the one bedroom apartment probably wouldn't do. Business was picking up and I was well on my way to saving for a down payment on a house. I was going to have to put this in high gear though, because while on our trip, Lynn told me she was pregnant. This news helped to cheer up Dad. He had a great idea. Why didn't we move in with him? It would give us more space and it would help him out with the mortgage. So, that's what we did.

Well, you remember how I told you about our trip to Atlantic City. The casino didn't pay off, but the lottery ticket did. I won $229 million. It was overwhelming. I took the lump sum payout option. I now had enough money to do anything I wanted. My first priority was my family, including Jimmy. I set out on a mission to try and free Jimmy. I was going to do whatever it took, even if it meant bribing the right people. My endeavor was futile. There was nothing I could do. I managed to get Keycoast privatized by paying off the right people and then I bought it. This way I could control how Jimmy's life would be spent behind bars.

Lynn and I moved out of dad's house. I remodeled one of the cottages for Dad but he didn't want to move. He felt that it was too close to Jimmy and that he would never have a break. I paid off his house, bought him a car and a bass boat but other than that his life remained simple. The press hounded me for an interview, after all I was one of the biggest lottery winners. I turned them all down, of course I had to agree to publicity photos for the lottery company. I did finally agree to do one interview. That's how I met you, Emily.

"Yes I remember that day," Emily states. "I knew that the other press agencies were always bugging you, wanting to know what you were going to do with the money."

"You took a different approach. You wanted to do a story on my purchase of Keycoast, how did you put it?"

"Brotherly love. I wanted the story of how you went to great lengths to help your incarcerated brother."

"I always felt that Jimmy was given a bum rap. He was put away for life in that place. Poor Jimmy didn't know what hit him or what it was all about."

"But the facts spoke for themselves Jack."

"People get put away all the time for murder, they cop a plea and after a few years they get out, but not Jimmy."

"I remember how bitter you were about Jimmy's sentence."

"Yes I was. It was a stroke of luck that I won the money and was able to buy the Keycoast resort and at least make his life seem normal to him. I was able to move him into the apartment that I had built for Dad, since Lynn was technically a staff member she took care of him. Jimmy felt part of the family again and was able to leave the 'bad place', as Jimmy called it.

Dad became more and more withdrawn; his visits with Jimmy became less frequent."

"In the interview," Emily states. "You unveiled a disturbing thought and a plan for the future. It was to unfold in front of the nation and lead you to where you are today. We'll be back in a moment with how Jack's fortune enabled him to carry out his plan."

"Break," Adam cuts in. "How's everyone doing in there?"

"I'd like a reprieve." Father Joe replies. "Do you mind if I step out for a while?"

The priest stands up and heads for the door where Seth is standing. As he approaches you can hear the mechanics of the door at work unlocking the system. Seth opens the door and Father Joe exits.

"Time for me to hit the little girls room," Emily replies and follows the priest out.

"Where's Jimmy?" I ask. I can see through the glass that he is no longer sitting with Adam.

"He was getting a little restless so the Warden took him out for a walk." Adam replies.

Jimmy finds the prison disturbing, probably because it reminds him of the 'bad place.' I stood up and stretched with the aid of Seth during the Netmercial.

The door opened and Emily returned. "I brought you a Coke, Jack."

"Where's Father Joe?" I asked.

"He's going to take a break for a while, he told me to tell you he'd see you at supper. He was going to catch up with Jimmy."

"That's good, he might be able to ease Jimmy a bit. I noticed that he was starting to twitch, he usually does when he's unnerved."

"We're back in five," Adam shouts.

"Welcome back. Okay, Jack, we were talking about your initial interview. What was the message you sent about what you were going to do with the money?"

"I bought a small island off the coast of Fiji that housed a quaint little resort. At the time it housed five cottages and a huge six-bedroom house. It was a luxury retreat where a lot of movie stars and business moguls went to get away from it all. My plans were to eventually move there once I freed Jimmy, with my wife, children and my dad, somewhere nobody would bug us and I could put everything behind us. Since I had sold my computer consulting business, I could just go to Fiji and play."

"What changed your plans?"

"There were several things. First I was unable to reduce Jimmy's sentence. My dad was sinking deeper into depression, and the stress was starting to get to me. I said I was going to use the rest of the money to hunt down and kill five people who had screwed me around. It could be anybody, and the revenge I seek could be for anything. I had had enough."

"During our interview I asked if there was any hint of who they might be."

"Like I told you at the time; that would take the fun out of it."

"But Jack, you were this loving devoted family man who always kept his nose clean, a son of a retired police officer, why murder?"

"Because I could, I had the money and I finally got tired of being screwed."

"Did you honestly think you could get away with it? The police were watching you like a hawk. Even your own father was upset with your statement."

"I know, in hindsight I deeply regret how much I devastated him. I knew he was becoming increasingly introverted but I had no idea it would lead to his demise."

"Your father was so distraught over the situation that he took an overdose of his medication and died only a couple of days after you made your statement."

"I know, like I said, I wasn't aware of his fragile state. Now I had lost my whole family except for Lynn, and that wasn't going so well. Even though on the exterior we looked great, internally we were falling apart. As her pregnancy moved along she was tired, and as she informed me, tired of having Jimmy around all of the time. Even though we had hired help he was still always there.

Weeks passed since I granted the interview, the media and police followed us constantly. We were safe at home because Keycoast had security features in place, but once we left the compound she would be hounded."

"So, with your mother, father and sister dead, your brother in jail and an unhappy wife, you still wanted to continue your plan."

"In my mind, I hadn't actually set out to kill anyone yet, I was still making the list in my head."

"Were you going to do it yourself or use a hired gun?"

"I wasn't sure, I had the money to hire anyone I wanted but

I was starting to relish the thought of doing it myself. I wanted the public to be aware of the whole thing, instill fright into people, kind of like a real life B murder mystery movie.

About a month later, I was having a poker game with some of the male staff. Lynn was getting ready for bed. She had just been soaking in the tub and was getting out when Jimmy rushed in the bathroom. I heard a scream and she came into the kitchen were the game was."

"Your brother has got to go," she screamed.

"What?" I said.

"I was taking a bath, I could hear tapping outside the door. Just as I got out of the tub Jimmy rushed into the bathroom with his pants off, masturbating."

"Now come on honey."

"Don't 'honey' me. He's a pervert. He always has been. That's why your sister is dead!"

I slapped her in the face. She stared at me for a second in disbelief. I couldn't believe I did it either, but it was too late, I had. She put her hand over her mouth and stomped out of the room. I tried to go after her but stopped when I noticed Jimmy in the hall. I went over to him and blasted him. I broke up the game and had the staff take him to the lodge. I also realized that it was time for him to move out. Lynn was going to have a baby in a couple of months and I couldn't afford to have Jimmy lurking around anymore.

As I was helping them get Jimmy out of the house I heard the garage door opener grinding the door open. I glanced out the window to see Lynn pulling out through the gates. I rushed out the door and ran the quarter mile to the guardhouse.

"Where was she going?" I asked the guard.

"She didn't say. She just honked, and I opened the gate."

I had the guard drive me back to the house, and I hopped in my Jeep and went after her. I drove the roads for hours but to no avail, so I headed back to the house.

I tried to think where she might go. She had no family here and only a couple of friends who I frantically called. When I returned home I sat and rethought my plans. Maybe I'm a fool for wanting to get revenge on people, maybe I should just let the staff take care of Jimmy and when Lynn comes back we'll head to Fiji and start our life over. I could have everything I want and more. These thoughts of leveling the score maybe should be put away and I should get on with my life.

CHAPTER 2

I must have dozed off. The guards pounding on the door woke me.

"Mr. Stevenson, open up." The guard demanded.

"What is it?"

"I have some news about your wife."

I scrambled to the door as fast as I could.

"What is it?"

"They've found Mrs. Stevenson's car sir."

"Where?"

"Twenty miles down the coast at Lovers Lagoon."

Lovers Lagoon was a local hang out spot years earlier. Now it was overgrown with brush and weeds and was a great breeding ground for gators. I hopped in the Jeep and tore down the laneway. The roads were slick from the rain earlier in the night, compounded with the morning dew; it was like driving on an oil-slicked road. It was 5:00 a.m. There wasn't a soul in sight on the roads. The fine mist glistened from the headlights like glitter falling on New Years Eve. I had gone about fifteen miles when I could see through the night air the faint glow of red lights. Through the misty fog they looked like coals dancing in a campfire. My forehead began to bead balls of sweat and my stomach felt like it was twisting itself into a knot as I approached the final curve in the road before Lovers Lagoon. As I rounded the bend I could see the brake lights of a tractor-trailer and a couple of cars. There was a small crowd of people standing at the side of the road. I stopped the Jeep, it lurched forward as I got out with it still running. I tore past the crowd and headed towards the tape the police had strung across the road.

"That's as far as you go," said a man in jeans and a navy blue windbreaker. I proceeded to duck under the tape, just as the gentleman grabbed my by the shoulder. "That's as far as you go," he said again. Clenching my shirt, he flashed a badge.

"That's my wife's car," I said, not even bothering to read his badge. I threw my arm up in a windmill fashion knocking his hand loose. I started to run towards the car. The officer ran after me.

"It's okay, Phil, let him come," said Chief Milner who had recognized me from when he responded personally to my father's suicide. He was walking towards me with his arms stretched out, he put his hands on my shoulders and stopped me.

"Is it her?" I yelled.

"It's your car, Jack, but there is no sign of Lynn."

"I want to see."

As I stumbled forward through the muck, I could see her car. It had slid off the road and rolled down the bank. The driver's door had been torn off and the car came to rest on an angle with the driver's side partially submerged in the swamp. There were several alligators dotting the surface of the water. Every once in awhile, they would submerge and then reappear.

"Jack, we've searched the land nearby hoping she was thrown clear, but no sign of her. Once we tow the car out, we'll go in with divers."

"Chief, come here," one of the officers said. "We've found something."

"You stay here, Jack," he said as he trenched his way through the muck, his feet making a suction sound with every step. I could see him pointing at something on the bank but I was unable to make out what it was.

"Jack, over here."

I made my way to the two men. On the shore there was a ripped piece of material and a shoe. I recognized them immediately as Lynn's clothes.

"Oh, my God! Those are Lynn's!"

"That's what I was afraid of. Alright, get this car out of here so we can search the area."

It looked like the clothes had been torn off of her. We cleared the way so the tow truck could do its job. The winch on the truck began to hum. The water started to stir as the car was dragged along the surface to the bank. The gators had now dispersed and were lining up on shore. Once the car was out of the water, the police started to look it over. While they were doing this they were installing a boom across the lagoon, the boom had a weighted mesh that hung down under the water. This would serve as a temporary gator-guard so the divers could go in. There were also officers with hunting rifles along the shore ready to nail any alligator that thought he might make a meal out of the divers.

They searched the water for about twenty minutes and came up empty. The divers made their way to the shore to change their air tanks. As they headed back in the water a shot rang out. Two of the alligators had started off shore and into the water. The shot was fired only as a deterrent and the gators retreated. A couple of them on shore got the message and left the area, although there were still about a dozen of them around.

The divers headed back under the water. The water had the clarity of soup stock, their vision was very limited I'm sure. The gators started coming again. Shots rang out, one of the shots hit one of the gators and he started to roll in the water, much like they do when they have captured prey. This sent all the others scrambling from shore. Sensing the danger, the two divers scrambled out of the water just as the boom broke and started drifting away from the crash site, allowing the gators to roam wherever they wanted.

"Okay boys, you're grounded," said Chief Milner. "It's too dangerous."

"What about Lynn?" I screamed. "You've got to find her."

"Listen Jack, we've done the best we can."

"Then do more. I don't care what it costs. Kill the fucking gators and get back in there."

"Jack we can't. We'd have every animal rights person from miles around down our throats."

"To hell with them—just do it."

"I know you've got the money and we could spend a fortune on capturing the gators and dragging the lagoon, but I don't think you'll find her."

"Chief, I found something," an officer said.

"What is it?"

"It looks like a partial dental plate and more of the red material."

"That is the shirt Lynn had on."

"Does she have a partial plate?"

"Yes, she had a fake front tooth from a swimming accident. She knocked her tooth out when she was a teenager when she hit the bottom of a pool."

Another officer was approaching us from the rear.

"Chief, we've got blood on the inside of the car. We've taken a sample."

"Send it to the lab. Jack, who was Lynn's dentist? We'll need her records."

"You don't think..."

"Yes I do. I think maybe the gators got to her before we did," the Chief explained.

As the police packed up their dive gear, I headed back to Keycoast. I never felt as alone as I did that night. I made a call to the dentist and the police station so they could pick up the records. I then fell asleep.

I awoke to the sound of the telephone. It was Chief Milner. He informed me that the plate and blood type matched that of Lynn's and that he had spoken to the Coroner's office and that he was sorry but Lynn was gone. He suggested that maybe I should think about funeral arrangements. I couldn't really see making too many arrangements. After all there was no body, only pieces of evidence. I had a small private service at the Keycoast Chapel, placed her plate, shoe and the scraps of red material in a small shoebox and buried it at the edge of the woods beside my dad's cremated remains. Dad's funeral was a little more elaborate. After I found his body in bed I called Chief Milner. He and the Coroner came to the house. Once Dad was pronounced dead, I had his body cremated. There was a huge turn out for his service mostly policemen. Dad's urn was wrapped in an American Flag and placed on a small pedestal at the edge of the woods. After the ceremony the flag and Dad's badge were presented to Jimmy. He still wears the badge now and then. Dad's ashes were then buried. Now with nobody left except for Jimmy, I was unsure what to do. I received several disturbing calls from the media and the police even investigated my whereabouts at the time of both my father and Lynn's deaths to see if I was involved.

"Well you did say you were going to kill five people," Emily interrupts.

"I know, I said five that have done me wrong. I loved them both, and I had no involvement. The police even confirmed my alibis. They were airtight. I'm insulted you even asked.

I took a few days, went to my island in Fiji. I went there to reflect on my life, on my statement about killing five people and I kept coming back to the same conclusion. I have nothing in life except money and Jimmy. Jimmy is basically, at times, a burden. I came to realize that I would leave Keycoast. I would let Jimmy stay there. He was getting accustomed to the routines. I could go and hunt the five bastards that screwed up my life."

"Cut," yells Adam. "Take a breather."

"Okay. The hard part is over. I can put my family out of my head and give you the details of the murders. I rehash them in my mind constantly. I have no regrets and I'm ready."

It is going to be a long three hours now, reliving the murders. I looked at the mirror on the wall, staring deep into myself, wondering if it was all worth it. The murders weren't the hard part. I wonder if my idea of a Webcast was right. Millions of people watching me flail about in the electric chair, some with eyes wide open, cheering the electricity on as if it were alive. Others will have their hands over their eyes asking if it's over yet. No matter what people think, it is going to happen. I shake my head vigorously like you would when you get to the stage where you're fighting sleep, trying to shake the neurons in my brain awake.

Adam was given full liberty to hire whomever he needed in order to re-enact any scene that he thought might be useful.

"Welcome back to *Death Row Diaries*," Emily says. "Jack, tell us about your first murder. Continue reading your book."

It all started in grade nine, I was small for my age. I had a hormonal problem as a kid. Everyone picked on me, mostly the guys. My locker was on the other side of the school and I had to walk past the 'Rad Rassers' at least twice a day. The 'Rad Rassers' was a group of seniors in the school, mostly grade twelve's that sat on the heat rads in the blue hall and made fun of people as they went by.

It was because of my small stature and the fact that I hadn't reached puberty yet that I hated Phys Ed. I tried every trick in the book to get out of that class. I was embarrassed to go in the change room to get dressed for it. I would often wear my gym clothes under my school clothes. One day during class I fell, and broke my nose. I was covered in blood. The Phys Ed teacher took me in the change room and insisted that I have a shower to wash up. The blood had stopped dripping from my nose, but I had blood everywhere. All the other guys were still in class so I quickly got undressed and got into the shower. I was going to be as quick as I could. Just as I was coming out of the shower, class ended early and all the guys came in the change room. There I was in all my glory, in front of the class, my scrawny little body, exposed to everyone. I was very conscious of the fact that I had no pubic hair and my privates had not yet started the journey to manhood. I regretted that day. If I could have crawled down the shower drain, I would have. It didn't take long before the whole school started to call me Shrimp. I would walk through the halls and get looks from everyone. The 'Rad Rassers' would throw raw hot dog wieners at me. Even the girls would point, stare and giggle. I could just imagine what they were saying. My only hope was that the year would end and the seniors would move on. I had to go to some counseling and I even went to the doctors and got hormone pills trying to push the puberty factor faster. I had to make sure that I always wore a belt, or the seniors would grab my pants and pull them down around my ankles, trying to expose me to have a good laugh. The year didn't end soon enough.

CHAPTER 3

I returned after the summer holidays without even growing an inch, anywhere, but grade ten started out different. There was a girl in third year that took a liking to me. We would walk to class together, hang out after school and even go on the odd date to a movie. Her name was Cheryl. She was able to ignore the taunting much better than I could. She made me feel good.

It wasn't a boyfriend-girlfriend situation but rather a damn good friendship. After about three months I was even comfortable holding her hand, of course I couldn't do this in public. I still felt a little uncomfortable and I was shy. She was a cute girl, long dark hair and brown eyes. She had definitely reached puberty. She had a nice body, you could tell by the tight shirts she wore that her breasts were firm and plump.

It was the annual Sadie Hawkins day dance on Saturday night and she asked me to go. My initial reaction was no, but she convinced me to give it a try. We could go for a bit and leave if I was uncomfortable. I agreed to go and she thanked me with a kiss. That was my first. Her lips were so warm and moist. I remembered leaving school that day on top of the world. I would have never initiated something like that. I saw her as a friend. I had no idea she wanted more. I tell you I knew that day that the hormone pills I had been taking were working. I could feel a twitch in parts I never knew I had.

That week leading up to the dance was extraordinary. I walked Cheryl home and she invited me in. We were watching TV when she reached over and gave me another kiss, this time a French kiss. I tell you, I came to attention in no time, and even though it was small I think it had a mind of its own. I was going to explode, literally. The next day at school I was floating on clouds. I didn't care what anybody said or called me, I had an older woman and she wanted me. Again I walked her home, I anticipated all day that I was going to make the first move this time, I was going to kiss her goodbye. When we arrived at her door, her mom was home and I chickened out and said I had to leave. Her mom invited me in. The three of us sat for a bit in the kitchen. Cheryl then told her mom that we had some homework to do and that we were going to her room to do it.

Her bedroom was all white and frilly, she had a four-poster bed and her comforter had little clowns all over it. Her walls were adorned with hundreds of posters mostly of guys with no shirts. It was very intimidating. We entered her room and I immediately went to her desk and opened my books. She pulled up a footstool and sat beside me. We worked on our homework for almost an hour when her mom yelled up and said that she was going to the store and she would be back in half an hour.

"I thought she'd never leave," Cheryl said as she put her hand on my thigh. "Jack, I think you're cute."

"I think so, too," I said like a dork. "I mean I think you're cute also."

She leaned over and kissed me, shoving her tongue halfway down my throat, at the same time she took my hand and put it on her breast. I don't know what was pounding harder, my heart or my pants. This was as far as I wanted to go, after all she was very well developed and I was still waiting for my pubic hair to fill in fully, I wasn't ready for this, what would she think? I knew she was aware of all the teasing that I took about the size of my penis. I'm not sure whether she had seen other guys, but judging from her forwardness, I am guessing she's been here before, but I knew I wasn't ready.

"I'm back," her mom yelled. "I forgot my purse."

Thank God I thought, I picked up my books and headed downstairs, Cheryl wasn't far behind me.

"I have to go now, my dad's expecting me," I said, heading for the door.

"Saturday night at the dance, let's do it," she whispered in my ear as her hand rubbed my crotch.

I almost tripped as I made a hasty retreat out of there.

That night I was torn on what to do. Should I back out of the dance or should I go and see what happens. I was only fifteen and she was almost seventeen, am I ready for it? The next two days went by in a blur and suddenly it was Saturday morning, the day of the big dance. I decided that I would go, after all we both wanted it. I may not be as developed as the guys in the posters, but I knew if called to action, my army would be at attention and willing to go in. My dad had brought an old 8mm dirty movie that he had confiscated from the police station home. I took it one day when he wasn't home and watched it. Looks pretty simple, put it in and pump. All I can hope was that it was her first time and she would have nothing to compare it to. In my mind, I doubted that.

It was 7:45 p.m. when I arrived at her door and she opened it. Her hair was in pigtails and she had freckles on her face that she made with eyeliner. I had on blue jeans, a checkered shirt and a straw hat. After all it was a Sadie Hawkins Dance. We walked the quarter mile to the school. The sun was just going down and it would soon be dark. We went into the gym and I found a small spot on the floor against the wall where we sat. On one hand I was proud to be with her, and on the other hand I was afraid of what people would say and how I would react to the teasing. The lights to the gym went out and the band began to play. We sat in the dark just holding hands and listening to the music. This seemed different tonight. People weren't teasing me or calling me *pencil dick*. I almost felt normal. The band began to play a slow song and I felt like it was my turn to make a move. I asked her to dance. I was finally coming out. We danced close and held each other tight. I could feel her breasts against my chest as we danced. Her hair smelled so fresh. I had never felt this comfortable with anyone before. When the song ended we went back and sat on the floor. Cheryl held my hand and put our hands in her lap, my fingers close to her crotch, we started to kiss. This was it and I was ready. We sat for a while longer, I looked at the clock on the wall, it was almost midnight. Cheryl then moved our hands from her lap to my mine. I could feel her hand against my penis, which was twitching at the thought. She leaned over and said, "Let's go outside." We walked hand in hand out of the gymnasium and on to the football field. The night was clear and smelled so clean. When we reached center field we sat down just holding each other. It was so peaceful. The air was quiet. There must have been a thousand stars in the sky. I don't remember seeing that many since I was almost six years old. It was in Algonquin Park in Northern Ontario in Canada. We went there on vacation once a year. Mom took me down to the beach about 1:00 a.m. to see the stars. As I lay in her lap, we stared up at them picking out as many shapes as we could.

Cheryl now laid back and pulled me with her, as we began to kiss she took my hand and placed it on her breast, with her other hand she started to undo my shirt.

"Are you ready?" she asked.

I could hardly hear her for the pounding of my heart. There I was on the football field and I was going to score, without out even making the team. I slipped my hand under her blouse, she stopped it at her waist.

"What's wrong?" I asked.

"Nothing, I'm nervous," she said.

"If you don't want to it's okay," I said like a gentleman, meanwhile wanting to rip her clothes off.

"No, it's okay," she said as she pulled my shirt off. We kissed for a few minutes and then I felt her hand tugging at my belt. With one flick of her wrist she had it and my zipper undone. She slid her hands up either side of the outside of my legs and grabbed my pants pulling them down to my knees. As she did, her wrist flicked my penis and I thought it would shatter. I had never felt it so hard. I reached for her top and again she stopped my hand.

"I'll do it," she said. "Take off your pants while I'm getting my top off."

I stood up immediately and stepped out of my pants like a marching soldier, lifting my legs and turning my pants inside out, my underwear tangled amongst them. When I had them off she stood up and embraced me with a kiss, she picked up my clothes and tossed them over her shoulder. She reached her hand down and grabbed my penis.

"Is your little guy ready?" she asked.

I took it as a sign of affection and not as a statement of size.

"Yes," I answered.

"Now!" She yelled as loud as she could. With that, the lights on the football field came on and momentarily blinded me, she started to run, picking up my clothes on her way. There I was standing at center field, butt naked except for my socks, the field was lit up like the Fourth of July. As I held my hand up to block the lights from my eyes I could see everyone from the dance standing around the field staring and cheering. I was never so embarrassed. I had been set up. A four-month plot by that bitch. I screamed, "I'll get you back." I ran towards the end zone, which was empty, and I never stopped till I got home. I was devastated, for a year I put up with the garbage. I finally thought it was over when I met Cheryl. I was wrong. The bitch was just toying with me the whole time. It seems the new crop of 'Rad Rassers' had paid her to do it. She was dating one of the football players at the time. It was quite obvious to me that when I made my list she would definitely be on it.

After the death of Lynn, I thought I would travel back home, to stir up some thoughts, to instill in me the desire to carry out my plan, Cheryl was just the first of two people I killed from high school.

It's amazing what you can find out when you're a computer geek. All you have to do is hack into files and you can find out anything you want about someone. When I was ready, I headed to Tucson. I knew the name of the theatre that Cheryl was acting in. I headed right over to watch the play. A nice mystery, a Who-Dunnit, only I had my own ending to the play.

Cheryl, it seems had moved to the Tucson area. Her aspirations of becoming a Hollywood actress or a model died when she became pregnant at nineteen years old by the football jerk she called her boyfriend. She kept the baby and her mom helped raise it. Anyway she was acting in this play, a play about a conniving mistress who got a lot of women mad at her by sleeping with their husbands. She is eventually hunted down by several of the wives who all had a motive to kill her. I sat and watched every performance for three weeks, and I memorized every line of one of the wives. As I said earlier I was into making masks, and I figured if Robin Williams and Dustin Hoffman could pull off playing a woman in a role so could I.

I set up a small office front in town, and posed as Hal Burton, Hollywood producer, again in disguise. I went to one of the dress rehearsals and started handing out business cards. I concentrated on hyping the talents of Cheryl and Lily. Lily was the one that eventually pulls the trigger in the play. I told them how talented I thought they were and that I would like them to get their portfolio together and come and see me. That I would soon be submitting names for a casting call in Hollywood and I wanted to see if they had what it took.

That night I received a call from both of them. I set up appointments with Cheryl in the afternoon and Lily in the morning of the next day. Lily arrived about 8:00 a.m. I had fallen asleep in the back of the office the night before and was startled when she arrived an hour early. I quickly threw on my disguise and make up and greeted her at the door.

"First things first, I'm going to need you to make a commitment of every morning for two weeks. We need to do some role playing and screen testing to check out your talents," I told her. This would allow me the time I needed to learn her character in the play. If I was going to double for her I needed to be convincing.

"Sure, it just so happens I'm a stay at home mom. I'll get my husband to work out of the house for couple of weeks."

"Okay, let's get started, here's the itinerary." I handed her a piece of paper with my plan of attack. A one-hour photo and make-up session, one-hour rehearsing the part she's already playing and one hour of new roles I would design as Improv roles to see her versatility. It all looked so convincing she fell for it in a minute.

"What type of part are you casting for?" she asked.

"A comedy about three young roommates in college, and I think you'd be perfect for one of the parts, but I've got to do a lot of testing." I was positive she was unaware of my motives and that this was all a hoax. I had to do a lot of acting myself in order to pull this off.

Lily was about twenty-four years old. You would never know that if you saw her in the play. She plays a forty something overweight wife, a kind of frumpy old gal, a Russian lady with a husky voice and an accent. That's why her role was perfect for my plan. I had no problem disguising myself for the part. Every morning for two weeks Lily showed up as bubbly as could be. I had hired a cosmetician to do her makeup, I was quite good at the final stage of makeup, blending latex to fit a person but I didn't think I could convince Cheryl or Lily that I knew what I was doing when it came to accenting their features, plus having some staff onboard gave my character more credibility. After makeup, I got out the camera. I took some glamour shots and extensive shots of her in the costume she wore in the play. I had to copy it exactly

We practiced her lines from the play and I videotaped every session. At night I would study her every move and mannerisms until I knew it well enough that I could play her part. In the afternoon I had Cheryl come in. We went through the same work out. Cheryl had changed since I knew her in high school. She had put on a bit of weight from her pregnancy and nature had taken some of the youthfulness out of her face. We spent more time on her role in the play. I would play Lily's part, asking Cheryl to correct any mistakes I made that Lily did different, after all I just had to be convincing. I had to be.

The two weeks went without a hitch. I had them totally convinced I was legit. The night of the big show was upon us, it was do or die, or should I say do and die. I had told Cheryl at her last session with me that I had called in a Hollywood scout to watch the show tonight. I had not told Lily anything, as far as she knew it was just another performance.

Lily was surprised to see me when I arrived at her home about eight o'clock in the morning. I wanted to make sure her husband was home. I had hired an actor to come with me to play the part of the Hollywood Scout. His role was to convince her that I needed her in Los Angeles that evening. She invited us in and called her husband to the dining room where we sat around a table. Donald McDonald, the acting Hollywood scout had brought Lily's portfolio. He showed the glamour shots to Lily's husband along with a preliminary scouting report, one I just so happened to make up.

"Well Lily," Donald said. "It's like this. I looked at your portfolio and studied the videos from your sessions with Hal. I am very impressed." Lily's husband, Tom, was leafing through the portfolio his eyes kept rebounding from the pictures to Lily and back.

"Impressive aren't they?" Donald commented.

"I know it's her, but wow she's beautiful in these!" Her husband said.

Lily gave him a look.

"I mean she's always beautiful but these pictures just highlight her beauty."

"Nice recovery," she said.

"So anyway," Donald interjected. "Like Hal was telling you, I'm casting in Los Angeles for a coed sitcom. I flew in from Los Angeles after Hal's call to see exactly what beauty he had found, after looking over your portfolio I have good news and I have bad news." He paused.

"Go ahead," she said. "Go ahead."

"You would be great for the part, but we are not going to give it to you."

Lily's eyebrows dropped and you could see the disappointment in her eyes.

"And the good news would be?" Tom asked.

"Well that was the good news," Donald told him. "The bad news is that I need you to fly out in an hour to Los Angeles to cast for a new feature film we're doing."

Donald put his hands behind his head and leaned back in his chair.

"Bad news?" she yelled. "That's great!"

"The film is about a working man who struggles to make ends meet when he stumbles across a lottery ticket, a winning one of course, that changes his life drastically, and you would be playing his mistress in a love triangle, trying to get your fair share of the money."

"Sounds corny," I said. "But that's Hollywood."

"I would love to audition for it but I can't leave in an hour, I have a baby and a performance tonight."

"It's alright honey," Tom said. "I'll manage. I've got some time coming to me, I'll take a couple of days off. Maybe your mom could come in from Chicago."

"Actually, Tom, it's about a three week casting call," Donald said.

Again Lily's head dropped in disappointment. You could see she wanted it but was unable to commit.

"Okay folks, I'll let you in on a secret," I said. "Tom, I've already talked to your boss. You're okay to go, he said you can work from L.A. just don't forget your laptop. I also talked to Mr. Smith at the theater company and the understudy will play your role in the play tonight. Your mom and the baby can go also. Your mom can baby-sit while you and Tom work. You'll have a private trailer on the set. I spoke to your mom last night and couriered a ticket to her. She will meet you in Hollywood."

They both looked at each other and said, "Let's do it."

The phone rang in the distance, Tom headed toward the kitchen and picked it up.

"Hello, Oh hi, Mr. Spratt... yes, actually they're here right now... three weeks... great, I will email you when I get there... yeah she's ecstatic... who knows maybe she'll win an Oscar and I won't be back... I will... you too... bye." Tom put down the phone and re-entered the dining room.

"That was Mr. Spratt, my boss."

"I know," Lily interrupted. "I heard. Should I call Mr. Smith?" she asked.

"No need to," I said. "I spoke to him last night. Besides you only have forty five minutes."

"This is for real right?" Lily asked. "It seems like a dream."

"It's not a dream my dear, it's Hollywood," Donald stated. With that we both stood and walked towards the door.

"The limo will be here within the hour, the driver has your tickets and he will fill you in on the way."

Donald and I left. I had to get back to the office and get ready for tonight. I arrived back at the office and called the airline to make sure everything was set. I felt terrible, lying to that innocent couple like that. There was no casting call, but they would find that out in a day or two, it'd be explained as a mix up in schedules, that the film has been dropped. Tom's leave of absence was legit. I did arrange it. All I really need is for Lily to be out of town for a couple of days. I don't want to ruin their whole life. I offered Mr. Spratt triple Tom's wages to let him work from California, that way Spratt would not be out anything. The couple, her mom and the baby would have a wonderful vacation. When they arrive and are told the news, there will be an envelope with return tickets back on the following Saturday, and $50,000.00 cash for their trouble. Of course, Hal would be long gone from here when they get back.

I phoned Cheryl.

"Hi Cheryl; it's Hal."

"Hi, Hal."

"Are you ready? Tonight is the big night, I've got the Hollywood scout here and he wants to see a performance of a lifetime. Make sure you go out with a bang, convince us you're dying."

"You bet. I'll be so good you'll think I'm dead."

"Oh, I'm sure," I said. "We'll see you in your dressing room after the show, bye."

"Bye."

With my plan now complete I went for lunch. It was about 3:00 p.m. when I finally got back to the office. The show was in four hours, I was to be there in two for dress rehearsal. I would have to get dressed at the office because at the theater there were only two dressing rooms, male and female, and I couldn't use either. Of course Mr. Smith was never notified, Lily would be there, only it would be me that would be playing her part.

I had taken Lily's costume after one of our sessions. After trying it on, I took several pictures of it and took them to a seamstress and asked her to make a duplicate. I knew Lily would be back for hers the next day. I proceeded to get dressed. I put on the shoulder pads and the padded bra. Lily was playing a frumpy old Russian lady whose stature was like that of an Olympic Wrestler.

With all the get-up on I didn't look too bad. All I had to do now was put on the latex accessories I made, the wig, and the kerchief and I would be all set. The wig was easy, it was an over the counter semi-curly gray wig, and under the kerchief you couldn't see much of it anyway. The latex took a few days to make. In the play Lily strictly used make up for her appearance and added a fake double chin. She looked like an old maid but close-up you could see her beauty.

During our sessions at the office, the cosmetician would take measurements of her face while she was doing Lily's make-up. I explained it to Lily as standard procedures for Hollywood, that it was needed for her portfolio in the makeup department to see how versatile her roles could be. I took my facial measurements and tallied the difference. The latex mask would be formed accurately to these measurements. Where her features were bigger I would add more latex, and where they were smaller I would apply glue and tape to my face to help tighten the area, I would then slightly increase the mask proportionately until it would fit me but still looked normal. A process I developed into a software program that would do all the calculations. Then a simple plaster mold of my face was taken, the latex added, and behold a mask was formed that fit skin tight to my face. The only drawback was that I had to apply a lot of anti-perspirant and powder to my face, because if I were to sweat, the perspiration would relax the latex and the mask would droop.

Once I was ready, I poured myself a good size glass of Coke and waited. I sat and practiced my lines. I had to concentrate on my accent, this was the one area that was going to be tough. I could look the part, but I knew I couldn't sound the part. I was going to use the excuse of a cold and sore throat and that's why my voice was a bit raspy. The lady Lily played did have a deeper voice than her regular voice anyway.

I arrived at the theater about fifteen minutes before show time.

"Where the hell were you," Mr. Smith yelled as I walked in. "Dress rehearsal was two hours ago!"

"Sorry Mr. Smith," I said. "I've been fighting this sore throat all day."

"Do you want to sit this one out? Should I put in the understudy? Sounds like you're straining your voice, I like it though, it adds character to the old bat."

"No, I'm okay, is everything ready? Where are my props?"

By props I meant my gun. The gun in the show was a real Colt 45 with the firing pin removed. I had gone and purchased one the first day I saw what they were using, this way I got by the five-day waiting period and I legally had it, well Hal had it. It couldn't even be traced back to me.

My big moment wasn't until the third act, about forty-five minutes into the play. I had to go on and offstage about ten times first for small parts. I kept the real gun in a holster under my dress, the curtain dropped and the second act was over.

"Are you okay, Lily?" Cheryl asked. "Your voice sounds a bit rough."

"I'm alright, one more act to go. Too bad you won't see the end of the play though," I said jokingly.

"Yeah," Cheryl said. "It's always the pretty ones that die young in the entertainment business, and I'm going out with a bang. Where are we to meet Hal and Donald after the show?" she asked.

"Over at the restaurant next door about 10:30 p.m.," I said.

"Okay, curtains going up, I'll catch you later. Remember, shoot to kill," Cheryl said.

"I will. Make your death look real," I said.

"I will," she replied over her shoulder.

In the play Cheryl's character, was just returning home from a date with my character's husband. That was the hard part of my role, prior to his rendezvous with 'Samantha', Cheryl's character, 'Ivan', my husband, had to give me a kiss goodbye, right on the lips. I had to kiss him back, it was to be about a ten second lip-locked session. I had never kissed a man before, and didn't want to, but it had to be done.

Samantha walked into her apartment. The phone in her apartment was ringing. In her hurriedness she left the door open and I entered and hid in the bathroom off of the bedroom. After her call, she hung up the phone, closed the door and went into the bedroom.

She slipped out of her clothes and into a housecoat, and then laid on her back on the bed for a nap. That was my cue to enter. The timing had to be just right. Cheryl's housecoat was lined with three small explosives that would go off as she grabbed herself where I had shot her. She would then pierce the balloons filled with fake blood that were underneath her housecoat. She had a small nail that was soldered to the ring she wore on her finger. This would give the effect of the gun shot wounds bleeding. A speaker underneath the bed was hooked to a computer that made the gun sounds. The computer also detonated the small explosives. I had loaded my gun with two blanks and four real bullets, one for Cheryl and the other three as backup just in case my exit got failed somehow. The third shot was the one that I would shove right into her housecoat at her heart and pull the trigger.

The prop gun had a computer lead on it. As the trigger is

pulled it activates the computer and the shots are fired. I pulled out the real gun, I had to keep the prop gun out of sight, I had to pull both triggers at once. I had to hope that in all the confusion nobody would see that my left hand was inside my dress. I had made a small slit by the waist so I could reach in and pull the trigger.

"Miss Samantha," I said in my raspy voice. "Out vith my husband again?" I said as I raised the gun.

"You don't understand, he means nothing to me," she cried from the bed.

"You must mean something to him. Vy vould he leave me to be vith you?" I said, the gun still pointed at my victim.

"I'm sorry, don't shoot me, I'll stop seeing him!" Her voice carried a well-practiced desperate tone.

"It's too late my dear, I vant you to die."

I pulled the trigger and fired the first blank. Cheryl grabbed her right arm and burst the balloon. Blood began to seep from her arm as she crawled to the head of the bed.

"No, please," she pleaded.

This was great. What a rush, I thought to myself. I was enjoying this. I was remembering how she had led me on back in high school. How she played me for a fool and embarrassed the hell out of me, even though I was pleased with the situation I had to keep in mind the task at hand.

"Vy shouldn't I shoot you, you whore, I vondered vy for the last six months he didn't vant me. I try to be romantic but he say he's tired, now I know vy."

I fired the second shot off. Cheryl grabbed her stomach, now her housecoat was drenched in blood.

"No! No!" She pleaded again.

Boy was she convincing, if there really was a Hollywood agent in the audience I'm sure they would've been impressed, she was giving quite the performance.

"He don't have you again, no one vill," I said in my raspy foreign voice.

I stepped forward, hopped on the bed and straddled Cheryl as she lay back in pain, I put the gun to her heart. "This is for all the vomen you hurt."

Just before I could shoot there was a knock at the door. It

was the neighbour who heard the shots and had come to rescue her. He would come in as I fired my last shot. I would get up and run past him, bumping into him, dropping the gun as I exited the scene. He would chase me for a bit out the door, wait behind the scenes for a minute and then go back in to aid Samantha. The play would continue in act four with my character on trial, there was only one problem though. My character wouldn't be there.

As the neighbour was knocking on the door and saying his lines it gave me the opportunity to lean into Cheryl. I had about fifteen seconds before he would knock down the door and I had to pull the trigger. I had my hand over her mouth so the neighbour wouldn't hear her screams.

"Cheryl" I said quietly so no one would hear me. "Remember back in high school," I said in my normal voice. Cheryl's eyes opened wide, she knew something was up. "Remember me, Jack, the Jack you dated and you took to the football field the night of the Sadie Hawkins dance, it's payback time."

She bit my finger just as the neighbour knocked down the door. I took my hand off of her mouth and slid it back under my dress and grabbed the prop gun's trigger, ready to activate the computer.

"NO! NO!" She screamed.

I pulled the triggers on both guns again, the bullet ripped through her housecoat splattering the fake blood and her blood all over me. I felt her tense body go limp as I jumped off of her and ran towards the door. I took out the prop gun and dropped it on the ground, at the same time I hid the real gun out of sight. I bumped into the neighbour and ran out the door with the neighbour in pursuit. All the stagehands were behind the door, the neighbour stopped behind the curtain waiting for his cue to return.

"I'm going to wash up for the next scene," I calmly said to Mr. Smith.

"Great scene," said Mr. Smith. "You've got three minutes until the fourth act."

I continued down the hall towards the bathroom. I entered the utility closet just to the right of the bathroom. I quickly disrobed and let the clothes fall to the floor. I reached over to a

VCR and ejected the tape. I had been in the theater two days earlier dressed as Hal. I told the stagehands at the time, that I was a Hollywood producer. I explained that I needed some footage from the angle of the director so I could capture the true essence of Cheryl's talent. They installed both the VCR and the camera for me, union rules.

I went back to the stage dressed as Hal. Everyone was milling about. I stayed long enough to see them find the envelope I had tucked under Cheryl's housecoat. Mr. Smith opened it revealing a recipe card with a large #1 written on it. This was going to be my trademark, every serial killer has to have one.

With the tape in hand I ducked out the stage door to where I had parked the rent-a-car. I drove one block down the street and pulled into the underground parking garage where I had left my own car and got into it, within minutes I was back on my way home.

I listened to the radio reports of the murder all night as I drove back. I couldn't wait until I got back home to watch the footage on TV. The police had no idea who committed the murder. They were looking for Lily but of course it would be awhile before they would find her, and there the trail would end. With Hal not existing they had nothing to go on.

Murder one down without a hitch.

It took the police over a week to locate Lily. Her alibi was so strong, I made it that way, I had to use her, but I didn't want to hurt her. Her story must have sounded bizarre; a phantom man named Hal that sent her off to California for a movie role that wasn't, $50,000.00 cash... was it a pay off? Her husband's boss confirmed the contact with Hal.

After a little digging, the police showed up at my door, they must have somehow found out about Cheryl's high school prank. That would give me a motive, plus I said I was going to kill five people. Unfortunately for the police, my alibi was steadfast. On the day of the murder my debit card was used several times throughout the Denver area. The card was even used to buy four tickets to an Avalanche game. Debit cards are great, they don't require a signature, all you have to do is give someone your pin number and tell them to go crazy, I think the whole day cost me $5,300 bucks. That was the last I heard from the police on that case.

CHAPTER 4

For the second murder, again it was those great high school years. I had basically been a quiet guy in high school, kept to myself. The ordeal with Moany had made me somewhat shy and reclusive. I didn't want to rehash it over and over and it seems that this is all that the kids in school wanted to talk about. I had found myself in with a little group of friends. Including me there was a total of eight, four guys and four girls. We hung out and did everything together. We met during one of the variety shows that the school put on. I had signed up as a stagehand. We all became part of the Audio-Visual Club. In the A-V Club we filmed all the sports and dramas put on by the school. It was more of a social club than a technical nerd club, as all of the other students referred to it. It got us out of a lot of classes; we traveled with all the sports teams to league games and participated in a lot of set up time with all the variety shows that were put on. Usually three-to-four shows a year, we also had the A-V room where we could go hang out at lunch and during our spares. In the A-V room we had three TVs and lots of videotapes. The girls could catch up on the soap operas and the guys could watch tapes of sports games. The A-V teacher was a cool guy, he wasn't really a teacher with credentials, just a guy who was hired for his technical skills, and therefore he wasn't as pompous as some of the teachers.

We hung out together all the time. Outside the school, we would get together every night. Most nights we would just go to someone's house and listen to music. We never drank or did drugs. We just had a good time being with each other. Even though there was the same number of boys and girls, Mark and Stephanie were the only ones to really have something steady going on, the rest of us would just pair up depending on the mood and be with each other for the day. The next day you might sit snuggled on a couch with someone else. There was never any real sexual electricity between us. You would catch the odd pair kissing during a movie when the lights were out. If we went out somewhere, we would hold hands as we walked. The guys formed a bowling team at the local alley and bowled there every Thursday night, two or three of the girls would usually show up to watch. Okay, now that I think about it maybe we were nerds, but we were tight, nothing could break our bond.

I told you about the area in our school called the Blue Hall where all the 'Rad Rassers' sat. Most of the time they were harmless, just taunting, no real physical abuse. In a way they were the ones everyone looked up to. They were the elite, and to be invited into the group meant you made it. They too had a bond, as a large group and even in the smaller groups. The small groups consisted of a few different fraternities. Now when you think of fraternities you think of your Ivy League Frats like those at Harvard and Yale. These fraternities were more like gangs. They weren't violent gangs on the whole, but every fraternity had their idiot. There was one in particular, Delta Zeta, the Tigers, as they liked to be called. Delta Zeta was the top dog, the fraternity to be in. In order to be a member there was a whole ritual, depending on the frat. First of all you had to be asked in, this usually took place by a member inviting you to a meeting. The meetings were more a drunk and/or drug night. Unless you were asked into Omega Epsilon Gamma, or the 'Grammas' as they were called, these were the real nerds, the scholars of the school. Their meetings were actually meetings. They decided how to help the community through volunteering their time. The other fraternities just hung out and partied. At the asking in meeting, you pleaded your case on why you should be a member. The next step was sandwich night, followed by initiation. Sandwich night was exactly that. You went to a meeting and you were served sandwiches made by the frat members. You had to eat three sandwiches. The 'Grammas' meeting was like a little old ladies bridge night, but for the rest of fraternities it was hell. The rule for the sandwiches was, anything goes. They were allowed to put anything edible that can be bought in a grocery store into it and you had to eat it, and keep it down for ten minutes. The trick to it was to starve yourself for a day and then load up on rice and Pepto Bismo to help absorb some of the disgusting things in the sandwiches. The final step consisted of a whip line. Fraternity members would line up in a row on the beach and you would have to run from one end of the line to the other, and back, while they whipped you with anything from canoe paddles to skipping ropes. Once you passed all three levels of the initiation you became a member and received your jacket and wristband. This meant you were in and could now take part in all aspects of the frat, including all meetings and doling out punishment at initiations.

It usually took until your fourth year of high school before anyone ever got asked into a fraternity. It was our third year, grade eleven, when we were all ask to be in a fraternity, the guys in the group that is. The girls had their sororities. The girls had been asked in three weeks earlier. Their initiation was a hell of a lot easier. They only had to be asked in and attend a parade night. The parade night consisted of them being paraded through town blindfolded wearing just their bras and panties.

We all figured we would be asked into a fraternity, because unless you were a total loser, you were asked. I figured we would be asked into the 'Grammas', the nerdy one because of our association with the audiovisual club, but much to my surprise we were asked into Delta Zeta, coolest of the cool. It came as a total shock. We debated as a group whether or not we should go, and knowing the stigma of not going and being black balled from all the other fraternities was reason enough, like I said, only real losers didn't join one. I was told that because my dad was on the force, and two of the other cops on the force had kids in the Tigers, was why we were even being considered.

"You're watching *Death Row Diaries*, the execution of Jack Stevenson. We'll be back in a moment," Emily breaks in.

"Great job Jack," Adam remarks over the loudspeaker.

"You sure? Am I going into too much detail?" I ask.

"No, we've got three more hours to fill before your last meal."

I barely have time to take a drink and stretch before I hear Emily say, "We're back with the live internet debut of *Death Row Diaries*."

Well the asking in meeting was a piece of cake, like I said it was a matter of pleading your case of why they should let us in.

All we had to do was make up some bullshit story on how cool they were, and that we thought their fraternity was the best. Now sandwich night that was another story. We all met at my house after school. We cooked up a whole box of Uncle Ben's Rice and chowed down. We only semi cooked it, so it was a little tough, we figured that the rice would absorb any liquid we consumed, and help us get through the night. The meeting wasn't until 7:00 p.m., we finished eating the rice around 4:00 p.m., this would give it time to work in our stomach. We headed to the grocery store and bought three bottles of Pepto Bismo to share between the four of us. We started drinking them as soon as we got outside. The cashier put them in brown paper bags. We must have looked like a bunch of winos on a Saturday night.

We arrived at Dave's house at 6:45 p.m. he was like the Grand Pooba of the frat. We were invited in and offered a drink, which none of us took. We were saving room for the goodies. The rules were explained. We had to eat three sandwiches and hold them down for ten minutes. If you barfed you were out. The sandwiches would be made in front of you so you knew what you were eating, and so you could see nothing was tampered with. Any cans, jar or bags were opened as they made your sandwich. We were taken into the kitchen one by one.

I drew last straw. It seemed like an eternity sitting there waiting for my name to be called. My stomach was already doing flip-flops. I walked in and sat at the kitchen table. Dave began to make the first sandwich, peanut butter, mustard, ketchup and mayonnaise. A little gross but it went down okay. Dave kept offering me a drink, but I figured I was better off without it. The second one was tuna, sardines, pickles and blue cheese dressing. Again it was gross but it also went down without taking a drink. Other than feeling a little full it wasn't too bad. One more and I was past stage two. The third sandwich was tough. I sat there as Dave put it together. First he poured Tabasco sauce on the bread and spread it around. Next he took out a tin of dog food, not the nice beefy looking stuff, but the kind that kept its shape as it made a vacuum sound when it plopped out on the plate. He knocked it over on its side with a knife and cut a one-inch slab of meat off. He then put the top slice of bread on it and slid it towards me. I reached out to grab it just as he pulled it back.

"Oops," he said. "I almost forgot." He lifted the lid of the sandwich and added half a can of this runny, and I mean runny, cat food. "Just one more ingredient." He pulled out a solid piece of chocolate bar and slapped it on top. "A little fiber for you," he said.

He slid the open face sandwich back towards me. I could see the word 'Exlax' on it.

"Yeah I thought tomorrow you could have a real shitty day," he said as he laughed.

Well it was eat or be eaten. I picked up the sandwich and started eating it. It was disgusting. The slab of dog food was like paste. It kept sticking to the roof of my mouth. I could hardly taste the Tabasco sauce. I think the rank smell of the cat food took away the taste. The chunks of cat food kept dropping onto my plate. I knew I would have to eat them, but I left them there for now. I pulled out the bar of Exlax and put it on the plate. I knew I would pay for it in the morning but for now I was going to save it for dessert. I kept gagging as I tried to force down the dog food. My mouth was dry but there was no way I was taking a drink, half a glass of vinegar and half a glass of prune juice. I was going to have a tough day tomorrow as it was with the whole bar of Exlax. I finally forced it down. I picked up the chunks of cat food that had fallen on my plate and threw them in my mouth. It wasn't that bad, it was quite meaty tasting. I knew now, I had made it. I finished it off no problem. The Exlax was actually pretty good and it went down very easily. I had done it and I was now on my way out the door to join up with the other guys. They were sitting at a picnic table chugging a beer and had a cold one for me. I grabbed my beer and took a big swig, not because of the taste in my mouth but to help remove the dog food that was stuck to my teeth and gums. I only had the one. I had enough Exlax in me that I didn't need anything aiding its actions. A couple of minutes later Dave came out and told us we were done.

"You can leave now. Saturday night at the lake, be there at seven."

We stood up and headed home. Once out of site I stopped along the path. I was feeling okay but I figured if I could make myself vomit I could get some of the crap out of my system and I'd feel even better. I stuck my finger down my throat far enough to make me gag. I threw up a little, but probably not enough to make a difference. As we walked we discussed what we all had to eat, it turns out that the other guys had all been given three peanut butter and jam sandwiches, not one disgusting item. It seems I was the scapegoat. Only I was given the garbage ones to eat.

I got home around 11:00 p.m. and went to bed. I slept quite soundly until about three. I awoke to a terrible pain in my stomach. It hurt so bad I could hardly move. My stomach was gurgling so loud I thought I was going to wake my dad. I had gas pains that doubled me over. I burped a couple of times on purpose and that alleviated some of the pressure. I went downstairs and made myself a glass of water with a couple of tablespoons baking soda and guzzled it down. I headed back to bed and again fell asleep. Even though I was asleep I could feel myself tossing and turning. Every once in a while I would clutch my stomach and curl up in the fetal position because of the pain. At one point I woke up doubled over, the pain was so bad I thought I was going to die. I tried to burp but I couldn't. So I did the next best thing, I let out the biggest, loudest fart I could, boy did it feel good, but the aroma was vile. I think the sardines had gone rotten on their way through my system.

Again I fell asleep. I don't think I was out long when I had another cramp attack. Well it worked before so I tried again. I rolled on one side, stuck my butt out and lifted my leg for maximum leverage and let it go. I let it go all right, pure liquid. My sheets were covered. I hopped out of bed and headed towards the bathroom. It was now about six in the morning and I could hear Dad in the shower. I had to head downstairs to the basement. There was a small bathroom off the rec room, just a two-piece, but I only needed one, and I needed it bad. I could feel liquid running down my leg with every step I took and I was leaving a trail. I landed on the main floor and I could feel another burst of gas ready to escape. I squeezed the cheeks of my butt shut and put my hand over my bum. I could feel the wetness of my track pants against my ass. I took the final four steps to the rec room all at once, and made the fifteen-foot sprint to the bathroom in one stride. As I went through the door I drop my track pants to my knees, whirled around on one foot, and landed smack on top of the toilet. I pushed with all my might. I let lose like a twelve gauge shotgun. The back splash of the water shot up like droplets of rain hitting a mud puddle during a mid-August thunderstorm in the heart of Kansas.

The coolness of the water was a welcome relief as it blast against my ass. I swear I could hear the water sizzle as it hit me. The burning ring of fire would last the day. I stood up to flush, I closed my eyes, and took a deep breath. As I headed upstairs my dad had just finished taking his shower and was coming out of the bathroom.

"You've got one hell of a mess to clean up," he said. He wasn't angry. As a cop he was well aware of the fraternities and their initiations. "If you're going to play with the big boys, you've got to take it like a man. Now clean up the mess and take it easy today," he said as he patted me on the back.

"Thanks Dad." I knew he'd understand. He always did.

I went back upstairs and headed right for the shower. I stepped in the tub with my track pants on and put the plug in the tub. I stripped off my track pants and threw them at the end of the tub on top of the plug and turned on the shower. I stood under the water letting it rinse off most of the shit, as the water filled the tub, it turned muddy brown, mostly from my track pants that were now semi floating in the water. I grabbed the chain attached to the plug between my toes and pulled it out of its nest. I picked up my track pants to let the water escape. I held them up to the showerhead so they could rinse. The jets of the showerhead and the soaking in the tub had rinsed them pretty clean. I rang them out, opened the shower curtain, and threw them in the sink on the vanity. The water that was thrown off in the process dotted the now fogged mirror like raindrops on a freshly waxed car.

I put the plug in and gave myself a good lather and rinse. I wanted to fill the tub again. I needed to throw my sheets in to let them soak while I mopped up the floor. Luckily when Dad bought the house he had all the carpets replaced with vinyl flooring, Jimmy wasn't the neatest person and with Mom gone it meant house cleaning would be easier. I finished my shower and stepped out of the tub to dry myself off. Dad was gone to work so I paraded to my room naked to retrieve my sheets. As I approached my doorway I could smell the stench. I held my breath and made it to the window, I drew up the blind and opened the window wide, there wasn't much of a breeze but enough hopefully to make a difference. I gingerly grabbed my sheets and carried them into the bathroom and dropped them in the tub, there they could soak while I cleaned the floor. Once I was finished mopping the floor, I threw in a load of wash, put new sheets on my bed and collapsed in it. The guys from the audiovisual club had called, and even Dave called to see if I was okay. I could hear the hesitation in his voice, it almost sounded sincere. The rest of the day I spent in and out of bed and on and off the toilet. That night I slept well.

The final stage had finally arrived, it was Saturday, the day I looked forward to, also the day I dreaded. I was leery about going through with the whip line, I wasn't sure I could handle it, I was also unsure what they would do to me, after all they nailed me good on sandwich night. On the other hand it finally meant acceptance.

I got up and ate a huge breakfast. My stomach was still upset, I'm not sure whether the pain was from it stretching or shrinking. At least my bowel movements were now solid again, although the burning ring of fire was still a bit raw, I had to watch how I sat down. Dad had joined me for breakfast. He wasn't eating much those days. You could see life was wearing him down. Every once in a while I would hear him sobbing in his room, but I didn't dare acknowledge the fact. I knew he hurt, losing Mom and Moany, and Jimmy being sent away. It was tough on him but he always played the tough guy. I guess it was the cop in him. I wanted to let him know that I knew he hurt, but I couldn't. That's how we handle things, us men, you know. You had to be tough. Show them that you are not afraid. That was his motto. That's why I had to see this fraternity thing through. As much as Dad was against the idea, I had made a commitment, and if I showed my fear it would probably hurt Dad more.

"You ready for tonight, son" he asked.

"I guess so Dad. There's really no way to prepare for it," I said.

"Well in my time on the force in this town, there had only been one or two, what you might call, major incidents from the whip lines," he said, stirring his coffee.

"Like what?" I asked.

"One year a kid cut his leg up pretty good, needed a few stitches."

"What did they hit him with?"

"Just the normal stuff, canoe paddles, one-by-six's, he actually cut it falling in the sand and landing on a broken beer bottle someone had left there."

"What about the other guy?"

"Broken wrist."

"How?"

"I guess he had put his hand behind his back to protect his ass and someone nailed him. The trick is, son, run like hell and don't stop; lift your feet high so you don't trip in the sand."

"Yeah, but I've got to go through it two times."

"Listen, Jack, from what I've seen it is usually not a problem."

"You've seen the whip line?"

"Hell yeah. It's great Saturday night entertainment for the guys on the force. We'll hang out every now and then just to make sure things are okay. Usually the guys doing the whipping have had a few beers, and they stand so close together that they can't even swing hard. The guys running have the advantage."

"I hope you're right Dad."

"You want me and a couple of the boys to show up? We could do a walk around about a quarter to seven, just to let them know that we're in the area."

"No, I think it might make it worse."

"You're probably right, son. I'll let the department know to stay clear tonight."

"Thanks, Dad."

"Well, I'm off to work. I'm working twelve so I'll see you when you get home. There are a couple of bags of frozen peas in the freezer, if you need them later."

"For what?"

"A cushion to sit on," he laughed as he made his way out the door.

I cleaned up the dishes and went and got dressed. I lay on my bed for a while just staring and thinking about everything. I wondered how Mom was doing, it had been a while since she was gone, was Moany with her? Could they see Dad and I? And know how much we miss them? Every once in awhile I would feel a cool breeze pass by me and I wondered if it was them, just letting me know they're there. I hope they are tonight, to push me through that line. I wonder how Jimmy is, locked away in that strange place, and Dad, what can I do to cheer him up? Probably nothing."

"Jack. Jack," I hear a voice faintly call.

I shook my head a couple of times.

"Yeah, I'm here."

"Boy, Jack, you can really take the viewers back. It's like we're all back in the eleventh grade," Emily says. "Have you ever thought of storytelling as a career?"

"It's kind of late now. I'll be dead in a few hours," I said sarcastically.

"I'm sorry Jack," she replied.

I wipe my cheek. It seems that it is moist from a tear that has trickled down my face.

"It's okay Emily, I'm caught up in it, too. Great job, Mark," I yell as I give him a thumbs up. Mark is doing the video feeds of the reenactment. I had left it in his hands. I had written a novel, an autobiography of sorts. The one I'm reading right now. Who knows maybe I will get on the bestsellers list when I'm gone. Artists are usually worth more dead than alive, at least the good ones. Anyway, Adam had full liberty to hire actors to re-enact the scenes I would be describing, and to film it. Mark would patch them through during the Webcast as I read the book aloud. That way the viewers wouldn't have to sit and stare at my face for hours while I told my story. That would be boring. He did a great job with the reenactment of Cheryl and I on the football field, but the interaction between the characters playing my dad and myself even got me.

"Back in three, two, one, go Jack," Adam yells at me.

So like I was saying, I was lying on my bed. I must have

dozed off. The next thing I knew, Kevin was ringing the doorbell.

"Wake up," he yelled.

I scrambled to get dressed and ran downstairs and opened the door.

"Come on in, Kevin."

"You all right?" Kevin asked.

"Yeah, just tired."

"You ready for this?"

"As ready as I'm going to be."

We headed out the door and down the street. The clouds had a puffy look but the sky was grey. We arrived at the lake about 6:30 p.m., nobody else was there yet. The water was a bit choppy. The odd white cap would roll in and then fold itself back into its surroundings. There were a couple of seagulls on the water's edge, making a meal of a dead fish. They were unmoved by our presence as they ripped pieces of flesh off the carcass and tilted their heads back. They would bob them up and down so the flesh could make its way down their gullets. Every once in while they would glance up at us, and make that sound, that shrieking laughing sound they make and then they would go silent as they pecked at the fish, like a jackhammer in cement.

"Where do you think Mark and Adam are?" I questioned Kevin.

"I don't know."

"I talked to them yesterday and they said they would be here."

"There they are. They're coming now."

The two of them were dredging along through the sand, it seemed deeper than normal, but then I haven't been to the beach in awhile.

"What's up guys?" Mark asked.

"Not much. Thought you weren't coming. What's in the bag?"

"I brought some old National Geographics, I thought we could shove them down our pants to soften the impact."

"Great idea," I replied.

I took two of them and stuffed them inside my underwear,

one over each cheek. I left my t-shirt untucked so it would help cover them up.

"Kevin, how's mine?" I asked.

"Yeah right, you just want me to stare at your ass."

"No really, can you tell?"

"They all look fine," Mark said. "Now shut up. Here they come."

Off in the distance I could see them approaching. They were lined up two abreast, jogging. As they got closer I could hear them chanting. Dressed in army fatigues they looked like a military squadron in basic training. They carried their weapons in one hand resting them on their shoulders. Their faces were blackened and almost seemed invisible.

"Company halt," Dave yelled. "Fall in."

They formed a line on either side of us, there had to be almost ten of them, they looked very professional.

"At ease," Dave shouted with great force.

They lowered their weapons and stuck them in the sand, still holding the one end of them. I could see canoe paddles, one-by-six planks of wood. Dave walked to the end of the line and pulled out four shovels that were inside a bag. He walked towards us and planted them in the sand at our feet.

"Pick them up and follow me," he shouted.

We each grabbed a shovel and followed him between the lines of guys. As we approached, they raised their weapons overhead and crossed them with the guy opposite them, much like a royal wedding procession. When we reached the end of the line we were stopped at a circle that had been drawn in the sand. The rest of the guys followed.

"At ease," Dave shouted.

The guys threw their weapons in a pile and sat down. They dotted the edge of the circle as they sat, like the numbers on a clock.

"Okay, rookies, here's how it works: we sit and drink and you dig a hole. I want it one foot deep." He tossed a tape measure into the center as he told us to go ahead.

A pickup truck had made its way through the sand, spinning its tires, creating a rooster tail two feet high from the back. It came to rest just outside the circle. All the members of Delta

Zeta got up and headed towards the truck. A tarp was pulled back revealing four or five coolers. They were plucked off the truck and carried off to a spot a few feet away.

"The sand goes in there," Dave said as he extended his arm towards the pick up. He then sauntered away and joined the group.

No questions were allowed, we started digging. As I started throwing the sand off my shovel and into the pickup, I noticed a barrel full of liquid in the one corner.

"Look at that; what do you think it is, Kevin?"

"I don't know, Dave's dad does own a pool supply company though. Probably has algaecide or something in it."

"Okay, hold it there," Dave yelled. "I thought I said no talking."

"Actually, you said no questions," I replied.

"Oh, a smart ass. Okay, rookies, strip."

"What?" I asked.

"Shut up and do it," Kevin said. "Don't make it worse."

"But the magazines," Mark said under his breath.

"Come on, guys, this is what we wanted. We've gone this far," Kevin said as he started to take off his pants.

"Now, not another word until I tell you to talk." Dave shouted.

The four of us proceeded to take our clothes off.

"What do we look like, idiots?" Dave asked.

I wanted to confirm his accusation but I knew better, he held all the cards.

"Magazines! Do you not think we've done this before? Why do you think we make you strip? Oh, National Geographic—figures! Now dig, nerds!"

Did you know that there's no dignified way to shovel when you are butt naked? I tried to turn different ways, but there was someone at every point of the circle. I took a peek at the other guys while shoveling, and even though I had gone through puberty later than them, I had caught up, (although it was hard to tell—it was a bit chilly.)

I shook my head to snap out of my daze as Dave yelled. 'Red, measure the hole.' We all looked at Adam, he was the only one with reddish brown hair, but his pubic hair was reddish orange. Adam grabbed the tape and measured.

"Thirteen inches," he said.

"Okay there, there and there," Dave said as he pointed to three different spots in the eight-foot circle.

"Twelve inches, twelve and a half inches and twelve inches," Adam said.

"Okay, you're all free to talk, but no questions." Dave said as he threw us some towels. "Cover up for now."

We all grabbed a towel and covered ourselves. It was the only relief we got from the cool night air. I put mine over my shoulders. My whole body was chilled.

"How about a cold one, boys?" Gerry, one of the other guys said as he handed us each a beer. I grabbed mine and walked over to the fire they had started, I could feel the warmth radiate off it as I got closer.

"*Death Row Diaries* will be back in a moment," Emily interrupted, reminding me where I am.

"Where'd you get these guys?" I asked Adam, referring to the guys in the video re-enactment.

"That's my brother and a bunch of his buddies, it's amazing what you can get people to do when they want their fifteen minutes of fame," Adam replied.

Emily staring at the video screen of the naked boys. I lean towards her and say, "They're just boys. Maybe you can see a man later." I turn to Seth. "Am I allowed a dessert with my last meal?"

Seth laughs, "Not that kind of dessert."

"Hey, get your minds out of the gutter," Adam interjects. "Three, two, one."

"Okay Jack continue with your story," Emily says as she points to me.

I went up to the fire to get warm with the other three guys.

"You guys ready?" Mark asked.

"I am," Kevin replied. "Let's just get it over with."

"As soon as you're done your beer we'll continue," Dave said as he walked towards us.

I took another sip and tossed the can on the fire.

"Let's go."

"Here are the rules: we will draw two lines in the sand. One at a time you will drop your towels and run forward through the line. Once you reach the end, you wait for the rest of the guys. You will then run backwards through the line. Once you've finished, you're done, and you're in. Oh yeah, and don't fall." Dave said as he walked away. "Two minutes and then one guy come forward."

"But..." I started to say.

"Remember, no questions," Dave yelled.

"What's with the hole?" Mark asked me quietly.

"That's what I was going to ask."

"I guess we'll find out if we fall," Adam said.

Kevin threw his beer can into the fire and headed toward the line. There were eight guys in total standing side by side. Dave was first. As president he got the first whack on the way down, and last on the way back. Kevin, who had volunteered to go first, dropped his towel as the three of us started toward him to join up. Adam still had his beer with him and started to sit down.

"It's better if you stand, Red," Gerry said. "Sand on your ass will make it worse—like pellets out of a shotgun when you get whacked."

"Okay, boys, choose your weapon," Dave commanded.

I could see the whole pile now, it was hard to see the arsenal of weapons when the pickup truck first pulled in. Dave grabbed a hand full of brush. The twigs were about three feet long and some of them had pine needles still attached. Gerry picked up a cricket bat. The other six guys picked up the rest. One grabbed a broken canoe paddle, two grabbed skipping ropes, one grabbed a tennis racket and the last two had one-by-sixes, all were about three-to-four feet long. They took their positions about five feet apart, four on one side and four on the other.

"Okay, rookie, you first," Dave was pointing at Kevin.

"I'm last," I said. I remembered what Dad had said about the drinking and I figured they would be a little worn out, and a little drunk by the time they got to me.

"Okay," Dave said as he put a whistle in his mouth. "On the whistle, you take turns and run through the line as fast you can, until you reach the other line over there."

You could barely see it in the sand, but it didn't matter I was going to go like a bat out of hell until I knew it was safe.

"Remember," Dave continued. "Don't fall...are you ready? Oh yeah, one more thing, you may want to cup your balls in your hands, just in case."

The sound of the whistle penetrated the sky like a screaming firecracker. Kevin took off running full steam. Dave missed him with the sticks, but Gerry caught him good with the bat right square on the ass, Kevin yelped like a defenseless puppy, you could see a white line across his already pink butt. The air was cool and we were all a little bit pink. Kevin stepped up the pace as he went through the line.

Whack!

The tennis racket nailed him. His ass now looked like a Do Not Enter sign. He got nailed once more by one of the skipping ropes. He let out a girlish scream. When he got to the end he was dancing up and down.

"That's why you cover your balls boys," Dave said as he blew the whistle again.

Adam took off. He wasn't as fast as Kevin. Adam got nailed by six of them, by the time he reached the end of the line I could see his ass glowing. He was now at the end marching in a circle raising his knees high as he went, trying to relieve the pain. The whistle went again. Mark sprinted forward. Dave hit him so hard with the sticks that he stumbled forward. I started rubbing my ass vigorously, hoping to restore some of the blood to my cheeks to warm them up. Cool night air was bound to compound the sting as we got hit. Mark regained his balance and kept running. He leapt at the last station and caught a skipping rope across his left calf muscle.

"Son of a bitch!" he yelled as he grabbed his leg and hopped towards the line and fell over it. I gasped and covered my mouth.

"It's okay," Dave yelled. "You got over the line."

I let out a sigh of relief for Mark. I did not want to see what was in store for us if we fell. The whistle went again. I dropped my towel and took off. I had no strategy, just to run hard and get there as soon as I could. Dave nailed me hard right on the ass. Boy it stung. I lost a stride but kept motoring. I made it to the canoe paddle before I was nailed again.

Smack!

I'm sure you could hear that one in town. It propelled me forward and I made it the rest of the way without any more contact. When I got to the end we compared asses, all of us commenting on who got it worse. The consensus was that Adam did.

"Okay, boys, five minutes until we do it again. Backwards!" Dave announced.

The four of us pranced around like we all had just returned from the proctologist's office. My ass stung, but the longer I waited, the better it felt. Five minutes flew by in a flash. Two of the guys, one with a skipping rope and one with a one-by-six had put down their weapons. The other six had now paired off across from each other and the distance was shortened.

"Twenty-five feet to go," Dave said. "Jeff, Todd," they were the two that had no weapons. "Grab their wrist bands and wait at the end of the line."

The wristbands were orange and black. Once you passed initiation you would receive yours. It meant you were officially a Tiger. The whistle blew. Kevin took off, digging his feet into the sand for better traction. He was hardly moving. I found out later just how tough it was to run backwards in the sand holding your balls. As Kevin approached the first two guys he stumbled and took a couple of quick steps backwards, he regained his balance just as he reached them. A one-by-six... Smack! He took one right across his ass. He stopped dead in his tracks, just long enough for another guy to wind up and swat him with a skipping rope.

"Holy fuck!" Kevin yelled as he dug in deeper and continued to backpedal. He made it through the next two guys receiving a glancing blow from both of them. His ass was as red as the crescent sun that was hovering above the lake ready to disappear into it for the evening.

"Come on, Kevin, two more," Adam shouted.

"Adam..." I started to say.

"It's okay, Red," Dave said. "You guys can cheer him on."

We all started cheering. Dave had nailed Kevin so hard, you could see the welts swell instantly. The pain in his face looked unbearable. He was now home free heading towards the line.

Todd and Jeff were the only two left and all they had in their hands were the wristbands. Kevin had three feet to go to the line when he reached them. The two of them were standing facing each other with their legs one in front of the other in a scissor stance. Kevin slowed as he left Dave's station, raised his arms in the air and let out a big YES.

"Way to go," Mark yelled.

Kevin started sprinting backwards again, rubbing his ass as he went. When he approached Todd and Jeff they both took a step backwards exposing a rope they had tied to one of their ankles. It shot straight out of the sand and became taut, sending sand pellets flying everywhere. The rope caught the back to Kevin's right ankle sending him scrambling backwards. He took a couple more steps and fell flat on his ass. We all gasped.

"Well?" Dave asked, looking at Todd.

"He's over," Todd replied.

Dave nodded at Jeff. Jeff bent over, offering Kevin a hand up.

"Congratulations," Dave said as he walked towards him. He extended his right hand.

"Kevin," he said, that was the first time he called any of us by name. "Welcome to the Tigers," he said as he grabbed the wristband from Jeff and handed it to Kevin.

"Get dressed, have a beer and relax, there's ice packs in the green cooler, it'll help with the swelling."

"Gee, you can be human," I blurted out without thinking.

"Hey rookie, once you are Tiger, you're family, no more bullshit. Red, you're next."

Adam lined up and was gone the instant the whistle blew. I was so glad for Kevin making it that I almost forgot how pissed off I was at them for adding another wrench to the game. Adam raced through the first two without them even taking a swing at him. It was almost as if they didn't try. Adam's ass was still beet red, probably because of his fair skin, being a red head and all. The canoe paddle caught him though. As it hit him he was turned askew a bit, colliding with a tennis racket. It made more of a thud, than a smack as it made contact. You could see the pain in Adam's face. He stopped and grabbed his ass.

"Right on the fucking cheek bone," Adam shouted. As he raised his hand off his butt you could see a trickle of blood running down the cheek.

"Come on, Red, keep going," shouted Dave.

"Come on, Adam, you can do it," Mark yelled as he kept pacing around trying to relieve his Charlie horse from the first round.

"Okay, boys, we've got blood, lighten up," Dave snapped.

"Blood!" Adam yelled.

"It's okay," I said. "It's only a little."

Adam dredged on as they all put down their weapons. Adam made it across the line with ease.

"Good work, Adam," Dave shouted as he extended a hand to shake Adam's. "Jeff, give him his wristband. There's ointment in the green cooler also. Grab a beer, you're a Tiger now. Next."

"I don't think I can go through with it," Mark said. "My leg hurts too much."

"Come on," Kevin said. "My ass is feeling better already, it's like having a baby, once it's out, the pain is gone."

"What does he know about having a baby?" Emily interjects out the side of her mouth. "I've had one and it hurts like hell."

I shake my head returning to reality. I look at Emily. "I asked him the same thing. He said his mom said so."

I continue telling my story.

"I'm serious Jack," Mark said. "I've got a cramp."

"Beer break," Dave said. "We'll give you five minutes to work it off."

Adam and Kevin came and joined us.

"Come on, Mark, we did it," Adam said. "Kevin's right, once you get the wristband the pain's a lot less. Hey, we're all going to make it. We are all going to be Tigers."

"He's right," I added. "We've come this far."

"All right let's do it," Mark shouted. He took his spot on the line.

"C'mon boys, let's get it done," Dave said. The whistle cried its high-pitched sound and Mark started to run backwards, he got hit with both of the one-by-sixes and the skipping rope.

"Yeah," he screamed as he kept going. You could see the determination in his face. Smack, went the canoe paddle. It nailed him square on the ass. Mark turned it into high gear and kept going. All of a sudden he began to hop and reached for his aching calf, he stumbled and fell flat on his back right at Dave's feet.

"Tough break rookie, go into the hole and wait." Mark got up and limped to the hole we had dug earlier and sat down. Adam and Kevin started toward him.

"By himself, he sits by himself. Tigers do not join the rookies," he said as he put his hand on Adam to stop him.

"But..." Adam started to say.

"No buts, rookies that don't make the whip line, sit in the hole, he'll get a second chance."

"It's alright guys," Mark said to Kevin and Adam. "Don't blow it for yourselves."

You could see the pain in his face as Mark sat massaging his calf muscle.

"He's not out yet," Dave said. "He'll just have to dig deeper"

It started to dawn on me why we dug the hole. Initially I had thought it was to zap the energy out of us before we started the line, but now I figure it also was a punishment for falling and all we'll have to do is fill it back in to become a Tiger. I took my position. Dave had wandered over to Mark with a beer and handed it to him. This gave me time to plan my strategy. Would I run like hell and run the risk of falling as I muddle through the sand, or would I go slow, take the whacks and hope I get cut up a little and get a bye into the Tigers. The whistle shrieked again and I started walking backwards I got hit with a skipping rope across the ass, only it wasn't that hard, for some reason he let off of it a bit. The whistle blew again.

"Hey Pencil Dick," Dave said. I hadn't been called that in over six months. "No walking or you're out. No second chance, start over."

"This is bullshit," I screamed.

"Your choice, you can leave now, you whiner, or you can toughen up and be a Tiger like the rest of your buddies, or should I say, ex-buddies, because Tigers only hang out with Tigers."

"Nothing will stop our friendship, we'll always be friends," I yelled.

"Suck it up, Pencil Dick," Kevin shouted. "He's right, Tigers don't hang out with wimps," he yelled.

The whistle went again, and I stood there.

"Your choice, move it or be gone, rookie."

"Come on, Jack, all for one, remember?" Mark yelled from the hole.

"Pencil Dick, Pencil Dick!" they all shouted. Even my three best friends joined in. I don't know whether it was the beer or the anger burning inside me, but I dug in deeper and took off like a rocket. The first two guys barely had time to react as I went by them. I got nailed with the tennis racket and dug in deeper. I headed towards Dave and got smacked with the branches. It hurt like hell. He hit me and then pulled them sideways scratching the hell out of my ass. I continued. As I approached Jeff and Todd I could see they were ready to pull the rope tight. I leapt into the air to hop over the rope just as they pulled it tight. Wham, I was flat on my back, the bastards had lifted their legs and took my feet right out from under me.

"In the pit," Dave yelled at me. I could tell he was getting angry.

"You two," Dave pointed at Adam and Kevin. "Grab those bottles out of the truck." They did and handed one each to Dave. He unscrewed the caps and threw the bottles at Mark and I.

"Second chance, boys, in or out?"

"In," Mark snapped before I could even open my mouth.

"What about…" Dave started to say.

"I'm in. I'm not going to lose to you no matter what," I said as the anger brewing inside me was now talking. "Bring it on."

"Fill the bottles with sand from the truck and come here."

Mark and I got up. He was still limping. We went to the truck, filled the bottles and headed back towards the hole. When I got to the edge I turned my bottle upside down and released the sand into the pit.

"What are you doing," Dave shouted, "I didn't say to empty them."

"I thought…" I started to say.

"That's your problem— you're not here to think, now here," he said as he threw us the caps to the bottles. "Fill it back up and put the cap on it, then go kneel at the end of the line. Oh yeah, no more talking rookies."

I refilled my bottle and capped it. We headed toward the

line. Mark struggled as we knelt down, you could tell by the line in his sandy face that a tear had trickled down it. You could feel the warmth of the fire increase as the other guys were throwing more wood on the coals. Dave handed us both a twelve-inch chain.

"Attach those to the caps on the bottles."

As we were doing this he walked about ten-to-twelve feet, dug his heel into the sand and made another line and then wandered back.

"I love it when there's two lame ducks," he said.

Todd and Jeff started to laugh. I wondered what was next.

"Well rookies, usually we skip this level but because there's two klutzes and we only want one screamer in the pit. We have to have a run off. The winner of the next race is a Tiger, the loser goes in the pit. Boys fill the spray bottles." The rest of the group including Kevin and Adam hopped on the back of the pick-up. Brian took off the lid of the barrel and submerged a topless spray bottle into it.

"The loser goes face down, butt up in the pit and we spray his tanned ass with salt water, hence, the screamer in the pit," directed Dave.

I looked at Mark and he looked at me, I could see another tear welling in his eye. I could tell by the look on his face without him even uttering a word, that he wanted me to let him win. I nodded. I didn't think he could take any more. I had to let him win. I knew he was hurting and was ready to break.

"You boys ready to become men?" Dave asked.

I nodded.

"Okay Jeff, Todd." They leaned down and attached the end of the chain to the wristband.

"Grab your dicks and pull them out, rookies. We want to give you your wristbands."

I looked at him with a puzzled look.

"Well what are you waiting for, are you in or are you out? All you have to do is stand up with the bottle dangling between your knees and cross the line, first one over is in."

I grabbed my dick and pulled it out as far as it would go. "Slap it on," I said.

Todd reached down and fastened the wristband around my

dick. I stood up slowly, very slowly.

"C'mon, Mark, it's not that heavy." I squatted and rested the bottle in the sand. Mark had trouble standing up his leg was cramping bad. He slowly got up and then squatted again.

"You're right," he said. "Ready when you are."

The whistle went. Mark stood up with a jerk. The bottle stretched his dick a couple of inches longer as he started to walk. I just stayed squatting.

"It's up to you, Pencil Dick, if you want to face the pit it's your choice."

I almost had to join the others in laughter, there was Mark waddling like a duck, a lame duck, as he limped his way towards the line. He had gathered a little momentum and the bottle was now swinging back and forth pulling his dick with every step. As he crossed the line I undid my wristband.

"Well, Mark," Dave said as Mark fell to his knees. "You're a Tiger now, grab a beer."

"Where are my clothes?" Mark asked.

"You'll get them later, when it's all over."

Mark undid his wristband, took off the chain and put the wristband around his wrist.

I got up and jumped into the pit, laid on my stomach and said I was ready. One more step and I'm in, I thought. Three more months and I'll be in grade twelve, and all these assholes will be gone. I'll be a Tiger, a sign of toughness, something I had never achieved before. I was getting quite warm as my adrenaline pumped. My ass was raw, and this was going to sting a bit, but in a couple of minutes it's over I thought. I could see them all armed with their spray bottles ready to go into action.

"Now," Dave announced, "once all the bottles are emptied it's over and we're all out of here."

I covered my face with my hands and laid down in the sand. I clenched my cheeks tight, my butt cheeks that is, and waited for what seemed like an eternity.

"Oh, yeah," Dave started to say as I could feel some of the water hit my leg, "remember Cheryl? Well, she was my girlfriend."

I could feel more and more liquid pounding up my legs towards my ass.

"She said that you actually kissed her and felt her up, this is payback time."

I started to lift my head when I felt a hand hold it down from getting any higher. I could feel the liquid now reaching my ass. Boy did it sting, and it was warm, which I thought was unusual since the air was cool, and it had a familiar odor to it that I just couldn't place. I could feel it coming from three or four different ways. As it hit more and more, my ass was burning so bad it felt numb. I struggled to get up, but was now also being held by my legs. The water kept coming in streams. They must have taken off the spray nozzles and were just dumping the water on me. I kept struggling until it stopped. I was still being held. I heard the engine of the truck start and I was let go as all the Tigers except for my three friends hopped in the back of it. Dave tossed me my wristband and said, "Well, you're in," he shouted.

The truck sped off. As I rolled over I could now distinguish the smell that was eluding from the puddle beside me. It was piss. Those fucking bastards pissed on me. I got up and ran towards the truck. It stopped. Dave stuck his head out and he yelled, "I hope we didn't piss you off."

I sped towards the truck, as I reached out to grab the tailgate I was shot in the face with a blast of salt water from one of the spray bottles. As I put my hand up to block it from hitting me again, I heard the engine rev, and I was now receiving a face full of sand from the swale of the truck tires. I wiped my eyes and spat out the mouthful of sand. I turned, in a fit of rage I headed towards Kevin. As I approached him I caught him off guard and gave him a fist to the side of the head knocking him into the pit. I leaned over him and yelled.

"What the fuck was that, you calling me Pencil Dick?" I pulled my leg back to give him a boot when Adam and Mark tackled me.

"Relax," Adam said.

"I had to, Jack. You were going to chicken out and I knew if I pissed you off, it would make you do it."

"Piss him off," Mark laughed. "Look at us, four naked guys rolling in a pool of piss. I think we're all a little pissed off right now." He started to laugh harder. We all started to laugh, an uncontrollable laughter that lasted several minutes. I laughed so hard my stomach was more sore than my ass or my eyes that were now burning from the salt water and the sand.

"Let's wash off in the lake, there is still beer in the cooler."

The four of us pulled ourselves out of the pit and ran to the lake and jumped in. We were hooting and hollering with joy of becoming Tigers, and with pain as the cool water caressed our battered and beaten butts.

"Back in a moment," Emily interrupted.

"Awesome tape Adam. I hope those actors were paid well."

"Thanks," Adam replied, "Can I keep that one for my brother's wedding? It'll be a hit at the reception."

"Be my guest. It's not like I'll have time to watch it again."

Mark leaned into the microphone.

"Jack, the chat rooms and emails are going crazy. You've got a mega hit on your hands."

"Actually, it's up to you Adam and Emily to see it through after tomorrow. It's yours from here on in. Take it and run."

"Will do," Adam replied. "Back in three, two, one," he points to Emily.

"We're back with Jack Stevenson on *Death Row Diaries.* Continue Jack."

The four of us took a quick dip, rubbed as much of the urine and sand off that we could without rubbing our asses too hard, we stood by the fire to dry off and warm up. We got dressed, finished the fourteen beers that were left and headed for home.

That Monday morning Dave, Todd and the rest of the Tigers met us at the front door of the school. Dave extended his arms. He was holding a black and orange Tiger jacket in his hand. He spread it out and showed us the back with a huge tigers head on it. He turned it around and showed the front with the lettering Delta Zeta and my name on it.

"No hard feelings," he said. "Three weeks and school's over and you'll be in charge, it's just part of the process. Now that I've got your jackets, I need your bracelets back."

We took them off and handed them to Dave.

"Like we would let you in the frat," Dave said as he shoved the bracelets in his pocket. "Maybe the 'Grammas' will let you in their frat. See you later, losers." He tucked the jacket under his arm, turned and left.

When I made my list of five to kill, Dave's name popped right in my head.

CHAPTER 5

For the second killing I knew I had to be in shape. Dave was a pro wrestler with the Florida Wrestling Federation. The FWF was huge, especially south of Tampa. Every Saturday night somewhere in the state there was a match with all the top names, it was broadcast throughout the state and even into Cuba.

Even though every move is well choreographed, it still hurt like hell when you have a three-hundred-pound guy jump on you from the top rope. I had set up a small gym on my island in Fiji and did some basic training. Once in shape, and by no means great shape, I bought a gym in Japan. Wrestling was huge there, almost as big as in North America, and not just sumo wrestling either. I had kept all the staff on including the managers and trainers on both the business and technical side. For the first three months I basically poured money into it to keep it afloat. I showed up occasionally to see the action but was more interested in finding someone with the same stature as Dave or should I say "The Playboy" as his stage name went. He had a good guy role. He wrestled in silk pajamas and always had two or three well-endowed women in his corner at all times.

One day I paid a visit to the gym in disguise as usual, a wig and some glasses. I kept a lookout for a wrestler that could foot the bill. I spotted my target. He was a six-foot-three, 250-pound guy by the name of Johnny Sashi. He was one of four siblings whose mother was Caucasian and his father was Japanese. He was pretty good in the ring, but what I needed more was his size and his determination. His father was an ex wrestler, both in North America and Japan. It was quite easy for a Westerner to make it big in the Japanese market. All you had to do was disgrace the Japanese culture, and you'd be an instant hit as a villain. Johnny's dad did well until he broke his leg in a free fall from the squared circle. He never got back in the ring so his popularity plummeted. He was now working in a fresh air fish market. He still gets asked for the odd autograph here and there but it's a far cry from the fame he once had in the ring.

After spotting Johnny in the ring, I went upstairs to Mr. Hashito's office. He was the man in charge of the business end of things. I told him that I was tired of pumping money into the gym and we needed a star attraction or I was going to pull the plug. I gave him two weeks to get it together or he was gone. I slammed the door as I left and yelled, "two weeks."

I returned to the modest apartment I had rented to prepare my plan. I took out my razor and shaved my head bald. I was getting quite hungry so I headed towards town. While there, I stopped in a store and picked up some supplies that I would need. While out scouring around, I found a small place that served battered fish and chips like back home. I picked some up and I trekked my way back to the apartment. I usually could eat what I wanted. I often traveled back and forth between my island in Fiji and the West in my jet. I could pick up good old North American food anytime I wanted. That wasn't the case for Lee Kitama. She was my neighbour at the apartment. We've spoken a few times. Last night, we had even gotten together for a couple of beers.

She had been in the country two weeks longer than I had. She was born in Canada somewhere near Toronto. Her father who was also Japanese had gone to school in Canada at the University of Waterloo. Before Lee was born he met his wife while at school, they fell in love and decided to stay. They got married halfway through the school year when Lee's mom became pregnant with her. They settled down in Kitchener, Ontario and Lee was born. She grew up in the area and even went to the same university. She got her teaching certificate and after a couple of years in a small rural school, she decided to go to Japan to teach English as a second language. She did not speak much Japanese at all. With her mom being Canadian, it was never spoken in the house except when her dad called home to relatives. She taught two mornings and three evenings a week to corporate businessmen. With the world now at the end of your fingertips thanks to the Internet, more business was being done globally, and English was becoming mandatory. I had recalled what she said she missed most about Canada. She said it was driving through the country on a Sunday morning just to see all the Old Order Mennonites in their Sunday best driving to church in their horse and buggy. The Mennonites lived a simple life without motor vehicles, indoor plumbing or even electricity. I looked up from the camera at Seth.

"I wish they didn't have electricity here," I said.

He just smiled a bit, but I knew he got it. The other thing she said she missed was going to the Fisherman's Wharf Restaurant on Friday nights for fish and chips. Once I saw the faded laminated sign in the front window saying they had authentic English style fish and chips, I had to get her some. Besides she seemed close to my age. I wanted to get to know her better. It had been a few months now since Lynn's death, I wasn't looking for a bed partner but could sure use a friend. Hopping from country to country was a bit lonely. I walked up the three flights of stairs, when I reached my apartment I fumbled for my keys. Lee must have heard me because she opened her door.

"Hi Lee," I said.

"Hi Mr. White," she replied.

That was the name I was using in the apartment, at the gym it was Mr. Brown.

"Nice doo," she said looking at my freshly shaven head.

"Why so formal? Call me Darryl. You like?" I asked as I rubbed my head. "I hope you haven't eaten yet, I have a surprise for you." I said even though it was only 4:00 p.m.

"No I haven't."

"Great, come and see what I've got."

"I'll be over in a bit. I have to feed the cat."

"Okay, I'll see you in about ten," I said.

I went inside and did a once around the place to pick up anything I had thrown around, and I gave a quick wipe to the bathroom sink to remove any whiskers that had been left from when I shaved my head. I also gave a wipe to the toilet and put the seat down.

"Come in," I yelled, as I heard a knock at door.

"It's me Lee, and I brought some beer," she said.

"Close your eyes," I told her as I placed the plate of fish and chips in front of her. "Okay, open them, they're probably not as good as the Fisherman's Wharf, but they do look good."

"How did you know?" she gasped.

"You said last night how you missed fish and chips and Mennonites. I looked all over for a Mennonite family but I just couldn't find one."

"You're so funny," she said as she slugged back a guzzle from her beer.

She always looked so prim and proper, and there she was slugging back a brew right from the bottle. The conversation soon died as we dug into our food. When we finished, we retired to the living room. We sat and drank three or four more beers, each one lasting longer as we drank. I could tell by her eyes that she was almost done in from the booze. Her words were becoming slurred and her movements seemed calculated as if she had to think to move every muscle.

"Well it's getting late." I said. "Should I walk you home?"

"Okay." She started to rise from the couch and fell back into it. "Looks like I had one too many."

I offered her a hand up and we headed towards the door.

"Oh," she yelled, "I love this song."

I had put in several CDs to play as we sat there, Stairway To Heaven was just beginning to play.

"One dance," she blurted. "One dance and then I'll go."

I turned and faced her and extended my arms, she leaned into me putting her arms around my waist, I could feel her breasts as they touched my chest. I wanted her badly. Even though I was drunk, I knew better. Getting involved would just complicate my plans. With me popping in and out of the country it would make things worse. I just held her tight and took in the moment. I felt like I was back in high school dancing in the gym under crepe paper decorations. That brought me to my senses, and the reality of my project. I had remembered how Cheryl had set me up, how we danced to this very song just before she hung me out to dry. I realized at that moment that I must act as soon as possible for the second murder, before I became too attached. The song ended and Lee plopped herself back into the couch.

"I thought you said you were going," I said.

"In a moment, I'm a bit dizzy," she replied, sliding down the couch.

"I'll help you in a second, I've got to see a man about a horse." I said.

I too could feel the beer as I made my way to the bathroom. When I was done I went to the sink and splashed some water in my face to wake up a bit. I re-entered the living room to find Lee passed out on the couch. I stood over her and admired her beauty. How peaceful she looked. Damn she was good looking. I leaned forward and gave her shoulders a shake.

"Lee wake up, Lee." She moaned and turned on her side to get more comfortable. "Lee, come on." I shook her again but to no avail, she was out cold. I headed to the bedroom and grabbed a comforter and a pillow off the bed and returned to the living room. I dropped them on the floor and grabbed her ankles that were dangling over the edge of the couch and lifted them onto it. She still looked uncomfortable so I placed a hand on both sides of her hips and gave her a push. This flipped her onto her back, straightening her legs out. I moved to the end of a couch and I undid both of her shoelaces. I slipped her shoes off gently. God I thought to myself even her feet are cute. The scarlet nail polish gave emphasis to the silver ring that she wore on the middle toe of her left foot. I bent down and grabbed the comforter off the floor and covered her legs. I then picked up the pillow and went to the other end of the couch. I stood over her head. Her hair was strewn across her face like she had just walked through a windstorm. I reached down and brushed it off her face, she licked her lips, which were covered in a scarlet shade of lipstick, and a small smile came to her face. I grabbed the comforter and started to pull it over her. I stopped as I reached her breasts. I could see through the shear blouse she was wearing, that she wasn't wearing a bra. Her nipples looked like a couple of sand dollars dotting the white sand at the beach. I moved to the side to bring the comforter higher, Lee turned slightly towards me, as she did her blouse fell open as one of the buttons made an escape from the hole that housed it. I could now see her whole breast, but only for a second, she then turned and was lying flat on her back again. I reached my hand toward her to fasten the button once more. As I did, my wrist caressed her right nipple bringing it to attention. I could feel the stirring deep within my groin. I wanted her. I needed her. But I knew better. I did up her button and pulled the comforter up to her chin. I picked up the pillow, raised her head and slid it underneath her head. Now was not the time. I headed towards the bedroom to retire. There was a knock at the door. Glancing at my watch, I could see it was just after one o'clock in the morning. I staggered to the door and looked through the peephole. Standing in the hallway, although she looked like an image in one of those carnival mirrors, I could see a tall blonde woman. Again my groin began to twitch. I opened the door.

"Hi, I'm Ursula," the tall blonde said. "I'm your neighbour, Lee's roommate. She left a message on the fridge that she was over here."

Boy, am I glad I behaved like a gentleman I thought to myself.

"Come on in, she's on the couch," I said.

I stepped aside and let her in. She was at least three to four inches taller than me.

"I'm Darryl," I said as I extended my hand for her to shake. She did.

"We had a few beers," I explained to her as she looked upon Lee's sleeping body.

"A few too many by the looks of things," she sat herself down in a chair. "I'll have one if you've got more."

"Sure," I went to the fridge and grabbed one. I also poured myself a Coke.

"Here you go," I said giving her the bottle. "Would you like a glass?"

"Nope. The bottle's fine. Aren't you having one?"

"No I've had enough, besides it's my last." It wasn't really but I wanted to sober up.

"I'm sorry, I didn't mean to take your last one," she said.

"It's okay I'll get more in the morning, besides its late," I'm sure she thought I was rude but I really didn't want her to stay.

"Lee had mentioned she saw you a couple of times, I guess our paths just never crossed," she continued.

"I've only been here a short time, and I'm not in a lot. Business you know," I said.

"Lee's the same way, she spends a couple of nights a week and weekends at one of her co-workers place," she said.

"Oh," I said, more disappointed than I intended.

"I don't think it's like that, he's older, more like an uncle. She goes to help him watch his kid while he works the swing shift."

Lee started to snore a bit, a quiet rumble.

"Sounds like she had a good time," Ursula laughed. "We've only been roomies for a short while, nice girl, very quiet."

"I'm from Texas, you?" I asked, making conversation.

"Washington State," she answered.

"What brings you here?" I asked.

"I work for a large computer company. I'm here to do some software development," she said and then finished her beer. "Well," she said as she stood up over Lee. "You look comfy, but it's time to go."

"Here let me help," I grabbed Lee by the shoulders while Ursula swung her legs to the floor.

Ursula swooped her up in her arms. At about six-foot-four, she was built like a brick shithouse.

"I've got her," she said.

"Thanks. See you later," I said watching Ursula carry Lee out of the apartment. I closed and bolted the door. I went to the bedroom and fell asleep.

I woke up about eight a.m., still a little dizzy and with a slight headache. I had a coat of fur on my tongue so thick I thought I might have to shave it. I grabbed a quick shower and got dressed. I went back into the bathroom grabbed a towel and wiped the fog off of the mirror. As I looked at the streaks the towel had made on the mirror's surface, it added wrinkles to my face and aged me about twenty years. I opened the bathroom window to allow the air to finish the job I started on the mirror. Now instead of the wrinkles in my reflection, my face appeared to have freckles, as the water droplets had turned to hazy spots as the mirror dried. I gave my teeth a good brushing. When I was finished I could still feel the fuzzy coating on my tongue, so I brushed it also. I stood there for a moment staring at myself. My head had such a shine. I wasn't sure whether I liked the new look or not. It made my head appear bigger.

It was time for me to head to the gym. I picked up my doctor's bag and headed out. I stopped at the couch and looked at it for a moment. I could still envision Lee lying there, I could remember her position, and exactly the way her blouse fell open exposing her creamy breast. Her face looked so sweet with that girlish smile on her lips. I shuddered momentarily. I wasn't sure whether it was a micro orgasm or not, but it felt good. I straightened the comforter on the couch. I noticed a strap tucked slightly under one cushion so I pulled it out. On the other end was a key. The strap itself was red and white with small red maple leaves and the word Canada on it. Knowing it was Lee's I stuffed it into my pocket, locked the door and headed to the gym.

"Cut. Cue commercial," Adam yelled.

I could see through the glass that Adam and Mark were working feverishly at the video terminal.

"What's up guys?"

"The VCR is acting up, we're getting some distortion," Adam states.

"Great. "Just what we fucking need, fix the damn thing."

"Relax Jack, we're trying," Mark said in a scolding voice.

"We're on a fucking deadline you know and the whole story has to get out!" I yelled back.

"I got it. Just a piece of lint."

"Thank God."

"Okay Emily, back in ten," Adam said pointing at her.

"Welcome back, please continue Jack," Emily said into the camera.

I stopped outside Lee's apartment debating whether to knock or not. I wanted to see her again so badly, but maybe later was a better time. I didn't want to have to explain the doctors' bag. For all her and Ursula knew I was a photographer. I took the stairs down to the street, hopped on the bus and rode it to the gym. As I sat there on the bus, I pondered my plan. This one hadn't even really started and I was getting confused. I was playing two different roles for this murder. The first was a gym owner from England, Mr. Brown with a wig, in the second role I was Mr. White, at the apartment with a shaved head from Texas, a photographer. But as Mr. White I was going to become a wrestling manager at the same gym that I owned as Mr. Brown. I'd have to remember two accents, two phone numbers and two sets of appointments, and to top it all off at the apartment my hormones were already taking control.

I bumped into the lady beside me as the bus came to a lurch and stopped. The driver opened his door and yelled something in Japanese to the driver beside him. I could tell by the expression on his face that it wasn't have a nice day. It was then that I realized I missed my stop. That was another pain in the ass. Having to use the bus as Mr. White while keeping the car for Mr. Brown to drive. I stood up and made my way to the open bus door. I exited while the bus driver was still yelling profanities, but this time I think they were directed at me as I exited the bus without it actually being a bus stop. It's amazing how no matter the language you can tell when someone is pissed off. I walked the three blocks back to the gym repeating to myself Mr. White, Darryl White, over and over again. I entered the gym through the front door, normally as Mr. Brown I would come in through the back door with my key and I would go up the back stairs to the office.

"Howdy," I said in my best Texan accent.

"Hello, may I help you?" Mr. Yamaha said. He was the towel boy. He was about fifty. In his prime, he was a manager, some twenty years ago in North America. He managed a tag team wrestling champion duo for a full five-year reign. His own men injured him in a fight. Once he recovered well enough to leave the hospital he returned home to Tokyo and bought the gym that I now own. With a sagging stock market he had to sell it to pay his debts. I bought it from him as Mr. Brown far below its market value. I kept him on staff.

"Yeah howdy, my names Darryl White."

"My name is..." he started.

"Hell, I know your name, you're Jay Pan, one of the rootinist tootinist managers Texas has ever seen, that's where I'm from you know, made my money in oil," by now everyone in the gym was looking at me. After all if you're going to be a wrestling manager you have to be loud and obnoxious.

"I'm here to find a wrestler to manage. I'm looking to have some fun. I don't really have to work you know, too much money for that."

"Actually Mr. White, they call me Mr. Yamaha," he answered.

"Yamaha, like the bike, oh yeah, and call me Darryl," I replied.

"Mr. Brown, the owner likes everyone to be called by their last name, it adds respect he says," Mr. Yamaha continued.

"Respect, obviously your owner hasn't seen North American wrestling, ain't no respect about that. Sex, lying and dirty dealings, that's what it's all about." I laughed my Texan laugh.

"Yes sir I've been there, I know what it's all about," Mr. Yamaha said.

"Anyway I'm looking for a young one. Who's that?" I said as I pointed to Johnny.

"That's Mr. Sashi, Johnny," he replied.

"Johnny. What kind of name is that for a Japanese guy? What's his wrestling name?" I asked.

"Johnny Sashi," Mr. Yamaha said.

"Johnny Sashi. No. We'll paint his face red or something and call him the Red Dragon." I headed toward him.

"Mr. Sashi," I said, putting my formal face on. "My name is Mr. White. I like your style. How would you like a new manager?"

"Well sir, Mr. White, I don't think Mr. Brown would allow it," he said.

"What do you mean allow it?" I asked incredulously.

"Well Mr. White," Mr. Yamaha interjected. "Mr. Brown says we must fight on our merit, not gimmicks."

"Where's this Mr. Brown?" I asked. "I'd like to talk to him."

"He's not here, he won't be in for a few days," Mr. Yamaha answered.

"Where can he be reached? Let's call him," I said.

"I'm afraid we can't do that. He doesn't want to be disturbed," was the reply I received.

"Mr. Brown, that's not a Japanese name either," I pressed.

"Oh he's not Japanese, he's British," Mr. Yamaha explained.

"Then he should know what wrestling is all about. Gimmicks, liars and cheaters. That's what the fans want, not merit. You of all people should know that, and to hell with the formalities. Johnny, don't make any plans for tomorrow night, I'm taking you to dinner. Jay would you like to come also?" I said.

"No thank you, I have plans," he said.

"Jay, you call your Mr. Brown, tell him I'll be here at 9:00 a.m. I want to see him. I'll change his mind or I'll buy the place and throw him out," I stated.

My last brainstorm came to me on the spot. What better way to end the confusion I face of trying to be two people at once, which in the end, would surely have to meet.

"I'll see you tomorrow at 9:00 a.m. sharp."

I left, pausing outside to stare into the gym. Sometimes I even amazed myself. I headed back to the apartment to redesign my game plan. I stopped at the one store that I knew sold American beer. Lee and I pretty well finished off everything I had back at the apartment. I guess in the back of my mind I was hoping for an encore of last night. Every time I closed my eyes I could see her breast, laying there, staring at me, calling me towards it. How I wanted to touch it, caress it, have it guide me to the rest of her creamy white body.

"One thousand yen," a voice said.

I snapped out of my daydream and looked up to see the cashier holding my beer.

All thoughts of sex had vanished from my mind when my eyes met up with the old clerk's wrinkly face. I threw the money on the counter, grabbed the beer and left. I arrived at the apartment, it was quiet as I entered the lobby. Usually there would be someone around. The building was huge, thirty-eight stories high and about three-years-old. It looks North American on the inside; it was like being in New York or L.A. I heard it was built that way to attract the business moguls that came here from North America and Europe. Feeling spry I thought I would take the stairs. I strolled up the three flights with ease. As I grabbed for the handle on the door I heard the elevator bell. A sound I knew well, my apartment was right next to it. You would think with all the research I did in setting up the second murder I would have picked one of the better apartments in the building. But I knew I had to be next to Ursula's apartment, after all she was going to help me with Dave's murder, even though she didn't know it yet.

CHAPTER 6

The camera in the prison is pointing at me. I can feel the warmth of the light that is illuminating the room for the camera. Adam sure has done his homework. He knows exactly when to cut to me, and when to cue Mark with the videos. As the light goes off, dropping the temperature a couple of degrees, I can see out of the corner of my eye the stairwell of the apartment building on the monitor behind Emily. From behind, the character playing me looks like Dr. Evil of Mike Myers fame. Of course it isn't—Austin Powers didn't hit the big screen until after the murder. Now that I think about it, maybe that 'Fat Bastard' got his inspiration from my Dr. Death wrestling character. Anyway back to my story.

I paused at the door peering through the glass. I still had Lee's key in my pocket and I wanted her to be alone when I gave it back. I only caught a glimpse of her flaxen hair, but I could see it was Ursula boarding the elevator. Once I heard the rumble of the car as it plummeted back to Earth, I stepped through the door. I walked the fifty feet down the corridor and paused outside Lee's apartment. I set down the beer and reached into my pants pocket and pulled out the key. It fell towards the ground, making a clinking sound as it grazed one of the beer bottles. The strap became tight. I swung it up, catching it in my right hand. I looked at the key and then the lock. Knowing Ursula had already left, I debated opening the door. It was Lee's day at work. The apartment would be empty. I fixed the key in my hand and reached towards the lock. I slid it into the tumblers, like a surgeon performing laparoscopic surgery. It clicked several times as its nubs banged against each tumbler as it went by them. It was almost erotic. I took a look over my shoulder as I felt a presence staring at me. I was just about to turn the key when my eye caught the black globe that entombed the security camera. I withdrew the key quickly. In spotting the camera I realized that anyone in the building could see me by turning his or her television to Channel 103. I picked up the beer, slapped myself on the forehead to give any viewers the impression that I had the wrong apartment and headed to my door, slid my key into the lock, opened the door and disappeared behind it.

Even though it was daylight outside, the apartment was dark inside. The windows had a special tint on them to decrease the glare on the computer monitors. I also kept my blinds drawn most of the time. I could see a flickering red light from across the room, there was a message on the answering machine. I reached over to the switch on the wall, and turned on a lamp that was stationed beside the television. I figured the call was from Mr. Yamaha, trying to reach Bill Brown, the owner of the gym. I walked over to the phone and hit the rewind button on the answering machine. As it reset itself to start, I yanked on the chain of the blinds and cracked them open, allowing a bead of light to split the room in two. The machine beside the phone made a click and then silenced again. I hit the play button and headed toward the kitchen to put the beer in the fridge.

"Mr. Brown," the crackling voice in the background stammered. "Are you there? It's Mr. Yamaha. I'd like to set up an appointment tomorrow morning to speak with you. We had a gentleman in today that wants to be a manager for Mr. Sashi. He would like to talk to you. I hope you get this message. I'll call you tomorrow, good-bye Mr. Brown." I headed to the bathroom. Just as I reached the bathroom door the machine started again, I paused.

"Hello," a woman's voice said. "Darryl, I hope it's Darryl. The machine said Mr. Brown was not in, I hope I have the right number. Anyway it's Lee, Kitama. Darryl if this is you, I think I lost my key at your place. I'm home sick from work today. If you have my key can you bring it over? Ursula is going to work around eleven. Just knock on the door, if no one answers, let yourself in, there's a table beside the door that you can put the key on. The door will lock behind you, thanks."

I walked back over to the machine and rewound the tape. I sat on the couch for a minute and flicked on the TV. I turned to CNN, thank God for satellite TV. I sat there in a stupor just staring at the TV, not really paying attention yet knowing what I was watching. I snapped out of it when I saw a picture of Lily up in the corner beside the reporters head, I turned up the volume.

"Lily Springwall, suspected accomplice of Hal, the unknown killer has been cleared of all suspicion in the death of Cheryl Hopkins, the actress who was gunned down in a theater in Tucson. Four months of questioning hasn't brought the police any closer to finding her killer. After the shooting of Ms. Hopkins live on stage, the killer who was standing in for Lily just vanished. The only lead the police have is an unknown man by the name of Hal. No one knows him or has seen him since. We go live now to Police Chief Crompton who has called a press conference on the matter," the reporter said.

Police Chief Crompton was now speaking on the screen. "I called you here to bring you up to date on the matter. Ms. Springwall who was never really a suspect in the case has cooperated fully with the police. Donald McDonald, a Hollywood agent has not been found. If you are out there we would like to question you. You are not a suspect. The female that Hal used as a cosmetician has not been located either. This composite sketch is all we have to go on. I urge you, wherever you are, to please come forward. You are not suspects; we just want to question you. We also have a composite of Hal. He's believed to be between twenty-five and thirty-five years old, about six feet tall, 160-180 lbs. white male. Anyone with any information is asked to call headquarters at 555-978-1212. I will now take three questions."

I sat there dumbfounded listening to the Police Chief. I thought the investigation would have ended by now. With no leads to go on, I figured the case would have turned cold.

"You, sir," the Chief on the television continued while he pointed toward someone in the crowd.

"Yes, Chief Crompton, is there any lead on the identity of the man named Hal?"

"I'm afraid not, the storefront that was used, was rented for a year and paid in full, cash up front. The only name used was Hal. Go ahead," the Chief pointed at someone in the crowd.

"What about the limo used to pick up Lily, and the airplane

used to take them to L.A?" The anonymous person asked.

"The limo used was from a rental agency, again cash up front and all we've got is Hal. Now the airline tickets, that's a different story. The suspect bought them online and used a MasterCard. We are currently checking receipts and locating the ISP used to purchase them."

"Look all you want," I yelled at the T.V. "I'm not that stupid. This is a very well thought out plan." I remembered back to how simple getting a MasterCard was. All I did was walk into an apartment building, grabbed someone's pre-approved letter sent to them saying they've already been qualified for a Platinum MasterCard with a $25,000 limit, fill in some of the spots on the form and sent it back, sure I had to keep an eye on the person's mail for awhile until the postman actually brought the card about five weeks later. First a security number came and then a couple days later the card came. Once I had both, I just called and activated it, easy peasy. Once I had it activated I went online and ordered the airline tickets. I used the address and phone number of the storefront.

"As far as the ISP goes, Chief Crompton, go and check out Joe's Spider Café," I yelled at the TV. I had gone to the Spider, sat there at the computer and ordered the tickets. Lily and Tom picked them up at the airport.

"Last question," Chief Crompton said as he pointed into the crowd.

"Is it true that Jack Stevenson could be involved in the murder?"

My ears perked up.

"Well it is a fact that Mr. Stevenson was known to the victim. They did attend the same high school in Florida. We are currently checking out that lead. We have it from a reliable source that Ms. Hopkins betrayed him back then, and since Mr. Stevenson went on national TV with his outrageous scheme, it is a possibility. Thank you for your time, that is all the questions for now," the Chief said.

The station then cut back to the reporter at the desk.

"Now on with the World News..."

I grabbed the remote and shut off the TV. I got off the couch and went to the kitchen for a can of Coke. I leaned into the counter to reach in the top cupboard for a glass and felt Lee's key press into my thigh through my pocket.

"Shit," I said aloud. I forgot to return her key.

I set the glass on the counter, reached in my pocket and took out the key. I put the keychain around my neck so I wouldn't forget, grabbed a can of Coke from the fridge and poured myself a glass. I drank about half of it. I set the half finished glass on the counter, grabbed my keys and headed out into the hall towards Lee's apartment. After seeing the CNN report I was even more aware of the camera at the end of the hall. I reached her door and gave it a firm knock and waited for a response. After about twenty seconds with no response, I knocked again. Still no answer. I knew Ursula was out, but Lee was supposed to be home. I remember her saying on the answering machine to open the door and put the key on the table inside. Still feeling watched by the camera I took the strap from around my neck and slid the key into the lock and turned it. With the forward pressure I had put on the key, as I turned it, the door opened slightly. I opened it far enough to quietly call for Lee. I wanted her to hear, but if she was sleeping, or should I say sleeping it off, I didn't want to wake her. I could hear a radio playing quietly from a room down the hall. Her apartment had the same layout as mine so I judged it was coming from one of the two bedrooms at the end of the hall. I called again, this time a touch louder. There was still no response. I could see the table just inside the door against a small wall. I had to enter the apartment if I was going to be able to set the key on it. I was still holding onto the key, which was still nestled inside the lock. I eased it out and stepped inside the apartment. It was a lot cozier than mine. They actually had some paintings on the walls and plants were scattered here and there. My apartment definitely paled in comparison. They had knick-knacks scattered throughout the place and it looked like a home, it had a warm feeling about it. The oak mantle above the fireplace was congested with picture frames. I couldn't really tell of whom, as I was too far away. A noise from down the hall caught my attention. A familiar noise but it wasn't coming from the radio. It was the shower. I could hear the water as it bounced off its surroundings. My heart started to pound faster. It was beating with excitement knowing it was probably Lee in the shower, my mind took me back to last night and the image of Lee on my couch, her breast lying exposed, I could feel my cock twitch inside my pants. I wasn't sure whether I should leave now or try to catch a glimpse of her in the shower. I know it sounds perverse, but my thoughts led me to the latter. I eased the door shut. Just off to the right was a hall where the two bedrooms would exit off, one going left and one going right. The shower was directly at the end, if you were standing in the bathroom doorway looking in, the sink would be to your left, the toilet and the bidet would be on your right, and the tub which housed the shower was straight ahead. I slowly crept forward and stopped where the wall ended. I turned and glanced to my right, the bathroom door was wide open. I pulled my head back as my heart began the race. Here I was in her apartment with Lee just twenty feet away, stark naked. I turned back and put my back against the wall. I was leaning on a coat, which was draped from the middle hook of a three-hook rack, actually all the hooks had a coat hanging from them. Judging from where I was I felt well camouflaged between them. I stared straight ahead trying to take deep quiet breaths to slow my heart that was pounding like a drum. It was so loud I'm sure if the shower wasn't drowning out the noise, Lee would be able to hear it. As I glanced in the living room I spotted a mirror on the east wall. In it I could see the reflection of the hallway. I maneuvered myself another six inches to the right, and there she was. I could now see directly down the hall into the bathroom, again my heart started beating faster. I could see her standing in the shower behind the clear glass doors. Her body was more beautiful than I imagined.

I put my one hand over my heart to muffle the sound, and with my other hand I pulled the coat resting beside me over a bit so I would blend in, my hand was aching from squeezing the key so tight. She grabbed a towel from her right and threw it over her head and began drying it. I could feel my penis going limp as the blood started to exit. I glanced back at the image in the mirror, when all of a sudden I dropped the key as something grazed my calf muscle. It was Lee's damn cat. It must have sensed I was feeling amorous, and came for some action, running its body back and forth above my ankle. I sure as hell was horny, but that wasn't the kind of pussy I had in mind.

I look away from the monitor as I say that and give Emily a wink. She just rolls her eyes as Mark continues with the tape. I can feel now, even as I watch the reenactment that I have a chub on. It's a good thing I am sitting at a table, I think to myself.

I had tried to grab the key as it plummeted towards the ground, but with no luck. It hit the floor with a bang.

"Hello, who's there, hello?" Lee's voice called out.

I shooed the cat away.

"Hello," her voice yelled again.

"Meow," the cat whimpered.

"Tabby is that you? What are you doing?"

"Meow," the cat said again as it started to wander down the hall.

"I'll be out in a minute," she said. It's funny how people talk to their animals as if they were human. Sometimes we expect them to answer.

I heard the roar of the hair dryer start up as I looked back in the mirror. There was Lee still naked rubbing her hands over her hair trying to dry it. Her firm breasts pulled even tighter with the extension of her arms. I bent down and grabbed the key and quietly opened the door. I snuck around it and exited to the hall. Pulling it softly shut, I glanced up the camera with a guilty look of a child being caught with his hand in the cookie jar. I headed back to my apartment. Once inside I finished the glass of Coke I started earlier. I could feel in my pants that my penis had shrunk. It was almost as is if it knew it was bad and was trying to hide. I grabbed a cigarette and lit it. I plopped on the couch and enjoyed it, right down to the butt before putting it out.

As I sit here in the jail watching the videos I can almost taste the cigarette. Since being incarcerated I have pretty much given it up. Twenty-three hours of isolation left only one hour a day that I am allowed outside in the yard to enjoy a smoke. Well actually about five or six smokes, and it wasn't actually in the yard. The other inmates have full access for eight to ten hours a day. The 'Fryers' are let outside in the 'kennels.' The 'kennels' are long fenced areas, like a dog run, hence the name. It is twenty feet long and six feet wide, completely fenced in on all sides and the top. The cement floor is painted green except for a one-foot area on each side and the end where it is painted red. The red is there to remind you that the fence is electric. There are four runs in all, each separated by an eight-foot area of grass, where armed guards patrol each grassy corridor, three in all. Even though they put us out four at a time we are only allowed to engage in some small talk. Anything more and we are whisked away inside and our time is up. The guards hand you a pack of smokes as you go out. Once inside the kennel the guards light you up a smoke using a gauntlet, much like they use in church for lighting the candles at Christmas.

Once your smoke is lit, you have to use it to light any more you want. Once it goes out, you can't smoke anymore. This is a real pain in the ass when it rains, because there isn't any shelter. We all smoke. You don't think much about cancer when you're going to die anyway. It just doesn't matter much. They yell, "clear one," five seconds later, "clear two," and then five seconds after that you hear the fence hum. You learn very quickly to get back to the green line before you hear the hum.

I shake my head and continue with my story.

I finished my smoke in my apartment and headed back to Lee's. I knocked on the door again and waited. I was just about to knock again when I could see the light through the peephole disappear and the doorknob turn.

"Hi Darryl," Lee greeted me.

"Hi," I said. Lee was standing in her housecoat. I could see that she was partially dressed underneath because I caught a glimpse of her bra strap. "Here's your key."

"Thanks, come on in."

"No, it's okay. I've got a lot of work to do." I wanted to, but the temptation to seduce her was becoming more and more apparent each time I saw her.

"I'm going to make some tea."

"All right, for a bit." So much for controlling myself.

I handed her the key and walked into her apartment.

"Grab a seat," she said pointing to the living room. "I'll put the kettle on."

I walked six steps in the living room, two more than I had ventured before.

- CRIMINAL JUSTICE -

"Nice place," I yelled.

"Thanks. Same layout as yours," Lee explained.

"I see that."

I ventured into the living room, funny thing, but I didn't notice before, she had no sofas or chairs, just low tables with cushions around them. I grabbed one of the cushions and sat down.

"Ursula's idea," she said. "She wanted to be authentic, and besides she was here first. I'm just a roomy."

It took a minute before it dawned on me what she was talking about.

"Oh the furniture, what a nice touch," I said.

"Speaking of nice touches, what's with the head, I didn't want to say anything last night, but now that we know each other better."

"It's for a job I'm doing."

"What job?"

"Have dinner with me tomorrow night and I'll let you know, and bring Ursula, I'm bringing my business partner. I'll fill you in then."

Lee returned with the tea.

"It's Tetley," she said, none of that Japanese stuff.

I started to stand up to grab my cup.

"Stay seated," she said as she knelt down and then sat on a cushion, she took a sip of her tea. "There's honey or sugar, which do you prefer?"

"Honey," I said as I grabbed the bottle.

"Yes dear?" she laughed.

"No I meant I'd take some honey," I said oblivious to her joke.

"Duh."

I loved her wit, it matched her face, cute.

"Damn cushion," she said as she fidgeted to get comfortable.

"So you were sick this morning?" I asked.

"Must have been something I drank," she said with a smile.

"Must have been," I said before sipping my tea.

We sat and chatted for bit, not really about anything, yet about everything.

"Listen I have to go," I said as I struggled to get up. "Tell Ursula about tomorrow night, my treat."

"Where are we going?" she asked.

"I haven't decided yet, it won't be any place fancy."

I put out my hand and helped her up. How I wanted to pull her close, but I didn't. I wandered to the door and opened it.

"I'll call when I'm ready to come by."

"OK it's a date then," she said as she closed the door behind me. I was unsure whether the date part was a joke or not, but I hoped not. I went back to my apartment and ran the tub, it was only mid-afternoon, I just wanted to soak and relax. While the bathtub was filling I went into the bedroom and stripped down and tossed my clothes on the floor. I walked back to the bathroom, shut off the water and climbed into the tub. I must have dozed off because it didn't seem like any time at all had gone by but the water was cold and my hands were wrinkled. I stepped out of the tub, pulled the plug and grabbed a towel and went into the bedroom. I threw the towel on the bed and fell into it. Another great sensation, air-drying, just lying there letting the droplets dry on your skin. It seems to tighten it, making you feel younger. The phone rang in the other room. I got up and answered it.

"Hello?" I said.

"Hi, it's Lee, tomorrow's great, Ursula can make it."

"Great, see you then."

"Oh yeah, I was going to ask you, who's Mr. Brown?" She questioned.

"Mr. Brown?" I said a bit confused.

"Your answering machine, I called and it said it was Mr. Brown," she explained.

"Must of been the guy that had the apartment before me, the answering machine was here when I rented the apartment," I answered easily.

"Oh," she said.

I could sense the disbelief in her voice.

"How did you get this number?" I asked.

"Last night, when I was in your apartment, I looked at the number on the phone."

"And you remembered, even after all those beers?" I asked,

impressed.

"What can I say, I've got a good memory."

"Okay, goodbye." I hung up the phone.

I went into the kitchen and made some supper, macaroni and cheese, the bachelor's delight. I sat on the couch naked and ate my meal as I watched a rerun of I Love Lucy in Japanese. Somehow it seemed funnier in a foreign language. I knew the faces but the show made no sense. I grabbed a pen and paper and started to write out the lines I would need to put in the computer's answering machine for tomorrow. I rehearsed it a few times until I got it right. I clicked on the machine and read the lines. I only had a few minutes, and I would have to time the pauses right. When I was finished I threw the dead bolt on the door and crawled in bed. I was exhausted, it was still early but I retired for the night anyway.

CHAPTER 7

The alarm shattered the silence. I stumbled out of bed, hardon and all. It's funny how I don't remember the dreams but five out of seven times a week I wake up with a hardon. The cool air in the apartment soon ended that. I got dressed, grabbed a big glass of Coke and headed to the gym. It was early, about 8:30 in the morning.

"Hi Johnny," I said as I approached him. "Where's Jay?"

"Not here yet Mr. White."

"I told you to call me Darryl," I said.

"Yes Sir Mr. White," he repeated himself.

I sat and watched him as he did his stretches, nice kid. I needed him for my plans, but he wouldn't get hurt. The same with Ursula, she too would play a key role, it's just that neither of them knew it yet. Jay arrived at a quarter to nine. You could see the worried look on his face. "What's up Jay? You look like you've lost your best friend?"

"Nothing Mr. White. I just don't think Mr. Brown is going to like the idea of a gimmick."

"That's why your gym is losing money. You need something controversial in this industry if you're going to make it. Whether it's Japan or the United States. Bullshit sells. Did you get a hold of Mr. Brown to tell him I was coming in?" I asked.

"No sir, I left a message."

"Okay well I hope he comes in, where's the office?"

"Right over there sir," he said as he pointed to the stairs.

"Okay I'll meet you up there in five minutes, I just have to step out and make a quick call."

I took my cell phone out of its holster and headed outside. The air was brisk and it really made me feel alive for the first time a long time. Lee had helped that process, but having my plans for murder number two kick-started me into gear, it gave me a renewed feeling. I dialed my apartment phone number on my cell phone.

"Hello," the voice with an English accent said, it was my voice and it didn't sound bad. A little James Bondish I think.

Emily rolls her eyes as I look up at her.

I just throw my hands in the air, "what can I say?" Even though we are allowed to talk in the room as the videos air, there is very little conversation apart from the odd banter back and forth. We are all enthralled with the story and I am hoping the whole world is, too.

The answering machine in the video continues.

"Hello," my cell phone echoed. I pressed the # key.

"Please enter your password," the sexy computer generated voice said. I hit my password buttons in order.

"To reset the machine, press 1." I started to walk back into the gym, hesitating, waiting for the right moment to press the #1 button. When I reached the bottom the stairs I hit the button. This reset the answering machine on the computer to standby. I wanted to make sure it worked. I headed through the door as I reached the top of the stairs.

"OK Jay, give him a call."

Jay picked up the receiver and dialed the number.

"Put on the speakerphone, I want to hear and talk to him as well."

Jay hit the speaker button and hung up the receiver. I could hear over the speaker that the line was busy.

"There's no answer, Mr. White."

"Try again." I yelled.

I pulled my cell phone out and pressed the end button. I had deliberately kept the line busy on the answering machine until I knew Jay was calling. Jay hit the speaker button and then redialed. The phone began to ring.

"Hello," my English voice on the other end said. It sounded okay but it would never fly in the U.K.

"Hello, Mr. Brown, this is Mr. Yamaha."

"Yes Mr. Yamaha what would you like?" The answering machine replied.

I raised my arm up to signal Jay to stop talking.

"Mr. Brown," I said. "This is Darryl White."

"What can I do for you Mr. White?"

"Please, call me Darryl."

"And you can call me Bob."

"Yes Sir," I said as I kept glancing at my note pad and stopwatch, I had started it as I started talking. I knew exactly what I had said on the machine and how much time I had allowed for a response. I had to make sure that I could finish my lines before the voice on the machine talked again.

"So why did you ring me?" the answering machine asked.

"Well Bob, I've come over here from North America with a pocket full of cash." I said.

"I like the sounds of it already."

"I found your gym while wandering one day. I have a flair for the dramatic, and I wish to incorporate it in the business world."

"How can I help?" the machine questioned.

"I found a young wrestler here at the gym and I'd like to change the way your gym runs."

"Continue."

"Well you see Bob, all the formalities and technical style of wrestling just don't cut it the real world. I'd like to change that."

"How would you suggest doing that?" my English voice on the recording asked.

"I'd like to add the dramatics of North America to your wrestling and make a name for your gym in the mainstream Japanese wrestling market."

"I've seen the North American style of wrestling and I'm not interested in all the sex that goes on. As far as the Japanese wrestling, it's alright, a little showy though."

"You think showy doesn't sell? Look at the revenue your gym brings in...."

"What revenue?" asked the machine.

"Exactly, you bring in approximately three hundred spectators a month. A match in Tokyo brings in three thousand, you do the math." I said, as I believed I was talking to a real person.

"Yes," the voice continued. "When I bought the gym I was hoping to see some profits, but I haven't yet."

"That's what I'm talking about, profits. I know I can turn this place around. I can make a name for it. What do you think?" I asked.

"I like the old style."

"Old style is for fish and chips, not wrestling."

"Fish and chips, now you're talking. You open a good fish and chip store here, and you can make money. I'm tired of all the raw fish these Japanese eat. It's certainly not England."

"I know this great place for fish and chips, only a few blocks away," I told the computer.

"Tell you what Darryl, meet me at the gym tomorrow around 11:00 a.m. and we'll do lunch at that restaurant you're talking about. I'll listen to your proposal. If the food is as good as you say and I like your idea, we'll work something out. What does Mr. Yamaha think about the idea?" the computer uttered.

"I haven't told him yet, I'll discuss it with him tonight if he's free." Jay looked at me and nodded.

"Okay it's a date Darryl, I'll see you at the gym. Tally-Ho." The computer said as its final line.

"Good-bye." I said and hit the speaker button on the phone and hung up. "Okay Jay, tonight at 7:00 p.m. can you pick Johnny up?"

"Yes sir, Mr. White." Jay replied.

"Alright then, I'll pick up the girls and meet you at the Tempura, oh yeah, and bring your wife," I said as headed down the stairs to ringside where Johnny was sparring. "Johnny," I yelled. He turned his head to look at me and was clothes lined by his opponent, knocking him off his feet. His head landed just short of the ropes beside me, there was a stunned look on his face. "Johnny, two things, first of all Jay will pick you up tonight for a supper meeting, and the second thing is, always keep your head up." I smiled and made my way to the door.

"Stay tuned to see how Jack pulled off his double identity." Emily breaks in.

I can see that Jimmy is getting edgy behind the glass. After all it is hard for him to just sit there listening to me talk. Even I'm having a hard time. Thank God for the videos.

"I'll take Jimmy for some ice cream at the cafeteria," Father Joe says, standing up.

Jimmy is now standing up, smiling, he knows the words ice cream. Wes slides open the bolt on the door. Father Joe exits.

"How's everyone holding up?" Adam yells through the microphone.

"Okay but I could use a bit to eat. Ice cream sounds good to me," I reply.

Rocco pops his head in the door. "Emily, do you want anything?"

"I'll have some ice cream too."

"Okay just don't spoil your supper," he adds. "Especially you, Jack, it'll be your last." He laughs as he shut the door. I hear the bolt engage as it shuts.

"It's been a long day, hasn't it?" Emily asks.

"Yeah, tomorrow may never get here I hope," I chuckle. I can see on the monitor the Netmercial is almost over. I would make millions in corporate advertising, I donated it to the housing project I started in South Dakota. I bought two thousand acres of land, construction is to begin next week. Seth, Rocco and Wes are moving there to run it. It's going to be set up like a large camp for troubled youth, a sort of halfway house, for kids in trouble with the law. They would be able to get an education and earn money while working the land and learn a skilled trade. Once they graduate they could be released. A job in the community would be guaranteed. It would be a locked down facility, only not as visible as in prison. The guards have been with me every minute of their shift, day in and day out. We've sat many a time looking through the bars of my cell, engaged in some very deep conversations.

The Keycoast facility is closing a month after my execution. Some of the cottages will be given to the Warden and Mrs. Howard. It will be turned into a retirement village. Five of the cottages are for Mrs. Howard's brothers and sisters, all of which are already in retirement. Mr. Howard only had one brother who died in the war. Of course the Howards will live there the rest of their life for free. Adam, Mark and their wives are going to move to one of my two islands in Fiji, rent free, they are going to turn it into a studio for their filmmaking. Adam and Mark are independent filmmakers and two of my best friends. They wanted to do a documentary on me from rags to riches. The large island off the coast of Fiji I'm giving to Emily. She jokingly remarked that it would make a great venue for a nude reality show. Emily, who was a freelance journalist from the Southwest, had tried several times to get my story. I granted her wish for the news conference that shocked the world. Once I started carrying out my plans, I became a little more elusive. I'd keep in touch now and then, never letting them know where I was.

"You're on in three, two, one," Adam says.

"Welcome back, continue Jack with your story," Emily says into the camera. The camera light goes off which is my cue to pick up where I left off.

I headed out of the gym and back to the apartment. I had to set up the computer for tomorrow's phone call. I wanted to pass my plans by Jay and Johnny first to hook Jay into believing that this was for real. All in all, I think I did well. When I was done I grabbed a beer and sat in the tub. Since Mom's death I preferred the tub to a shower, it gave me a warm nurturing feeling. Now there's a topic for Freud. I must have dozed off, because the clanking of the pipes between the walls suddenly awakened me. It was a great apartment, but whenever one of the girls next door shut their shower off, the pipes rattled between the walls. I glanced at my watch, it was a 5:45 p.m. I pulled the plug and got out of the bathtub. As I reached for the towel I could see how wrinkled I was. I must have been in the water for a long time. I threw a towel around myself and called Lee.

"Hi Lee, It's Darryl, you girls still on for tonight?"

"Yep," Lee said. "Ursula just stepped out of the shower. We'll be over in about forty-five minutes. Are you going to drive?"

"No I thought we'd take a taxi, after all we may be drinking." I guess that was my next step. I'll have to rent another car so Mr. White could drive one.

"You can count on that, good idea," she said.

I picked up beer today, if you want you can come over for one."

"In forty five minutes I could down three!" She laughed.

"I don't doubt that."

"I'll let Ursula know and I'll be right over. Where are we going anyway? Is jeans and a T-shirt alright?"

"Sounds good to me."

"OK see you."

"Bye," I hung up the phone, sprayed on a little cologne, got dressed and went to the fridge and cracked open a couple of beers. There was a gentle knock at the door. "Come in," I yelled, as I walked towards it, it opened.

"Hi Darryl."

"Hi, here you go." I handed Lee a beer.

"I'm starting to like you," she said.

"I'm glad for that," what a lame response I thought to myself.

"So, where are we going?"

"The Tempura, a buffet on the east side of town."

"Isn't it all the east side over here?"

"Ha, Ha," I chuckled. "I've asked a couple of friends from the gym, I hope you don't mind."

"What gym?"

There was a knock at the door. I got up and answered it.

"Hi," Ursula said.

"Come on in, would you like a beer?"

"Sure."

"Grab a seat and I'll get you one."

When I came out of the kitchen I noticed that Ursula had taken my spot next to Lee on the couch. I set her beer down and grabbed mine.

"I'm sorry, were you sitting here?" she asked.

"It's okay stay there, this chair's fine," I said.

This was actually a better seat, the two of them looked so beautiful in their jeans and tight T-shirts.

"So Darryl, you were saying you've invited a couple of friends from the gym?" Lee asked.

"Yeah I've been doing some photography down there for a local magazine."

"Sounds exiting," Ursula commented. "Sexy too, all those hard bodies."

"No, it's a wrestling gym."

"Wresting, I love wrestling," Ursula stated.

Like I didn't know that I thought to myself, that's why she was here.

"Any cute ones?" Ursula asked.

"Well there's one, he's around your age, the other is older and is bringing his wife."

"What does he look like?"

"There she goes again," Lee said. "Talking about guys."

"Just because you're not looking doesn't mean that I can't."

"What's the occasion?" Lee asked. "Social or business?"

"Business," I said. "I'll fill you all in tonight." I grabbed another beer each and called a cab. We sat drinking, engaged in idle chitchat. Ursula kept pressing me for details about Johnny but I kept changing the subject.

About ten minutes later my buzzer sounded. I got up from the chair, pressed the little black button beside the door, "be right down," I yelled into the speaker. "Drink up girls, your chariot awaits."

Ursula set her beer down while Lee guzzled hers back. "Ready," she said.

They both stood up and we all left. When we reached the lobby, the doorman held the door open. The cabby had the back door of the cab open. The girls climbed in and he shut the door. I grabbed the handle of the front passenger door, opened it and got in.

"The Tempura please," I said to the driver, he nodded and drove off. The girls talked and giggled most of the way there. I just kept looking out the front window of the cab. It was almost seven when we arrived at the Tempura. The sky was gray and drab, much like I was feeling. I'm not sure why I was in a glum mood. It could have been the two beers I had. They left me feeling kind of bloated. It could have been the anticipation of the meeting, or maybe it was just life itself, the dilemma I have created. Even though the bastards I was going to kill all deserved it, I often wondered if I was doing the right thing. Who was I to control life, just because I had the time and the money to do whatever I wanted, should I? What about their families, their loved ones, people that would be affected, people that I'm not even aware of. I remember after killing Cheryl, watching the broadcast on the news of the grieving family members pleading for the killer to give himself up. That's something I've always wondered, why is it mostly men that are murderers.

"Darryl, you coming?" asked a voice in the distance.

My gaze became focused as I snapped back into reality.

Ursula called my name again, this time pointing at the little old Japanese man holding the door open and bowing at me. I reached in my pocket, grabbed a couple of bills and handed them to him as I bowed. Lee was already inside talking to the hostess. The Tempura was a Japanese-American restaurant. They catered to the North American market with their steaks and burgers, but they were expensive. The inside wasn't very glamorous. There were more luxurious places just down the street, but I felt this place would make most of tonight's gang feel right at home. Jay and his wife were the only pure-bred Japanese, and on his income, I'm sure he hasn't had a good steak in a while. As far as his wife goes, from the research I did, all I really know is that they've only been married five years.

I had made reservations and I figured Lee must have known as she now had the hostess leading us to our table. We had a small room in the back that I had requested. It was adorned with football memorabilia, they also had a room for hockey, baseball and basketball. I was always a Buccaneers fan, not living too far from Tampa. We sat down and ordered three beers. From where I was sitting I could not see the front door, but I'm sure Johnny and the Yamahas could find us. I had called them and told them I made reservations under my name and to dress casual.

"So where's your company?" Ursula asked. "What do they look like?"

"Well Jay's about five-foot-four, I'm not too sure about his wife, all I know is she's Japanese, and Johnny, he's tall, half American and looks Hawaiian."

"I think they're here now," Ursula said as she cocked her head out the door.

I stood up and made my way to the room opening to greet them. As they arrived it suddenly dawned on me that I had never told Jay or Johnny that I was a photographer, well not really, but that's what the girls thought. Jay knows me as an American loud mouth. I had told Lee that I had some money, but not to the extent that I had told Jay.

The hostess walked through the door and extended her arms towards the table and bowed, Johnny entered first, he was dressed in a pair of creamy colored dress pants, a black shirt buttoned to the neck and a blazer. Jay who was in a suit followed him. Behind him was Mrs. Yamaha I assumed. She looked like she just stepped from the pages of *Geisha Daily*. She was petite and beautiful. She had on a lovely kimono and her hair was done up on her head and held their by a couple of chopsticks, I'm sure they weren't chopsticks, but they looked like it. I bowed as she entered. She smiled and bowed back.

"Jay, Mrs. Yamaha, Johnny this is Lee and Ursula, my next-door neighbours." The girls rose and bowed, Ursula smiling at Johnny. "Have a seat," I said as I pulled out the chair to my right for Mrs. Yamaha. She bowed again, didn't say a word and sat. "Jay," I said as I pointed to the chair beside his wife. "Johnny that put's you at the other head of the table opposite me." I purposely arranged it so I had Lee to my left and Ursula and Johnny would be near to each other. As we got arranged the waitress came in with our beers. "What will the rest of you have?" I asked.

"I'll have a Coke," Johnny said.

"Coke?" Ursula said. "Have a beer."

"I'm not much of a drinker, Coke is fine for now."

As the video plays I see Emily watching Adam eat his bowl of ice cream. She looks at him, holds up her arms and mouths, "Where the hell is mine?" Just then the bolt on the door slides open. Rocco enters carrying two dishes of ice cream. He sets mine down in front of me and hands the other to Emily.

"You're having a beer," the actress playing Ursula said on the video.

Johnny just smiled.

"We'll have two green teas please," Jay said to the waitress. Mrs. Yamaha just nodded.

I was beginning to think she couldn't talk, it was probably because she couldn't speak English.

"So Jay, what's with the duds? I thought I said casual."

"Respect, Mr. White. Respect," A voice from the doorway snapped.

I looked at the doorway to my right and there was Mr. Hashito. I forgot about him, he was the manager of the gym. He hadn't been there for a couple of days and I completely forgot about him, he was totally unaware of what was going on.

I had not met him as Darryl yet.

"And you are?" I said as I stood up.

"Mr. Hashito, the gym manager. What's going on?"

Jay cowered in his chair a bit.

Sit up I thought, you used to be his boss before I bought the gym. Hashito was a robust man. A hard ass. That's probably why he was in management.

"What do you mean sir?" I asked.

He took a step back out of the doorway, reached behind him and grabbed a chair. As he pulled it around in front of him he stepped towards Johnny. "Move over Mr. Sashi," he said as he set the chair down.

Johnny slid his chair from the end of the table to his right beside Ursula. She moved a bit towards Lee, who moved closer to me. I didn't mind.

The waitress came back with the drinks for Johnny and the Yamahas. She turned, and asked Mr. Hashito something in Japanese. Whatever it was, I could tell he said no by the way he raised his hand and shook his head. "I'm only going to be a minute," he said. "I just want to know what's going on, why am I left in the dark about this stunt you're trying to pull?"

"What do you mean?" I asked again.

"My club will not submit to your pranks and gimmicks. I run a professional gym and it is known for its respect, not its gimmicks."

"I thought Mr. Brown owned the gym?"

"Yes, but I run it. I say what goes on." he said as he turned to Jay. "How come I have to hear this from Mr. Khaki?" Khaki was a wrestler at the gym.

Jay sank in his chair, drank some of his tea and said, "Well sir, we weren't trying to hide anything, you just haven't been in the gym the last two days."

"You have my number."

"Yes sir, but...."

"It's my fault," I jumped in. "I sprang this on him yesterday. He's not even aware of the facts yet. That's why we are here now, to discuss them."

"No need for that," Mr. Hashito said. "I make all the decisions, not Mr. Yamaha."

He started to stand, pointing his finger at me as he did.

"Now you, I'll meet you at the gym at eleven tomorrow morning, when Mr. Brown comes in we will discuss it. But don't get your hopes up. Enjoy your meal," he said. He went to the doorway, bowed to us and left.

"What the hell was that about?" asked Lee.

"I'm not sure," I said. "I brought you all here to tell you my plans and to see what you thought. I didn't know about Mr. Hashito. I thought you were in charge Jay?"

"No sir, Mr. Hashito is in charge." Jay said as he lowered his head in shame. "The gym was struggling and I needed more money. Mr. Hashito lent it to me as long as he could be in charge. When Mr. Brown bought the business from me, most of my money from the sale went to pay Mr. Hashito back. I had to convince Mr. Brown to keep all of us on."

"Enough of the past," I said. "Let's get on with the future. I brought you here as friends and co-workers. Some of you know me as a photographer and some as a rich Texan. Well I'm not a photographer. I do have a fair bit of money. It was left to me when my parents died. I am from Texas. The only part I lied about was being a photographer."

Johnny stood up to pull his chair back to his spot at the end of a table.

"It's ok Johnny," Ursula said as she grabbed his arm. "You can stay here."

I was glad to see it. A very important part of my plan was to have the two of them hit it off.

"Well the real reason I came to Japan was to fill a childhood fantasy. I want to become a pro wrestling manager. If my plans go right, there's a lot of money in it for all of us."

"I like the sounds of that," Ursula said as she snuggled closer to Johnny.

"I don't know Mr. White," Jay said. "Mr. Hashito doesn't seem to like the idea."

"To hell with Mr. Hashito, Mr. Brown is the one I have to sell on the idea, that's why I wanted to get together with you all to discuss my idea and work out any bugs before my lunch date tomorrow." The waitress came in and I ordered another round for all of us. "Let's go grab some grub," I said as I stood up.

"They've got a smorg as big as Texas here."

Mrs. Yamaha looked at Jay, and with a mousy voice said. "Smorg?"

Jay said something back to her in Japanese and they both stood up. I headed through the doorway followed by the rest of them. The food at the bar looked great. Like the others I had not eaten here before. I had heard about this place from two of the guys in the apartment building.

I headed right for the hot food table, grabbed myself a huge rack of ribs and a steak and went back to the table. The waitress had already been back, and I had a cold beer sitting right in front of me. The others trickled in slowly, first the Yamaha's, each with only a bowl of soup. Lee was next, followed by Johnny, they both had a plate of salad. Ursula pulled up the rear with a plateful that made mine look like an appetizer. There wasn't much talking for the next few minutes as we all ate our meals. The food was excellent, I hadn't had ribs in a long time, in fact I haven't had a really good meal since Lynn died. Damn I miss her I thought to myself as I watched the video. Only a few short hours and I'll be with her. That is if I get headed in the right direction. I wonder if there really is a heaven or a hell? How big is it? Are there different areas? Like cities and stuff. Will she recognize me without a body? What does a soul look like? These are things I often wondered about as I laid in my cell at night staring at the ceiling.

The actress' voice that was playing Ursula brought me back to reality. "I'm going for seconds," she said as she stood up.

I had only eaten half of my food, "That's what I like, a girl with a Texan appetite, go ahead, I'm not going to discuss the plan until we have dessert. Ursula exited the room followed by Lee and Johnny. It took about an hour before we all finished our main courses.

"Grab desert and a coffee and then we'll start." I got up, the rest of them followed me. I grabbed a piece of pecan pie and four brownies. I was a sucker for both of them. I noticed a soda dispenser and I filled the largest glass I could find with Coke, another one of my vices. The others all joined shortly after. Ursula and Johnny had their plates piled high, while the Yamaha's had a small plate with two pieces of cake on it, they proceeded to each eat a piece off the same plate.

"Now," I started. "On with my idea. I want to sponsor Johnny and become his manager. I will pay for all the traveling, meals and rooms while we travel throughout Japan promoting him. It will be very American and somewhat controversial, but in the long run Johnny will be the number one wrestler in Japan, and very wealthy. I hope to take him to North America and make him a star there, what do you think Johnny?"

"Okay I guess, I'm not sure I can live up to your expectations."

"What do you think Jay?" I said as I turned and looked at him. "Does he have the talent?"

"Yes Mr. White. I see great potential in his wrestling ability, but Mr....."

"I don't want to hear Hashito's name again tonight, I will sell Mr. Brown on the idea and he can deal with Hashito."

Jay gave a sheepish nod. He had really become docile. I assumed it was the shame of losing his gym.

"I know wrestling," Ursula said. "So what's the gimmick gonna be?"

"Johnny will be known as the Disease and I will be Dr. Death. Johnny will wrestle in the ring while I do my job outside, dirty tricks and foul play, distracting the ref, getting the crowd going, and then finally delivering the death serum to Johnny's opponent. His challenger will thrash around in the ring with convulsions until death finally sets in. We will run out of the ring and into the dressing room. While in there, we will be on the big screen as the paramedics come in and try to revive the opponent in the ring. They will take his pulse, shake their heads in sorrow, and then cover him with a sheet. They will then load him on a gurney, transport him to a hearse and then drive away."

"Sounds bizarre," Lee said.

"I like it," Ursula replied.

"Johnny how about you?"

"I don't know. I don't want to kill people."

Ursula slapped him on the arm. "You don't really kill them, it's all an act."

"That's right, once they put him in the hearse and close the back door, they'll drive off. He'll hop off the gurney and exit through the side door and join us for a beer in the dressing room. It's like you're in a big movie."

"Jay, what do you think of the idea?"

"Well I'll admit, it's very American, it's a fresh idea and it will sell. What is my role? Why am I at this meeting?"

"You're going to be my assistant behind the scenes. I need someone to co-ordinate the matches, deal with the press and make traveling arrangements. I will pay you a salary of twice what you are making now."

Jay turned to his wife and spoke Japanese, she turned to me with a huge smile. I guess she liked the idea.

"What about Mr. Has..." Jay started.

I raised my hand and cut off his conversation.

"I mean, what about the current manager of the gym, isn't that his job?" Jay said, rethinking his words.

"I'll let Mr. Brown decide what to do with him. I will tell him of my plans and he either goes with it or not, if he does, then he goes all the way. Hashito can still run the other dealings of his gym, we can set up a small office, put in another squared circle that will be strictly for our use and that will be that."

"And if he doesn't?" Lee questioned.

I never gave it much thought, I thought to myself. I was Mr. Brown and I knew I wanted to go for it.

"Then we simply rent an empty warehouse and set up there," Ursula blurted out.

"Perfect," I hadn't even thought of that scenario, that way I would never have to worry about playing two characters. I could have Brown close the old gym because he's losing too much money, and me, as Mr. White, would just open a new one. "Perfect Ursula, waitress another round please."

"Not for me or my wife, we have to go, I just have a few questions."

"What are they Jay?"

"I'm ready to retire in two years, something like this could take a long time?"

"Not really, Johnny's already got the skills, all we have to do is line-up a few matches. I'm sure some of the boys at your gym could be used as opponents in the beginning. We'll hold some of the wrestling matches in our gym. We'll give free admission and invite the media. It won't be long and the Japanese Wrestling Federation will be knocking our door down, after that it's a matter of making the American media aware of it and trying to line up a tour in the US. What's the question?"

"You did say twice my salary?"

"Yes sir, for the next two years. That will put you into retirement. I'll also cut you in for thirty percent of all profits on our sales, both for the fights and merchandising for as long as the popularity lasts. Johnny is young, I figure he'll have an eight-to-twelve year reign. You go home, talk it over with your wife and I'll see you in the morning at the gym."

Mr. and Mrs. Yamaha both bowed and left.

"You said your parents left you some money, but I had no idea you had that much," Ursula said.

"It's not really that much, is mostly hype that sells, all I have to do is sell the media on the idea, the rest will fall in place. Like I've said before, sex and bullshit sells."

"You're from Texas, you should know," Ursula remarked.

"Grab your drinks and let's head to the bar to celebrate," I said as I grabbed my beer and stood up.

"I'll meet you there," Ursula said. "I have to hit the little girls' room."

"Me too," Lee added.

"C'mon Johnny, we'll go find a table," I said as I pulled Lee's chair out so she could stand up, Lee and Ursula both exited the room. We made our way to the bar and grabbed a booth. Johnny and I stood up and allowed the girls to sit. Ursula made the first move and sat on the same side as Johnny. Lee sat on my side. As she crossed in front of me I got a whiff of her perfume, it reminded me of the perfume Lynn used to wear. Just as I went to sit down the waitress plopped the pitcher of beer and four mugs on the table that I had pre-ordered from the bar.

"So Johnny, what do you think?" I asked.

"If Mr. Yamaha thinks I can do it, and if he is coming in on the deal, then I will do it."

"So why the hell did you invite us," Ursula blurted out and then belched. "Excuse me."

"Well I need one of you..." I started to say.

"Oh my God," Ursula yelled. "Oh my God, they've got a mechanical bull." She was pointing a finger on her outstretched arm between Lee and I. I turned around and looked at the bull.

"I want to do it, I want to do it," she said now visibly drunk.

"That's enough of this," Lee said as she grabbed Ursula's mug. "Sober up and you can go on it in a while."

"So like I was saying, I need one of you girls as my assistant."

"But I thought Mr. Yamaha was going to do that?" Lee questioned.

"Yes he is, I mean at ringside."

"I'll do it, I'll do it." Ursula blurted out.

"Are you seeing double too?" Lee asked Ursula.

"Why?"

"Because you're saying everything twice."

"I need a woman to assist me at ringside, to help me with my gloves and to prepare the needle. Of course you'll have to wear a nurse's outfit. I know you're willing Ursula, what about you Lee?"

"I can't, between my work and taking care of Mr. Campbell's grandson, I don't have the time. I could quit my job but Mr. Campbell needs me more and more. He's even made me an offer to stay with him, to be a live-in nanny."

"What about his family?" I asked.

"No, the child's parents and Mr. Campbell's' wife were killed in a house fire, only he and Liam escaped."

"That's so sad," Ursula replied. "Hey what about me?"

"I know you're interested, but you work full time, Lee only works part time."

I really wanted Ursula to do it. I needed her if I was going to pull this murder off. She had the connection in the U.S. I needed.

"I can work on the road. I'm a computer programmer. I can just write the programs and upload them from my laptop, all I need is a phone line."

"Well, I'm not sure, maybe it's the beer talking, why don't we all think about it until the morning."

"I don't have to think about it, I haven't had too much beer, besides, I grew up around wrestling, I know the business."

"What do you mean, you know the business?"

"Wrestling, I've been going to matches since I was young, my uncle is Mike the Mouth."

"Mike the Mouth who's that?" Lee asked.

"My uncle."

"No shit, you said that," Lee stated. She turned to me and said, "she's had way too much to drink."

"I have not. Mike the Mouth is a former wrestler who is now the president of the FWA, and he's my uncle."

"Your uncle," I said. "I never would have guessed."

I had already known that from the research I did. That's why I picked Ursula and the apartment beside her.

"Maybe he'll be able to help us set up a match in Florida. We'll call it Pearl Harbor, the invasion of the Japanese or something. Hell, we could even get it moved to Hawaii," I said.

"Maybe I underestimated you, you do sound like you know the sport," Ursula replied.

Lee moved her hand down on the bench. Her fingers now touched the outside of my thigh. I too put my hand down on my lap, my baby finger now touched hers, she smiled when I looked at her.

Johnny now started to point and laugh, I turned so I could see behind me, as I did I moved my left leg up on the bench a bit and rested it on Lee's right hand. As she turned around to see, she put her left hand on my knee. I think this might be a big step in our relationship.

"You think you could do better than that guy? Go ahead big boy," Ursula said to Johnny. "Let's see what you are made of."

"What do you mean?" he asked.

"Try the bull, it's only eight seconds that you have to stay on," Ursula stated.

I knew how tough that was. Those bulls were murder depending on who was on the controls. It's fun at the time, but you sure feel it the next day, your neck, your back and even your balls. "Go ahead Johnny, give it a try." I told him. Johnny stood up and made his way to the end of the platform. There was one woman waiting in line in front of him. She climbed aboard and a bell rang, the bull began to buck. It thrashed back and forth and from side to side. I could tell the control operator wasn't giving it his all. She lasted the full eight seconds and jumped off when the horn sounded.

"Go get'em cowboy," Ursula yelled as Johnny climbed up on the hunk of leather. I waved to the control operator and made a motion with my hands like turning a dial. He must have figured it out because once the bell sounded, Johnny was flat on his ass within two seconds. He sauntered back to the table wincing, desperately wanting to rub his balls. He was red with embarrassment.

"What happened big boy? Too much for you?" I asked.

"I've never seen anything like that before," he said.

We sat for a while, drinking jugs of beer and watching people ride the bull.

"Okay guys, let's call it a night." I threw some cash on the table to cover the bill and headed outside, it was a beautiful night.

"Let's walk back," Lee suggested.

We headed out, Lee and I were in front, Johnny and Ursula staggered behind, well Ursula staggered, and Johnny sort of swaggered, like a cowboy who just came in from riding a very long day on the range. I motioned to Lee to look back. There were the two of them, arm and arm, limping along. I wasn't sure if it was because they had feelings for each other, or whether it was to help each other walk. Lee stepped in front of me to the curb and stuck out her arm. A taxi stopped. She grabbed the back door handle and opened the door.

"There you go guys, hop in," she shouted.

They made their way into the cab. Lee reached in her purse, grabbed some cash and told the driver the address. Lee slammed the door and the cab sped off.

"We'd be all night if we had to wait for them," she said.

"I think you're right," I answered.

I then stepped to the curb, whistled and motioned with my arm. A rickshaw driver across the road grabbed his rig and came running over.

"There you go ma'am," I said to her as I extended my arm to the open carriage. I assisted Lee in the carriage and then I climbed in. The runner sped away. Lee reached over and grabbed my hand. We enjoyed a beautiful ride, holding hands the whole time. Now that we were alone she was more relaxed. The driver stopped in front of the apartment, I paid him and he was gone. We entered the lobby and rode the elevator to the third floor. We approached my apartment first. Lee had released my hand when we exited the rickshaw and never regained it.

"Would you like to come in for some tea?" I asked.

"Sure, but just a quick one, I should go check on Ursula."

"She's okay, she's with Johnny."

Lee followed me into my apartment. I went into the kitchen and put on the kettle, I grabbed a can of Coke for myself. "Is tea okay? Or would you prefer something else?" I shouted to the living room.

"Tea's fine."

I could hear the stereo start up. Mellow music filled the apartment. I went into the living room and set my Coke down. "I'll be right back," I said and headed for the bathroom. I flushed the toilet, washed my hands and headed back to the kitchen to make her tea, but Lee had beaten me to it, she was just stirring in the milk as I arrived.

"I could have got that."

"It's okay."

I escorted her back to the living room, she put her teacup on the table.

"I'm so glad my plans are going well," I said.

"I'm glad that you're glad," she said as our eyes locked on one another. I leaned forward and gave her a kiss, a long passionate kiss. She put her hand behind my head and held it ever so gently. I didn't want it to end, but it did.

"Listen," I said. "I'm going to be pretty busy for a while, so I won't be around a lot."

"That's alright, I've got to spend more time with Liam, he needs me more and I'm beginning to miss him a lot."

I reached into my pocket and took out a spare key. "Here," I said as I handed it to her. "Come and go as you please, I need someone to water the plants now and then." I only had three.

"Thanks," she said as she tucked it into her pocket. "You've got a lot to do to carry out your plan, I would only get in the way and distract you."

"I don't mind these kinds of distractions."

"No really, you need to stay focused," she said as she stood up. "I've got to go and make sure that Ursula is okay. I'll see you tomorrow."

She let herself out of the apartment. I hated to see her go, but she was right. I had a lot of work ahead of me if I was going to do this right. As much as I wanted and needed her to stay, I knew she was right. I locked the door and went to have a shower. It was getting quite late and I had another big day ahead of me, with decisions to make. How was I going to handle the gym situation? I figured I'd sleep on it, and go with my gut feeling in the morning. I shut off the shower, grabbed a towel and dried myself off, brushed my teeth and headed for the bedroom.

"Ursula put a coat hanger on the door, so I guess I sleep here tonight."

I looked in the bedroom and there was Lee, naked as a Jaybird. I dropped my towel and ran to the bed.

"Cut," said Adam.

"Good timing," Emily replied. "I have to excuse myself for a minute."

"May as well peak their interest," I replied.

It wasn't long before Emily was back.

"Okay Adam roll the tape, this is my favourite part." I smiled at Emily, who just rolled her eyes.

Mark started the video and I continued the story.

"What was the hanger for?" I asked.

"She's got a date for the night. I've never used it, last time she did I just spent the night with Liam and his grandfather."

I lay there on the bed and brought her close. Even though it was warm in the room her nipples were as erect as my penis. We kissed passionately, my tongue exploring the inside of her mouth. She smelled so pretty. I lowered my hands down her back, clutching her closer until her breasts were flattened against my chest. Our thighs intermingled. I could feel her pubic hair brush against my thigh, her toes caressing my calf muscle. How I had longed for her, waited for her. I never wanted it to end. For the last two months I had dreamt of this night and how I was going to cherish it. Now with my plans

almost set, I could relax a bit, knowing that in due time Dave would be dead. We made passionate love for what seemed liked hours. Exhausted, we rolled over, pulled up the sheets and fell asleep.

CHAPTER 8

When I awoke the next morning Lee was gone. I turned and looked at the alarm, it was 8:30 a.m. I climbed out of bed and grabbed the damp towel that I had dropped on the floor the night before, and threw it around my waist. As I passed through the living room I picked up my half full glass of Coke off the coffee table. I paused for a second and stared at Lee's empty teacup, remembering last night, I admired how rejuvenated I felt, how wonderfully alive I was. I cracked open the blinds, drew them back and opened the French doors that led to the balcony. I took a deep breath. Man I felt good. I grabbed a big Cuban off of the TV and sat down in a huge Adirondack chair. I lit the lighter that I had left on the arm of the chair for such an occasion. I shoved the end of the cigar in my mouth to moisten it. I slid it in, slowly turning it until my fingers hit my lips. The aroma of the tobacco was overshadowed for a moment by the aroma of Lee. Her scent was still present from the night before. I lit the cigar and took a huge drag, inhaled it for a second and then expelled the smoke from my mouth. There's nothing like a night of wild sex, a good sleep, and a great cigar to make a man feel like he can take on the world.

"Is that you or your smelly cigar Darryl?" I heard a voice yell out. Ursula poked her head around the retaining wall that separated the two balconies.

"You look awful perky today," she said.

"I had a very good night, have you seen Lee?"

"No, not at all, I just got up."

"Johnny up yet?"

"He's not here."

"But the hanger...."

"Oh that, I had great expectations, he came in for a night cap, and we sat for a bit. We got a little hot and heavy on the living room floor, so I put the coat hanger out. I then went to the bedroom to slip into something more comfortable.

"Now there's a cliché."

"But I must have passed out, because the next thing I knew I woke up, still in my clothes from last night and Johnny was gone."

"Sucks to be you."

"Quit gloating."

"Don't worry, once we start rolling with my plans, you'll see him enough, besides, I still think he's a virgin."

"Oh I can change that quick enough."

"So listen, I've got my meeting in a couple of hours, I'll fill you and Lee in tonight."

"Sounds good," she said as she ducked back behind the wall.

I sat there for a little over half an hour, enjoying my cigar and even my warm, flat Coke. I grabbed a shower and got dressed. I made some toast and sat at the computer. I set it up to have my computer fax my cell phone at 10:45 a.m. The connection noise will be irritating until the computer realizes that the cell isn't a fax machine. It will then disconnect. It will be long enough to fool them at the gym. I headed down there and was met at the door by Mr. Hashito.

"I'm coming to your meeting," he said. "I will talk Mr. Brown out of this foolishness."

"I don't think Mr. Brown..."

"He'll listen to me, I'm in charge," he interrupted.

"Your choice. Morning Jay, how's it going?" I said turning my back on Hashito.

"Good morning Mr. White," Jay said as he bowed.

"Johnny," I said as I raised my hand to get his attention. Johnny looked over from canvas, he was in a sparring match. His opponent had him pinned to the mat as I approached. Jay yelled something in Japanese and the two wrestlers stood up. Johnny came to the near rope. "Almost got lucky last night, eh cowboy?"

"Lucky?" Johnny said with a puzzled look on his face.

"His name is Mr. Sashi not cowboy," Hashito blurted from behind me. "We don't go by...."

The ring of my cell phone silenced his stammering. "Hello," I paused and listened to the irritating blurbs and beeps through the receiver, trying to cover it so Hashito wouldn't hear. "Well howdy Bob. Feeling great, yourself? My appetite? It's as big as

Texas. I'm here now. Mr. Yamaha and Mr. Hashito. Ten minutes?
Okay, I'll tell him. I'll go now and get us a table. Okay see you in
a bit."

"Tell who what?" Hashito demanded to know.

I clicked off the phone. "He told me to head over to the
restaurant, he'll be here in ten minutes."

"I'll get my jacket," Hashito said.

"He told me he's coming to the gym. I'd wait here."

I slipped my right hand, which was holding my cell phone,
into the pocket of my track pants. I fondled the keys until I felt
the raised Braille dot on the #5 key. I moved my finger up and
pressed the #2 key and held it down. I had reserved that key as
my speed dial number for the gym. The phone in the gym office
began to ring. Hashito took off for the stairs like a greyhound at
the track trying to catch the mechanical rabbit. As soon as he
was halfway up the stairs I exited the gym. I pressed the end
button as soon as he reached the top of the stairs. It was quite
amusing. I stepped around the corner and into the alley. I
slipped off my running shoes, took off the track pants which
were over top of my khaki colored dress pants and pulled off my
sweat shirt to reveal a light beige buttoned down collared shirt.
I opened my briefcase and took out a pair of loafers, grabbed Mr.
Brown 's wig and put them on. I reached inside the flap in the
top of the briefcase and grabbed my spectacles and centered
them on my nose. They weren't real glasses, the lenses were clear
glass, my eyesight was nearly perfect. I gathered up my
belongings and put them in a shopping bag, which my briefcase
also held. I set both the bag and the briefcase behind a dumpster
in the alley. I picked up an empty cardboard box that I was lying
in the alley and headed back into the gym. Just for the fun of it
I stood outside peering through the window, I could see Jay and
Hashito talking at ringside. I'm glad I stopped because I
remembered that I had left my cell phone in the pocket of my
track pants. I went back and grabbed it. I pulled it out and
depressed the number two button as I turned the corner. As I
reached the door Hashito was making another mad dash up the
stairs, this time tripping and falling halfway up. I laughed as I
hung up the phone.

"Cheery O," I said in my English voice as I entered the gym.

"Good Morning Mr. Brown," Jay said as he bowed.

The gym went quiet. As I looked around, everyone bowed as my head turned their way.

"Now that's what I call respect. Now carry on, let me see some of those skills. Respect and skills, Mr. Yamaha, that's what wrestling is all about," I said.

Hashito was scrambling to get down the stairs as fast as he could. He caught up with us as we approached the ring.

"Mr. Hashito, nice of you to join us. What kind of gym are you running here?" I asked.

"What do you mean sir, I mean Mr. Brown."

"I called you twice, no one answered. How are we going to get new clients or publicity if you don't answer the phone? I sure hope no other gyms have called looking for matches, and you missed their calls."

"Well I uh...."

"No excuses, when the phone rings, it's your job to answer it."

"Yes sir, Mr. Brown."

"So Mr. Yamaha, how was your dinner meeting last night?" Jay looked stunned that I knew.

"Mr. White called me this morning. He said he had you, your lovely wife, and Mr. Sashi out to the Tempura. Nice place, did you ride the bull?"

"No, Mr. Brown," he said with his lips quivering.

"So did he discuss his idea with you?" Jay looked like a schoolboy, caught cheating on a test. "Don't answer, I'm meeting with him shortly."

Jay's shoulders dropped as he breathed a sigh of relief.

"Yes, Mr. Brown, I wanted to talk to about these plans Mr. White has, I think..."

"Right now I don't care what you think," I said cutting him off mid sentence. "Respect, Mr. Hashito. Is that not what we teach around here?"

"Yes Mr. Brown."

"If I asked right now to speak to Mr. Yamaha privately, would you respect that?"

"Yes Mr. Brown."

"If I was having a party and didn't invite you, would you

show up to my house?"

"No Mr. Brown."

"Then why in the Queen's name did you go to the Tempura last night and interrupt a private dinner meeting, especially one with a potential customer? Is that showing respect?"

"Well, Mr..."

"Answer the question!" I shouted.

"No, it's not Mr. Brown. I did not show respect."

"Jay, when I bought this place from you, I had to keep Mr. Hashito on staff, you said he was the business manager. You just wanted to be a trainer. Well I'm changing my plans."

"Mr. Hashito," I said as I shoved the box into his stomach. "Go upstairs, clean out your desk. You're fired!"

Hashito bent quickly as he fumbled the box that I had let go unexpectedly. He stood there for a moment, "GO!" I screamed.

"Mr. Yamaha you're in charge," I bowed.

Jay looked confused.

"Thank you sir uh, I mean Mr. Brown."

Jay went over to the water fountain and got a drink. I felt sorry for him right now, but I knew I had it all worked out.

Hashito had come downstairs, with the box in his hands. "Here are your keys Mr. Brown. Thank you, you have taught me a great lesson. Respect." He bowed and was gone. I never saw him again.

"I'm going to my meeting now, Mr. Yamaha." I started across the gym. "I'll be back after lunch." Jay bowed once more. I left the gym and went for lunch. I ordered some rice and chicken dish, I think. It came after a few minutes. I'm not sure what was in it, but it was good. I took my time and enjoyed it. I didn't want to get back to the gym too quickly. I had to make it look like a real business lunch. I struck up a conversation with a Canadian woman. It was so nice to talk in my own voice, not having to think about the accents. We talked for about ten minutes until her husband joined us, which is where she then focused most of her attention. I paid the bill and left. I went back to the gym. Jay jumped from his chair as the bell rang on the door as I pushed it open. I think I caught him napping. He looked scared.

"Mr. Yamaha, how's it feel to be in charge again?"

"It feels a little funny."

"Well Mr. Yamaha, I made a deal with your Mr. White, he can fill you in. He should be here any minute. I've got to go to the loo, I'll be out in a bit."

I made my way past the ring and through the locker room to the bathrooms. There were only two of them, each in a separate room. I locked the door behind me. I opened the window above the toilet and stuck my head out. The coast was clear. I took off the wig, glasses and my shoes and left them on the floor. I stepped on the toilet, through the window and climbed onto the dumpster that was below the window and jumped to the ground. I put on the blue sweatshirt and pants and stepped into the running shoes I had left there. I picked up the briefcase and made my way through the alley to the front of the gym. I bent down and set the briefcase on the ground and grabbed a red file folder out of it and ran through the door.

"Jay," I yelled waving the file folder. "I did it, I did it. We've got a deal." Johnny was standing outside the ring stretching. "Hey Disease, come hear," Johnny looked around. "Disease, Johnny that's you. Get over here."

Johnny slowly walked towards us. I ran to him with my arms outstretched and gave him a big hug.

"We're partners Johnny, we're partners."

Johnny hugged me reluctantly.

"It's all right here," I pulled out a copy of the contract, signed by both myself, and myself.

"Yes I heard," Jay said. "Mr. Brown just told me, he's in the washroom."

"We've got six months to get it all together, all we have to do is train, promote and sell out Yokohama stadium for one night."

"That's ninety thousand seats," Jay added.

"Piece of cake, and if we do, the gyms mine for a dollar, and if I can't sell it out, I have to leave and never set foot in his gym again. There were a couple of things we had to come to terms on though. First of all, he had to fire Hashito."

"He did that this morning before you went for lunch."

"Yes I know, Hashito showed a complete lack of respect for our meeting last night."

"That's why Mr. Brown fired him this morning."

"Secondly, he has to give me full reign of this project, he's not to interfere for six months. Third, if my plan fails, he has to reinstate both you and Johnny back in his gym without any repercussions. And fourth, I have to pay him $10,000.00 U.S. a month for six months up front. Lastly, if I fail, I have to give him $100,000.00 U.S."

"But..." Jay started to say.

"No buts. I'm not going to fail. Be here at seven, we've got a lot of work ahead of us." I handed Jay the folder.

"I'm going to tell Ursula and Lee," I said as I bolted out the door.

I ran around the corner, back into the alley one last time. I damn near leapt onto the dumpster all in one jump. I stripped off my shoes and tracksuit, opened the half lid of the dumpster and deposited them inside. I scurried through the open window into the bathroom, put on the wig, shoes and glasses, tucked in my shirt and flushed the toilet. I turned on the taps and immersed my hands under the water. I twisted the handles the opposite way and stopped the flow, reached over, clicked the dead bolt, opened the door and exited the washroom. As I walked back through the change room, I shook off any loose droplets of water I still had on my hands.

"There's nothing like a good visit the loo after a big meal. Oh I see Darryl's been in," I said as I pointed to the folder in Jay's hand. "Where is he?"

"He just left sir. He went to tell his friends."

"Well chap, you can see it's all signed, sealed and delivered," I said as I stuck out my arm and patted Johnny on the back. "I'm going to England for a holiday, I've got $60,000.00 and six months off," I said as I held up the check. "Jay," I said as I put my moist hand out for him to shake. "I'll see you in six months, good luck." Jay glanced at our hands as we shook.

"Oh yeah, you need paper towels in the bathroom."

Jay released my hand and wiped his on his shirt.

"Tally ho," I said as I exited the gym. I walked a block down the street and threw the wig and glasses in a garbage can.

I hailed down a rickshaw driver and caught a ride home. I enjoyed the ride with Lee last night and thought I would give it another go. I arrived at the apartment and went to the parking garage. I got the car and drove it back to the rental place and exchanged it for another one. This way I didn't have to worry about wanting to use it when I played Darryl. I drove the new one back and now parked it in my spot. I rented two spots before and kept Mr. Brown's car in the other spot, that way Lee or Ursula couldn't question why I never used the car that was in my spot. I rode the elevator from the car garage to the third floor, passed by my apartment and went right to Lee's. I knocked but there was no answer so I went back to my place. There was a light flashing on the answering machine. I walked over and pressed the play button.

"Hi it's me, Lee. Sorry I wasn't there when you woke up. I got up early and called to check on Liam. Last night was great. I haven't had sex like that in a long time. Liam has been quite upset lately that I haven't been around. He misses me. I've talked to Ursula and I'm going to move out. I need to be here with Liam. You've got a lot of work ahead of you and I will only compound the confusion if I live right next door. I have your number and your key and I will stop in now and then. Give me a call and we'll get together for supper. For now it's best if I stay here, better for all of us. Concentrate on your plan. You're going to need to spend a lot of time with Ursula and Johnny, and it's better if I'm here. Liam needs me more and you need to stay focused on what you're doing. Call me, goodbye."

I shut off the machine and unplugged it. I disconnected the phone that was attached. Now that Mr. Brown was gone I had no need for that line. I could just use the cell phone. I grabbed a cigar and sat out on the balcony. I picked up my cell phone and called Lee. She answered on the third ring.

"Hi its me," I said. "I got your message. You're probably right. We can't get too close. I do have a lot of work ahead of me. I've disconnected the number you have so you'll have to use the cell number, it's..."

"It's okay I've got it on call display."

Shit, I thought to myself, my cell phone was under Mr. White's name. I only bought it a couple of weeks ago. I've had to buy one for each murder under an assumed name because the authorities could trace one registered to Jack Stevenson. I never thought about it when I used it to call Hashito, it was listed as

Darryl Whites', not Bob Browns'. I'm not even sure if the gym had call display.

"Listen Lee, I'm not going to be able to make it for supper tonight. I have to talk to Ursula and I have to be at the gym for seven o'clock in the morning."

"No problem, I'm coming by in the morning to get my stuff at the apartment. I'll see you there, if not, I'll leave the address on the counter. You can swing by tomorrow night."

"Sounds good, see you then."

I hung up the phone and finished my cigar. Ursula showed up a couple of hours later. I told her the good news and asked her to come to the gym in the morning. I vegged out most the night watching TV and fell asleep on the couch.

CHAPTER 9

The morning sun woke me as it cut through the open blinds. It was around six o'clock. I pulled myself off the couch, changed my clothes and headed for the gym. Jay was already at the gym when I got there.

"Morning Jay."

"Good morning Mr. White."

"Enough with the formalities, from now on, I'm Dr. Death.

"Yes sir."

"And Johnny is the Disease, and I'm not sure what we'll call Ursula yet. She'll be here later."

"Where is the Disease?"

"He's not here yet. Dr. Death."

"Very good, you learn fast, Dr. will do. How did your wife take the news?"

"Very happy, double income."

Jay and I went upstairs to the office and rearranged it. Hashito's old desk was empty. I gave that one to Jay.

"Four hours a day I need you to coach Johnny, I will spend two hours a day with him choreographing his moves and the other two he will be spend on jogging and practicing the moves. You will spend the afternoon in the office promoting and trying to set up matches. It will be slow in the beginning, but once we get going it will pick up."

"Yes Dr. Death."

"Rearrange the other desk in the office so it's workable. I'm going to have Ursula use it. She can do her job from here. I will pull her down to the ring when I need her. I'm going down to wait for Johnny."

I left the office, went downstairs and grabbed a chair. I set it down in the middle of the ring and waited for Johnny. He finally arrived around twenty minutes to eight.

"Good morning Johnny," I said as he walked in.

"Good morning Mr. White."

"From now on its Dr. Death, why the hell are you late?"

"I got a slow start this morning."

"Did I not say to be here at seven?"

"Yes sir."

"When I say seven, I mean seven. I'm docking your pay for half a day."

"But I..."

"I don't want excuses, when I say to be here, you be here."

"Yes sir."

"You know the little market on the other side of town?"

"The one that's two miles up the road?"

"Yes, I want you to go there and buy me a banana. I want you to jog. You have half an hour. That means quarter after eight. You'll have to run at least a six-minute mile there and back, and it should take you twenty-four minutes. I'm giving you an extra six minutes to spare, now move it, and don't be late again. If you're not ready for this commitment, then don't come back. I'm sure I can find lots of wrestlers willing to be a star. Now go!"

He took off like a bat out of hell. The poor kid. I had to let him know that I was serious about this plan. I could easily find another wrestler, but it was his stature I needed. I got up from the chair, crawled through the ropes, and went to the store down the street. I bought a Coke, the New York Times, and a banana. I didn't really want a banana, but I had to teach Johnny a lesson.

When I arrived back at the gym, Jay was folding towels near the change room.

"Jay, that's not your job. You're a trainer and a promoter. Grab a chair and come in the ring."

Jay finished folding the towel he had in his hand, picked up a folding chair and slid it along the canvas.

"What are we doing?" he asked as he unfolded the chair.

"I'm teaching Johnny to be on time."

I opened my Coke and started to read the newspaper. I looked at my watch and it was ten minutes after eight. Jay just sat there. I didn't really care if Johnny was on time. He was still going to receive the same treatment. My eyes looked up from the paper as I heard the bell on the door ring. Twenty-four minutes had past. He made it I thought.

"The least you could have done was give me directions, I had to call Johnny last night to get them," Ursula bellowed.

"Sorry Ursula, I never thought."

"And you're the mastermind behind this plan?"

"Who shit in your Corn Flakes this morning?"

"Nobody, but if we're going to pull this off, we have to work together."

"I like the attitude."

"My Uncle Mike taught me well, where's Johnny?"

"He's on an errand, he'll be here shortly. Come on up and have a seat." I reached over the apron and pulled a third chair in the ring. "When Johnny gets here, I need you to give him the same attitude, follow my lead."

The three of us sat there for a few more minutes before the door flew open and Johnny rushed in.

"Here's your banana sir."

"It's too late, you're late. I had to get my own," I said as I started peeling the one I had. "Twice in one day you're late."

"I'm sorry Mr. White. The traffic..."

"Who cares about the traffic?" Ursula piped up. "You were told to be here at a certain time and you weren't."

Johnny was bent over, his hands on his knees huffing and puffing, trying to catch his breathe.

"Are you going to be late tomorrow too?" Ursula asked.

"No ma'am."

"Don't call me ma'am."

"Yes Sir, I mean ma'am, I mean Ursula."

It was obviously working. We had him rattled. I don't think he'll be late again. Damn she was good.

"Now get your ass in the change room. You be back out in five minutes and give me a hundred push ups." Ursula snapped.

Johnny disappeared through the doorway.

"Good work girl," I said. "Come on up to the office."

I pointed the way and followed her upstairs. Jay removed the chairs from the ring. We stood in the office and peered out of the window at the ring. Johnny showed up momentarily and started his push ups.

"I thought you might need a desk to work at. Are you sure you can do your work from here?"

"I'll just bring in some of my computer stuff tomorrow. I will need a separate phone line."

"No problem, I'll have Jay call around today, we'll see what we can get."

"It's too bad about Lee," she said.

"I talked to her last night, it seems the little guy is having a hard time."

"She spends a lot of time there now, she may as well live there, why pay rent, when you can get paid to live somewhere else?"

"How will you manage?"

"It's okay, my company pays for the apartment. Lee's money was just extra income, besides we're going to be too busy to spend any."

"You've got that right, listen, make yourself at home, I'm heading back to the apartment. Lee's stopping by and I want to see her. I'm going to her new place for supper. You can come and go as you please, there's a key to the back door on your desk. It'll be a good couple of months before we're ready for a match. We'll decide on your role later. We've still got to come up with a name for your character."

"I'll work on that. Say hi to Lee for me."

"Will do," I said as I exited the office. I walked over to the ring. "I'll be gone the rest of the day and I'm not sure what time I'll be in tomorrow. What time are you going to be here Johnny?"

"Seven o'clock Dr. Death, seven o'clock."

"Good, I'll see you tomorrow."

Traffic seemed especially heavy. It seemed I hit every red light, it's always like that whenever you're in a hurry. I parked underground in my spot and rode the elevator up. I put my key into the lock, as I did the door swung open. I was frightened at first that someone had broken in, but when I laid eyes on the little toddler in my living room, my fears were soon laid to rest.

"Liam, honey, what are you doing?" Lee's voice said off in the distance.

"Hi, it's just me," I yelled.

"Oh hi," she said as she entered from the kitchen. "I was just leaving you a note."

"I thought I'd come home early and surprise you."

I leaned over and gave her a kiss, she kissed me back, hard.

"I've got all my stuff from next door. We were just going to head home."

"I've taken the rest the day off. Are we still on for supper?"

"Sure."

"I'll come now then, I'll follow you."

Liam seemed undisturbed by my presence. He was concentrating on how to get the remote to work.

"Come on honey," she said as she picked him up. "Let's go see papa. I've got his truck, I'm parked out front," she told me.

"I'm in the garage, I'll swing around and catch up with you."

I locked the door and we took the elevator down, Lee and Liam got off at the lobby, I rode it down two more floors. The garage door opened as I approached it. I made two quick rights when I exited and was soon behind the pickup truck. I followed her for five or six miles to the edge of town. She stopped in front of a small house. I stopped and shut off the car. She got out and went to the passenger side to take Liam out of his car seat. I grabbed a couple of boxes from the pickup and followed her in.

"Darryl, I presume?" a voice said from a lazy boy chair.

"Mr. Campbell, isn't it?" I put the box down and shook his hand.

"I'll help you get the rest in a minute," Lee said.

"It's okay I'll get them," I replied.

I made three more trips to the truck and I had it all in.

"Sorry, he started to get fussy so I laid him down."

"Who? Mr. Campbell?"

She hit me on the arm jokingly. We sat around for the afternoon and talked. Time passed quickly. Lee started to get up when she heard the baby start to stir over the monitor.

"I'll get him sweetheart, you stay and chat," Mr. Campbell said.

"Thanks papa."

"Papa?" I questioned.

"You can call me Papa too, everyone does. Papa's coming," he yelled down the hall. "How's my baby?" his voice came over the monitor. "Someone's got stinky pants, pee-ew! Come here you little rascal."

Lee reached over and shut the monitor off.

"I'm taking Liam out for a while so you kids can be alone," Mr. Campbell stated.

"It's okay," I added.

"You like spending time with your papa, don't you?" he asked Liam as he closed the door behind him.

I moved over to the couch and Lee and I started kissing, we held each other tight.

"How long do you think it will take you to see your plan through?" Lee asked.

"It won't take long and with Ursula's help we'll set up a title match in Florida, once we win that, I'm done. Time to move on."

"Sounds like a long time."

"It'll go fast."

"But I won't see you much."

"You've got Liam and his papa to keep you company, you must know by now that I'm a bit of a wanderer."

"Where does that leave me?" she asked tearfully.

"Let's cross that bridge when we come to it, right now enjoy the time we have."

She got quiet after that for a bit. When supper was ended she perked up, probably because Liam was home.

"Did you two have a good time?" Mr. Campbell asked.

"Yes we did," Lee stated.

"Good, let's have a drink. Who wants a beer?"

"I'll have one," I answered.

"Not me, not until Liam is down for the night."

We played with Liam for a while. He wasn't shy at all for a toddler. He was constantly crawling all over me. My beer took a while to drink, but I finished it. "Well I think it's time I got back. I've got an early day tomorrow." I said my goodbyes, gave Lee a kiss and left. It was going to be tough. I wondered if I had bit off more than I could chew. On the drive home I wondered if I should pack my plans in and just head home to Fiji. There I was with all the money in the world and I had to masquerade around so nobody would know it was me. I got back to the apartment and went to bed.

Morning came quickly. I didn't sleep very well. I dragged

myself off to the gym anyway. As I drove past the gym to turn into the alley, Johnny was waiting out front. I guess my antics yesterday worked. There was no way he was going to be late. I parked my car in the back and went in. I flicked all the lights on and unlocked the front door for Johnny.

"Your here bright and early."

"Yes Sir, I learn quick."

"We've got a lot to do over the next two months. We'll pick out an opponent and practice the routines so we've got it down for the match. You'll be the title match, we'll put six or seven other fights on the same card."

"Good morning gentleman," Jay said.

"Morning Jay," I answered.

"Ah Mr. Sashi, you're here early."

"I think I scared him yesterday."

"Yes sir," he replied.

"Jay, I want you to call around to the other gyms and line up a match. We'll need the wrestler here two weeks before to choreograph it. Let them know I'm paying the card that night and there will be extra if it's a big name star. Explain that Johnny is going to win and there will be a contract to sign so there's no double crossing. We'll set up the other matches later. Rent some bleachers, enough to hold a thousand people. We'll work out the ticket details later."

"Yes sir."

I was going to work with Johnny from twelve until two every day, after Jay and Johnny did their four hours of tactical stuff and had lunch. My time could be better spent at the apartment planning and researching my next murder or spending time with Lee and Liam, but I guess I had to immerse myself in this if I wanted it to go right. I went back to my apartment.

Every day was the same routine. Get up, go to the gym, come home, lay on the couch watching TV and going to bed. What a life I've dragged myself into. I could have just taken my lottery winnings and forgot about trying to make it easy for Jimmy. He would never have pissed Lynn off. She would've never stormed out and had the accident. Instead I'm sitting in an apartment half way around the world by myself. The days seemed like years. I talked to Lee almost every night. I saw her now and then but it wasn't the same. I wish she was still in the building, at least it gave me hope. She spent more and more time with Liam. I never saw him enough for him to even notice when I was around.

There was a knock at the door. I opened it after seeing Ursula through the peephole.

"What's up Tex?" she asked all bubbly.

"Not much, come on in."

She made her way to the couch as I closed the door.

"Sure I'll have a beer."

"Okay," I said and grabbed two out of the fridge.

"You seem kind of down lately and I'm here to cheer you up."

"You are, are you?" I questioned.

"Yep, we're going to sit and drink your sorrows away, we're going to laugh, we're going to cry and then we're going to flush that bad feeling right down the toilet, and when you're done, you'll feel a lot better."

"I don't think I'll get that drunk."

"Trust me. The cure for depression is to feel sorry for yourself, then laugh at yourself and when you're all done, stick your finger down your throat and barf until there's nothing left. Barf so bad that your sides ache for days. It works."

"We'll see. I'll start with just one."

"One my ass," she got up, put out her arm and pulled me out of my chair. "Change of scenery cowboy."

She pulled me towards the door.

"Where are we going?"

"My place, that way no one will bug us. Johnny's out for the night so he won't call and no one can call you." She pulled me out into the hall by one arm, I shut the door with the other.

"Shit, I forgot my key."

"You're spending the night at my place, you won't feel like going anywhere."

I was unsure about this. I know Lee and I aren't that close, but I really didn't need another woman to complicate my life.

"What about Johnny?"

"Nice try Tex, you ain't getting lucky, I'm just a friend

helping a friend. No sex involved. Too bad for you, because I'm good."

She shooed the cat away as we entered her apartment.

"Grab a pillow and sit down," she said as she went into the kitchen. I felt like a schoolboy being bossed around by the teacher. She returned and plopped down a cooler with ice and about a dozen beers in it.

"Okay Buckaroo, here's the rules. We chug three beers each, no talking until they're gone and then we start."

"Start what?"

"Uh Uh, I said no talking." She poured one beer each in a glass. She chugged her first beer, mine was only half gone. I put the glass to my lips to take another sip, she put her hand on the bottom of it and tipped it up and held it there. I drank as fast as I could, but I still spilled some down the front of my shirt. She cracked open two more and poured them. She handed me my glass. She drank her second one, only stopping for air once. I started to chug mine to avoid wearing it again. She let out a large belch while pouring our third. I could feel a bit of a buzz. This time I beat her. She stood up and took both glasses into the kitchen. She returned with two bottles of Crown Royal, four shot glasses and two plastic tumblers and four rolls of quarters. She opened up a beer each, put one on the coffee table beside me and one beside her, she opened the whiskey and poured one shot each into two of the shot glasses and slid mine towards me. She sat about eight feet away, spread her legs straight out in front of her and put one of the tumblers on the floor in front of her crotch.

"Sit like this," she said as she threw me a tumbler. I spread my legs and put the cup on the floor between them. "Fill your other shot glass with beer."

I did.

"Have you ever played quarters before?" she asked.

"No."

"You are now." She laid on her back and put her hand in her front pocket. Her jeans we so tight she could barely reach in. She sat back up and tossed me a quarter.

"Here's how it works, we take turns throwing our quarters at each other's glass. If you miss you drink a shot of beer. You get it in, and I drink a shot of whiskey. We go until both of us have used our two rolls of quarters."

"Sounds easy."

"If you're good, if not you're drinking eighty shots of beer."

"That's only seven bottles."

"In less than an hour."

"Oh."

"Plus any whiskey if I'm a good shot."

"Now it sounds tougher."

"Okay one practice shot each."

I threw my quarter. It landed on the floor about two inches from her glass. She threw hers right in my cup.

"Good thing for you this was a practice shot," she said.

I unrolled my two rolls of quarters and spread them on the table. She did the same.

"You first," she said.

I tossed a quarter and hit her in the chest and it fell right into the cup.

"Nice shot. Very titillating," she drank a shot of whiskey and poured another. She threw hers and missed. She took a shot of beer.

"I like this game already," I said.

"We've only just begun."

Over the next ten shots, I missed all of mine, and also drank three shots of whiskey.

"The worse you are, the more you drink, the more you drink, the worse you are," she said with a smile.

We fired off the next twenty in about ten minutes. I did a little better getting eight in. Ursula meanwhile hit for ten.

"You're right, this is tough," I said with a slur, the booze was really starting to hit me and we had fifty more quarters to go, each. Ursula started to cry.

"What's wrong," I asked. "I'll get you a Kleenex."

"No stupid. This is the part where we feel sorry for ourselves."

"Oh," I said, even though I was unsure if I understood.

"Look at me," she continued. "I'm pathetic, sitting in a lonely apartment playing drinking games. And I'm also fat."

"Your not fat, you're in good shape. Hell, you could even be one of those wrestling Diva's you see on TV."

"That's another thing," she said as her tears made her mascara run down her face.

"Just because I'm blonde and have big tits, everyone thinks I'm a Bimbo."

"I didn't mean it that way."

"I know you didn't, you're a nice guy. I have a brain, but nobody sees it."

"What about Johnny, he knows you're smart."

"Johnny, the Disease, what the fuck does he know?"

"I thought you two were an item?"

"He must think I'm the disease. He's got hands that could cover a basketball and hasn't even touched these yet," she said as she squeezed her breasts. "Do they look diseased to you?"

"No. They look very healthy to me," I could sense that I was getting drunk. I'm not sure if I wanted to continue. I have to be very careful what I say about my plans.

"You're just saying that."

"I don't know what to say. If I say you have nice tits, you'll think that I think you're a Bimbo. If I say they're not nice, I'd be lying."

"I know it's hard to think sometimes. I think you should throw another quarter."

We threw another fifteen or twenty each. I lost count. All I know is I opened another beer that time. I was getting very drunk.

"What do you have to be sad about?" Ursula spit out. "You've got money, you're living your dream, you've got it made."

"Made? Right, I sit alone every night until I fall asleep on the couch. In school they called me Pencil Dick." I said as I started to cry. "I never had a girlfriend until I was out of school, not until I met my wife." Shit, I thought to myself. I knew I had too much a drink.

"Do you really have one?"

"No, she was murdered."

"Your pencil dick was murdered?"

I looked up and caught her staring at my crotch. I don't even think she heard what I said about Lynn.

"I was a late boomer."

"How was your wife murdered?"

I started to really sob. "Someone broke into our house when I was at work and killed her." I wanted to get it out but I couldn't tell her the truth. "I hated being called Pencil Dick. It all started after this one girl set me up. Got me naked and took some pictures. Damn I hate her. Look at me now. I've got money and I still sit alone every night. I've lied and deceived people just to get even. I'm such an asshole. I should just give it all up."

"I'll take the money."

"No, you dickhead, my plan." Oh-Oh, watch it I thought, but I was too drunk to even remember what I said and I couldn't stop crying. My emotions just poured out. "My whole family has been screwed, and I'm sick of it. I am so drunk and so confused I don't even know what's real and what's not. I'd better shut up." I said out loud trying to convince myself to stop. "Why don't we stop the stupid game?"

"It's not a stupid game. I feel better letting it out, don't you?" she asked.

In all reality I truly did. I hated having my plans being bottled up inside me with no one to vent it to. But now was not the time, nor the place.

"It's your turn Ursula."

She threw another quarter and got it in my cup. I downed another shot of whiskey. We threw about ten more each. I'm not sure whether I missed them all but I sure did drink a lot that round. I looked at Ursula and started to laugh.

"What so fucking funny?"

"Your face," I laughed even louder.

"What's wrong with my face?" she asked.

"Look for yourself." I pointed to the mirror on the wall. Ursula struggled to get up, as she did she stumbled a bit. She raised her head and looked in the mirror.

"You look like Alice Cooper in drag," I roared.

Her mascara had run down her face, right from her eyes, past her mouth and down her chin. The top of her T-shirt that her breasts held up were covered with black dots that were deposited as her mascara dropped off her chin. She also started to laugh hysterically as she broke into a very bad rendition of *Only Women Bleed*. I was laughing so hard I thought I was going to piss my pants. I rolled on the floor and used the table as a crutch to stand up, knocking over my beer as I did. I tried very quickly to grab it. It exploded with foam instantly, the foam running down the neck of the bottle and over my hand. I stumbled over to Ursula and put my arm around her.

"It's okay," I said. "I like Alice Cooper."

She started wiping her cheeks to try to get some of it off.

"Here let me help," I said as I set the bottle on the mantle. I wiped her face with my hand that was still wet from the beer. It smeared her mascara even more. I looked in the mirror and started another round of laughter.

"Look," I said as I grabbed her chin and pointed it to the mirror. "Don't you look purdy?"

"My T-shirt," she laughed. "My tits have freckles."

"This will help," I said as I grabbed my bottle off the mantle and poured it on her top. Her white and now black spotted shirt morphed into two mounds of flesh as her T-shirt took shape around her braless boobs.

"Hey you freaking cue ball," she said as she stumbled over to the cooler, grabbed a beer and opened it.

"I think more of a bowling ball, look at the holes." I said laughing, putting two fingers in my nose and one in my mouth.

She poured some of the beer in her hand and wiped it on her face and blackened it. She then rubbed her hand on my head making it black.

"There, now you look like a bowling ball."

"I think you're right."

She held up her left hand and motioned to me. "Come here," she said still holding the bottle in her right hand. I swaggered over to her, as I did she stumbled back a bit. I reached out and caught her left arm. She reached for me and grabbed the waistband of my track pants. We both caught our balance. "I knew this guy," she said. "We went skinny dipping. The water was ice cold and when we got out of the water, you know what I called him? Pencil Dick," she said. Still grasping the waistband of my pants she pulled them out and emptied the near freezing beer into my pants. "There you go Pencil Dick." I fell as I jumped backwards, pulling Ursula to the floor with me. We laid there, her on top of me, laughing and giggling for a few minutes.

"It's your turn," she slurred. "By the way, your head looks like a bowling ball."

"My turn for what?"

"The game, were not done the game."

She rolled off of me and we both scrambled to our spots. I threw my quarter and missed, I poured a shot of beer and drank it down.

"Fuck it," she said. "You win." She threw all the quarters she had left, all at once. I did the same.

"Don't you feel better now?" she asked.

"I do," I replied, and fell on my side. "I'm so drunk I can't even move. I feel like a gutter ball."

"Good one," she said. "Good one. Feel any better?" she repeated herself. "We've laughed, we've cried, all we have to do is puke and we'll feel like a million bucks."

"I'm not going anywhere, I'm fine right here."

"Me too," she said tiredly.

Soon I heard snoring. She was lying flat on her back, her arms and legs stretched out. Even though I was drunk out of my gourd, I knew I couldn't leave her on her back. I turned her on her side. I made it to my knees again and crawled down the hall to get a blanket from the bedroom. I never made it. I awoke a minute later. I know it was longer because as I lifted my head from the rug I could feel the corrugated design on my cheek, wet from my drool. As I glanced back at Ursula I could see she hadn't moved an inch. I got up, still a bit wobbly and wandered into the bedroom and grabbed the duvet off the bed. I glanced at the clock radio. It was ten after four. I walked back down the hall dragging the duvet behind me. I took it to the living room and covered Ursula with it. She didn't move

The place was a mess and the aroma of stale beer filled the air. It started to make me nauseous so I stood up. My thighs were all sticky from Ursula's beer. I headed to the kitchen to get a glass of water. I stopped and looked at Ursula. Damn she looked terrible. I opened the fridge when I got there and took out a small bottle of water, screwed open the top and drank it down. Boy was it cold. I could feel it go all the way down to my stomach, where I swear I heard it splash as it landed. I sure was bloated. I took my hands and placed them on both sides of my stomach and shook it. I could hear it swooshing. Either that or my bladder was bursting at the seams. When I got in the bathroom I looked in the mirror. I had black smeared all over my head from our earlier episode. I took some water and washed my face and head. I dried them, turning the towel a shade of gray as I did.

My stomach started to growl, actually it was rumbling. If I listened close enough I could hear the liquid as it traveled its course through my intestinal track. I burped and threw up in my mouth. It was gross. I turned and spit it into the toilet, my stomach started to do a war dance. I knelt down beside the toilet, the aroma made it easy to throw up. The more I did the smellier it got. My stomach cramped, the pain was unbearable. I wasn't sure which end it was going to come out of. I turned and sat down. I gagged again. I spun around and threw up again, this time with so much force that I shit myself. I sat on the toilet again. I felt another gag coming on, and I turned sideways on the toilet, slid open the shower doors and threw up in the tub. I kept throwing up until there was nothing left. Although I felt like shit, my eyes watering from the effort, it all came back to me. Sandwich night, only I think this was worse. But it took my thoughts back to that bastard Dave, and why I was here. It put everything back into perspective. If anything, the beer that had clouded my mind was now making it all clear and focused. I grabbed the showerhead, turned on the water and rinsed the tub. I flushed the toilet while sitting on it. I let the hand-held shower head go and closed the doors, it danced in the tub like a Cobra. I shuffled over to the bidet and rinsed my backside. When I was done I climbed into the shower and took a long hot one. I dried myself off, wrapped the towel around my waist, gathered up my clothes and opened the door. I could see Ursula's lifeless body still flaked out in the living room. I walked up beside her and listened for a breath. Not hearing one I pushed her gently with my foot. She stirred but never woke. I made my way to her apartment door, opened it and turned the dead bolt to prop it open. I stuck my head out and looked both ways down the hall and then up at the camera. I ventured down the hall and tossed my clothes in the garbage chute. I went back to her place. I stood there just inside for a minute after releasing the dead bolt, I closed the door and locked it again, contemplating what to do next. It was too early to call the super to let me into my place. Lee would shoot me if I called her. It dawned on me that I hadn't locked the patio door after my last cigar. I reached through the blinds, unlocked the sliding door and opened it. I parted the blinds and stepped out onto the balcony. I went to the end that housed the retaining wall that separated her apartment from mine. I removed the towel that was restricting me from climbing the railing and threw it over my shoulder. I climbed to the rail, shimmied my way along it and hopped back over it once I was on my side. I went inside, got dressed and brushed my teeth, twice. It was now five-thirty. I grabbed a cigar, a glass of Coke and sat on the balcony catching the sunrise. I now felt like a million bucks. Ursula was right. Her therapy worked, only I didn't have to stick my finger down my throat to throw up, or maybe it was the rejuvenation of being focused again on my plan. Whatever it was, it worked.

CHAPTER 10

I grabbed a pound of bacon, whatever eggs I had left in the carton, and a jug of orange juice and headed to Ursula's. I got about halfway there before I realized that I had locked her door. I went back through my place, set the stuff on the railing and climbed back to her balcony. I emerged through the blinds after grabbing the items and made my way to the kitchen. I turned on the stove and poured two glasses of juice. I laid the bacon in the pan and put a lid on it. I walked back through the living room and drew open the blinds to let sun in.

"Rise and shine," I yelled.

I could now smell the bacon cooking. I wasn't the only one, out of nowhere came the cat.

"Rise and shine," I said again poking Ursula in the back with my foot, she stirred. The cat made its way to her face and started rubbing against it, purring. Ursula made a spitting sound, as the cats' fur must have entered her mouth. She pushed the cat away.

"C'mon on sunshine, get up."

"What time is it?"

"Six-thirty. Now let's go, we've got to get to the gym."

She brushed her hair away from her face as she sat up. "What's that smell?"

"Bacon, eggs, toast and orange juice. Do you want me to make coffee too?"

"God no. Your very chipper today."

"Therapy my dear. You said it would work; a little laughter, a few tears, a good vomit. And it did. You're a good nurse, speaking of which, did you come up with a name yet?"

"Yeah, Nurse Nasty, for the way I feel."

"I like it. Go have a shower. Breakfast will be ready in a few minutes... but don't look in the mirror."

"Why not?"

I started to laugh. "Because it will ruin you're appetite."

"Shut up," she said as she made her way to the bathroom.

I continued to cook the bacon, laying them on a sheet of paper towel when they were done to soak up the grease.

"That feels better," she said as she entered the kitchen in her robe.

"How do you like your eggs?"

"I'm just going to have toast and orange juice thank you."

"I want you to go buy a nurse's outfit, a sexy one."

"Why don't I stop on the way?"

"Okay," I said as I handed her some bills.

We ate breakfast together. I ate a lot; I was starving. When we were done I started to clean the plates.

"Leave them I'll do them later. By the way, thanks for last night," she said.

"Thanks for what?"

"The laughs, the tears. I think it really helped me too. And thanks for not taking advantage of me. Most guys would have."

"Listen, nothing personal, I think you're very attractive, but I respect you and Johnny. Sex would have only ruined our partnership in all of this. I'll see you around ten," I said as I left.

When I arrived at the gym, Johnny was already stretching in the ring.

"Take it easy for a bit Johnny, I'm giving you a reprieve. I want to finalize our plans, let's go see Jay."

Johnny climbed out of the ring and followed me upstairs.

"Howdy Jay, how's it going?"

"Good Dr. Death, I've found an opponent: The Tiger. He's from the Mitsui gym across town. He's got a good following."

"Is he willing to lose?"

"For $10,000.00 U.S. he's willing to be adopted," Jay laughed.

"Give him a shout, have him pack his stuff and get here in three days. We need to choreograph. The fight is in less than three weeks. Jay, have you ordered the bleachers yet?"

"Enough for a thousand people. It will be tight, but we should be able to squeeze them in."

"Great. Ursula should be here around ten. Has Mrs. Yamaha made Johnny's suit yet?"

"It will be ready in two days."

"Good. Jay, call a photographer and ask him to come here next Monday. He can take the photos for the fight card. The Tiger will be here by then. All we have left to do is to get a ring announcer and we're all set."

"Mr. White Sir, if you don't have anyone in mind, my father would love to do it. He used to be a wrestler, and he misses the ring very much," Johnny said.

"What the hell, tell him he's got the job."

"Thank you sir," Johnny replied as he bowed.

I bowed back. "Okay boys back to work."

I did some paperwork while Jay and Johnny went to the ring and practiced. Ursula came in a short while later.

"Good morning again," I said. "How are you feeling now?"

"Pretty good. I picked out a costume."

"Go try it on and let's have a look."

She left the office and went to the change room. I went down to ringside and waited. She emerged from the change room looking great. Johnny stopped in his tracks and stared. She had on open-toed white sling-back heels and her legs were clad with white mid-thigh nylons. The left one had a black garter around it. She wore a white garter belt that held them up under a very short mini skirt that showed off the bottom part of her buttocks from under the thong she was wearing. Her top was skin-tight, tapered at the waist and only buttoned up to her navel. Her breasts pushed back the sides of her top and were held in place by her lacy push up bra. She had lightened her face a bit with powder and had on the reddest shade of lipstick I had ever seen. Her blonde hair was done in tight curls, Shirley Temple style, and on her hair sat a white nurse's cap with a black band that had NASTY written on it with white letters.

"You said sex sells," she said as she made her way to the ring.

"It's perfect." I thought Johnny was going to pass out from panting so much. "Carry on guys," I said. I wanted to see if Johnny could keep his concentration in the ring. I went back up to the office and put on my outfit. It was a lot simpler looking than hers. I wore a pair of running shoes, covered with those green booties that doctors wore. A green two-piece surgical suit and a headband with a round mirror attached. I also had a black doctor's bag. I went back down and joined the others.

"Okay Jay, grab Johnny an opponent and put him in the ring."

Jay whistled to one of the other wrestlers working out and told him to go into the ring.

"Okay just spar for a while, when I give you the word, Johnny, put him in a Full Nelson and hold him there."

I set the black doctor's bag on the edge of the apron in Johnny's corner. I let them wrestle for a bit while I explained to Ursula what I wanted her to do. When she was ready, she dramatically opened the bag, and took out a large latex glove. Holding it in one hand she closed her other hand around it. She pulled it through her hand and waived it overhead, much like a stripper would a boa. In a real fight, hopefully this would get the crowd going. She grabbed the open end with both hands and stretched it open. I put my left arm out and she slid it over my hand. I pulled it so it fit tight. It came almost to my elbow. We repeated the process with the other glove, sliding it onto my right hand. I held my arms out with palms up, as if trying not to contaminate their sterility. She reached back in the bag and took out a small rubber topped medicine vile, filled with a green liquid. It was water and food colouring. She held it up to eye level and shook it. She then set it on the apron beside her. She reached back in the bag and took out an oversized hypodermic needle, held it gingerly in both hands and turned a 360-degree circle showing it to what would be the crowd. I had picked it up at a novelty shop. It had a button on the handle that would allow the needle part to retract slowly into the handle when pressed against someone's arm. Ursula picked the bottle back up and inverted it. She then eased it over the needle part piercing the rubber circle on the top of the bottle. She held the handle in her left hand, letting the bottle dangle on the end. She slowly and dramatically pulled back the plunger drawing the liquid into the cavity of the shaft. When it was full she tossed the empty bottle back in the bag and handed me the needle. I yelled to Johnny, who whipped his opponent into the turnbuckle above me. He ran into him with extreme force. His opponent took three steps forward and Johnny seized him in a

Full Nelson. I climbed the stairs behind him. I stood outside the ring and held the hypodermic needle up in the air, showing it to the invisible crowd. Johnny turned his opponent and faced the corner. Ursula slid on the canvas under the bottom rope, her skirt raising up to please the crowd and walked to the opposition's corner. Jay, who was acting as the referee, went over and tried to convince her to leave. This would drive the fans wild, as the ref was not paying attention to Johnny and myself. I tapped the needle in a flicking motion with my middle finger so it would collect all the air bubbles at the top. I depressed the plunger a bit, expelling the liquid into the air. I turned and faced the wrestlers. I grabbed Johnny's opponents left arm, took the needle, pressed the button on the handle and drove it into his arm. His opponent was shaking his head vigorously back and forth yelling "No!" The needle retracted and as I pushed the plunger the liquid released into a concealed area of the handle giving the effect of the liquid releasing into the opponents bloodstream as the chamber emptied. I hopped off the ring.

Ursula exited at the other side allowing the referee to return to his job. I threw the needle in the bag, picked it up and left to go to the change room. The crowd would be yelling with excitement, trying to convince the referee of the wrongdoing. Johnny released his opponent, pushing him into the centre of the ring. The opponent ran in circles and collapsed, convulsing on the canvas long enough for me to make my exit, and then he went still. Jay went towards him, bent over and felt for a pulse. He picked up his arm and then let it go. It fell to the canvas, limp. He did this three times. The crowd would be counting- one, two, and three. Jay then pointed to where the timer would be and the bell would sound. Jay stood up and raised Johnny's arm in victory.

"Perfect," I yelled from the doorway. "Perfect. That will get the crowd going. We will then have the paramedics rush in. A doctor with a stethoscope will listen to his chest, shake his head, and cover him with a blanket. They will carry him off on a stretcher and load him into a hearse; all of which will be shown on the big screen. The hearse will drive away past a curtain, and then the cameras will go off. Once out of the view of the

camera, the opponent will get out of the hearse and we'll all have a beer in the dressing room. What do you think?"

"Very good," Jay said.

"I like it," said Johnny. "Some will love me and some will hate me."

"Sounds good," Ursula said. "Even my Uncle Mike would be impressed."

"Speaking of him, we'll invite him once we get a title match. Hopefully then we can convince him to set up a match in the U.S."

"Right on," she said.

"Okay everybody, four days till Monday. Take a break and we'll see you then. Be back at 10:00 a.m. for a photo shoot, full costume. Pack your suitcases because after the shoot we're taking a working vacation in seclusion so no one can see our show. We'll be gone for ten days. Jay, unfortunately you'll have to stay back to keep the promoting going."

"That's okay, my wife wouldn't want me to go for that long."

"Okay see you on Monday."

I went back to the office as they all left.

CHAPTER 11

Monday came quickly. I slept until eight o'clock and made my way to the gym for ten. The others were already waiting.

"Morning y'all. The photographer will be here in an hour. Everyone suit up."

A gentleman I didn't recognize also stood up. He came over to me.

"Damn," I said to him. "You're even bigger than Texas."

He bowed and looked at Johnny.

"He doesn't speak English," Johnny said to me turning to the gentleman. He spoke to him in Japanese. I don't know what he said but it ended with Dr. Death. The man bowed at me again.

"Who is that Johnny?"

"He's the Tiger, my opponent."

"Where is your father?"

"I didn't know he was to be here. I can call him."

"It's okay, he really doesn't need to be here until the day of the fight."

We all exited to the changeroom to get dressed. Ursula had a little corner of it where we had strung up a shower curtain for a makeshift change room. We never had a women's change room before. Johnny pulled his costume out of his bag. It was white with a molecular model design on it.

"Cool outfit, Jay tell your wife she outdid herself."

The Tiger pulled out his outfit. It was a black and orange striped spandex suit. It also had a cap complete with ears and whiskers. We all got dressed. Ursula pulled the curtain back when she was done.

The Tiger looked at her with his mouth gaping and said something in Japanese. Johnny hit him on the arm and responded to the Tiger pointing at himself. I heard the bell on the door ring and I went to see who it was.

"Mr. White?"

"Yes," I said.

"I'm here to take some photographs."

He looked like a typical Japanese tourist with his camera around his neck.

"You can set up over there," I pointed to the ring. He whistled and two guys entered carrying lights, boxes and tripods. It took half an hour before they were ready. He took about a hundred different shots, some of us together and some individual ones.

"I want the proofs back this afternoon."

"But I..."

I handed him some cash.

"Yes sir," he replied.

"Jay you pick out the ones you want. Get the posters and tickets printed and get them out there. Give a bunch to the schools and the local merchants to display. That goes for the tickets also. All one thousand of them are at no charge. I want to pack this place. We'll be back a couple of days before the fight. Get your stuff guys, let's go."

"Where are we going?" Ursula asked.

"I'm not telling," I replied like a child. The four of us left the gym.

I drove to a small airport where my jet was waiting. Kevin was already in the cockpit. I had all the windows blackened so they didn't have a clue where we were going. I was becoming very fond of all of them. Well except for the Tiger, I didn't even know his real name. The jet landed on the airstrip I had built on my island in Fiji.

"Wow, look at this fuckin' place," Ursula screamed. "Is it yours?"

"No, it's my friend John's."

"Some friend," Johnny said.

"Make yourself at home. There's a pool and spa around the back, get a good tan. We want to look healthy for our debut. There are six bedrooms. Mine is the last one on the right."

Some of them unpacked and went straight to the pool. I checked the place over. I hadn't been here in a few weeks. I had the staff order in enough supplies for ten days. There were only two of them: Manny and his daughter Maria. They were living in a homeless shelter in Miami when I met them at a breakfast I volunteered at. He was a maintenance man. When I bought the island he begged me to take him and his daughter with me. She made a living as a prostitute, dependent on drugs and he wanted to get her off the streets. My island is definitely off the streets. I let them live in the smallest cottage on the island. He is a good worker and a good man. He takes care of everything. She's now the cook and maid. As the others slowly trickled to the pool, I introduced them to Maria.

"Whatever you need, Maria will get you," I said as she followed me outside with an armful of towels. "Manny is around here somewhere. He can show you the island if you want to go for a walk. Just have Maria give him a call. He's got a GPS if you want to venture out without him."

I had several of those little walkie-talkies. The range was good for a couple of miles. The only link I had to the outside world was Ham Radio. I hadn't bothered to see what satellite connections I could set up for the computer system. I didn't spend much time on the island.

The airstrip was fairly new and provided just enough room for my small jet. I also had a helicopter. Kevin was my other staff. He was my pilot, chauffeur, and right-hand man. After high school he got his license to fly airplanes and helicopters. He lived on the mainland with his wife. I call him when I need him. He doesn't spend much time on the island. I don't even think he's ever met Manny, who was also always working somewhere. Even though Kevin and I were best of friends in high school, we didn't spend much time together now. He had two sets of twin boys, eighteen months apart. When I didn't need his services, he was at home helping Debbi with the boys. There would be plenty of time for socializing when I finished my plan and I didn't need him as often. By then, the boys would be a little bit older. The first two days we all sat around the pool working on our tans and discussing strategies. Johnny and the Tiger practiced moves in the field. I never bothered to set up a ring since all they had to do was run through the routine and act it out the best they could. We would have a couple of days when we got back to see if it all worked. When the ten days were over we headed back to Japan tanned and relaxed.

I arrived at the gym three days before the fight. Jay was already there. I walked in and looked around. I could hardly recognize the place. Jay had the bleachers in and had even made a makeshift confectionery stand.

"Looks great Jay."

"Thank you sir. Everything's all set and the tickets have been distributed. Did you see the posters?"

"I saw them in the window, good job."

"The TV station is coming in at one o'clock to do some promo shots. I bought some local airtime," Jay said.

"Now there you go Jay, it didn't take you long to get back into the North American way of thinking, did it?"

"No sir."

Johnny and the Tiger arrived.

"Johnny?"

"Yes Sir."

"From here on in, you and The Tiger can't be seen together. You are enemies now. Explain that to him, will you?"

Johnny turned and spoke to the Tiger in Japanese, he bowed at me, I bowed back.

"Tiger," he said as he pounded his chest with his fist and sneered.

I noticed his tiger jacket for the first time. It hadn't donned on me until then. I should have been a Tiger, back in high school that is. Ironically that's why I'm here; to avenge that night. The bell on the door rang and a man entered.

"Father," Johnny said and bowed.

"Ah, my announcer has arrived," I went over and greeted him. Ursula came in behind him.

"Suit up guys. Let's practice what we've learned," I said.

After changing, the guys went into the ring. The rest of us went up to the office. Jay and I filled Mr. Sashi in on all the details. Shortly after lunch the TV crew came in. We spent a couple of hours doing interviews and promo shots. Everything was ready to go.

"Jay, is everything set with your wife? She doesn't have a problem with the Tiger does she?"

"No sir," he said. He turned to the Tiger and explained to him that he was going to spend the next couple of nights at the

Yamaha's. I was unsure whether or not I could trust him. After all, I'd only known him a couple weeks. He seemed committed. My reason for going to Fiji was to alienate him from any affiliates he might have. I wanted fight night to be a secret.

"Johnny, you're going to stay with me until Friday night. I need you close to Ursula and myself in case we missed anything."

"Okay Sir."

Ursula looked at me, pointed to her chest and mouthed "my apartment." The two of them had become quite close while on the island. The last four days they shared a bedroom. I think they were now an item.

"I don't care," I responded back to her. "But if I need you, you guys need to be available."

"Shhh," Johnny said pointing at his dad.

We all left for a couple of days, not arriving back at the gym until five hours before the fight. We did last minute preparations, including covering the windows with paper. Even though all the tickets were handed out free of charge, I wanted to peak the interest of anyone who did not get one. The TV crew arrived and finished setting up their equipment. I had bought a three-hour block of time on the most popular station in Japan. I paid a small fortune for it, but if I was going to take Johnny to the top, I had to spend money to make money. Jay was going to take the tickets at the door, more for crowd control than anything else. Mrs. Yamaha was going to sell the snacks. Jay could help her once everyone was admitted. Johnny, The Tiger, Ursula and I watched from the office.

Jay opened the door and they filed in. They came in droves. Within half an hour the stands were full and I was relieved. Even though my plan was sound, I wasn't sure whether it would work or not. The bell sounded and Mr. Sashi started to announce. The crowd was quiet for the first two fights. Some of them didn't even pay attention.

"Ursula, come with me," I said.

We went down to ringside as the third match began. She strutted her sexy body around the outside of the ring, grabbing the attention of the males in the crowd. The two fighters in the ring were from another gym. They were fairly well known fighters. They were given second billing on the card as a drawing feature to make sure people would show up. I had paid their managers for their rights for the night. Jay had arranged it all. We didn't care who won or lost. I only cared to know who the winner was going to be. I motioned to the office for the Tiger to come downstairs. The good guy put his match ending sleeper hold on his opponent who fell to the mat, pretending to be asleep. The referee bent down to do the three-count. He counted one, two... Ursula climbed in the ring and distracted the ref, taking him into the far corner. The good guy followed.

The crowd started yelling. I climbed in the ring with my doctor bag, knelt down beside the bad guy, and took out some smelling salts reviving him. He sat up slowly shaking his head dramatically and stood up. The fans were going wild and shouting in Japanese. I crawled over behind the wrestler arguing with the referee. Ursula dropped her nurses' hat. As she bent over to pick it up, her skirt rose exposing her tanned buttocks that had swallowed her thong. The good guy craned his neck to get a better look. The crowd was pointing and laughing. Ursula caught him looking. He withdrew his head quickly. She started to accuse him of looking at her ass. He raised his hands in denial. She slapped him across the face and sent him reeling backwards. He fell over me and landed on his back, his legs rising in the air as he fell. The other wrestler jumped on him and held his legs over his head, pinning his shoulders to the mat. Ursula pushed the referee towards them. He laid down and counted one, two, and three. The bell sounded to end the match.

The Tiger came running to the ring and slid under the bottom rope and went to the referee, crying foul and pointing at Nurse Nasty and myself. Ursula went over to them. I snuck behind the Tiger and knelt on all fours. Ursula pushed him in the chest with both arms. He went ass over teakettle landing on the mat. Ursula and I ran out of the ring to the change room. The crowd was yelling and throwing objects at us. The referee held up the bad guy's arm in victory. The crowd was booing. The Tiger grabbed the bad guys arm out of the ref's hand and pulled it down, at the same time raising the arm of the other wrestler. The fans were cheering. The referee pushed the Tiger, raised the bad guys arm and left the ring under a hail of empty soda cups. The wrestlers left the ring and met up with us in the change room. We all shook hands, and congratulated each other. Ursula and I went back upstairs. We watched the next few fights from the office, making an appearance every now and then at ringside just to egg on the fans. They were hysterical, yelling and throwing things at us every time we went down there.

It was finally time for our match. Johnny's dad entered the ring, followed by the Tiger. The crowd cheered. Our names were called and we made our way down the gangplank into a barrage of crumpled soda cups and insults. I entered the ring first. I stepped on the bottom rope and pulled the middle one upwards as high as I could, Ursula bent down and stepped through exposing her thong to the crowd. Johnny entered next. His outfit looked even better now that he had his mask on. It was skintight and covered his whole face. The only holes in it were those for an airway and his eyes.

Ursula and I made our escape from the ring as the bell sounded. As the match ensued in the ring we continued to taunt the fans, driving them more and more wild with every gesture. The match was nearing the end. It was playing out just like we choreographed it. Johnny and the Tiger made it look so real. Nobody in the stands had any idea of how it was going to end. Johnny picked up the Tiger and threw him out of the ring. That was our cue to get ready.

As the Tiger reentered the ring, I opened my black bag and took out the syringe. I dramatically held it to the audience. They went crazy. Better than I could have expected. Ursula grabbed a pair of latex gloves. As she held them open, one at a time I slid my hands into them, snapping them on at the cuffs. I put the bottle of death serum on the end of the needle and retracted the plunger, drawing it in as slowly and methodically as I could. I let my eyes go blank as if I were hypnotized. Once the chamber was full, I discarded the empty bottle back in the bag. I held the syringe in front of me in an upward position as I paraded around ringside, sporadically giving demented stares to the crowd. I picked out the loudest and most fanatic fan and headed towards him. As I got closer the more boisterous he became, yelling and pointing his finger at me. I approached the guardrail that was holding him back, and standing a safe distance away, I maneuvered my extended forefinger and drew it across my throat, mimicking a slicing motion. I pushed the plunger of the needle and some liquid ejaculated into the air. The overzealous fan fell over his chair as he darted to avoid contact with the serum, the rest of fans in the vicinity gasped in fear.

I headed up the three steel stairs and stood on the apron behind the turnbuckle in Johnny's corner. Ursula mounted the canvas and climbed over the second rope in the opponents' corner and entered the ring. This not only caught the frenzied crowd's attention, but also that of the referee who was now on his way to see her. She maneuvered herself so the referee's back was to the wrestlers.

This was Johnny's and the Tigers cue. Johnny grabbed the Tiger by the arm and flung him into the ropes. As the Tiger rebounded, Johnny locked him in a Full Nelson to my left. With my left hand I grabbed the tricep side of the Tigers arm. I took the needle and stabbed it into his arm and pressed the plunger. I eased it slowly, allowing the green water to descend into the handle. When it was emptied, I retracted it allowing gravity to force the needle part to drop, making it look like the needle was withdrawing from under his skin.

Johnny released him as Ursula and I left the ring. The fans were yelling at the referee trying to make him realize what had happened. The Tiger thrashed around long enough for Nurse Nasty and I to make our way to the dressing room. He then collapsed on the canvas, made a couple of dramatic twitches, and then laid flat on his back. The referee fell to his knees and slapped the canvas three times. The bell sounded. The referee raised Johnny's arm in victory. Johnny left the ring. The referee tried to raise the fallen warrior but to no avail. A well-dressed distinguished man appeared from behind the curtain and made his way to the ring. He set his black doctor's bag beside the Tiger and knelt down. He felt for a pulse. Feeling none, he took a mirror out and held it between the Tigers upper lip and his nose. The Tiger exhaled through his mouth ever so slowly so as not to fog the mirror. Jay's brother who was playing the doctor then shook his head, pulled out a sheet from the doctor's bag and covered the Tiger. The crowd was silent. A hearse slowly made its way into view. The driver got out and went to the back of the vehicle and opened the door. He pulled out a gurney and made his way down the ramp to the ring and climbed in. He assisted the doctor with the Tiger's body, dragging it from the ring and putting it on the stretcher. The fans that were previously silent started yelling and screaming as the big screen TV now showed Johnny, Ursula and I laughing in the dressing room. They got out of control. They started throwing anything they could find. The ring became quite littered. Jay and his wife made a hasty retreat to the dressing rooms to seek shelter.

"Great work guys," I said as we headed out of the dressing room.

"But Mr. White, look at this place," Jay said.

"Isn't it great, look at the reaction we got from the fans. Just watch TV tonight. With all the media's attention we're going to get it will put us on the map."

"But the place, it will take forever to clean up."

"Not to worry. In the morning make a few calls and have someone restore it, whatever the cost. I'm going home. I'll see you all Monday, have a good weekend," I said as I left.

I went home that night and basked in all the glory. The media carried the after-fight incident all night.

We were in demand everywhere. Jay set up fights throughout Japan.

"Good morning Ursula," I said as I came into the office.

"Good Morning Darryl."

"You're looking awful chipper today," I said.

"Johnny asked me to marry him, we're getting hitched the day before the big fight."

"That's great, no wonder you're smiling."

"Not only that, my Uncle Mike called."

"Your Uncle Mike?" I questioned.

"The wrestling uncle from Florida."

"Oh yeah," I said as if I didn't know. "What did he want?"

"He saw me on CNN. He said it looked like we had quite the success the other night. He would like to come here and see us. He says that if we are as big as he thinks, he would like to set up a match for us in the U.S."

"Give me his address and I'll send him a ticket to both the fight at the stadium and his flight. Will he need a motel?"

"No, he can stay with Johnny and I. That way we can catch up."

"What about a honeymoon? You will be at the fight, won't you?"

"Sure will. We're going to wait to see what Mike can set up in the U.S. Once Johnny wins there then maybe we'll take a couple of weeks and go to Africa. I've always wanted to go on a safari."

"You're pretty cocky in assuming Johnny can win a U.S. title."

"You said it yourself Darryl, bullshit sells. After all it is a very well choreographed soap opera. Besides, my uncle's in charge of the FWF and Johnny is going to marry me."

"Okay, okay I get your drift."

The next couple of weeks were spent on the road wrestling twice a week and training the rest of the time. We were hot. We packed the stands no matter where we fought.

Ursula arrived at the gym, three days before the wedding.

"Good morning Darryl, I'd like you to meet my Uncle Mike."

"Howdy," I said as I shook his hand.

"You've got quite the show going on here in Japan," he said.

"Yep, I was unsure whether we could pull it off or not, but we did. Your niece has been a great help."

"I've seen the footage, great concept."

"We've got a huge title match on Sunday, are you able to stay?"

"No we've got a match the same day. By the way, where is the champ to be?"

"He's down there in the ring," Ursula said as she pointed to him.

I stood up from the desk, opened the window behind my chair and yelled, "Johnny, come up to the office."

"Isn't he cute Uncle Mike?"

"I guess so... nice build, good size... you should do well."

"What do you mean should?" she asked. "He's doing great."

"Yes, but can he cut it in North America?"

"You're the boss, Uncle Mike. You tell me."

"You wanted to see me Mr. White?" Johnny asked.

"Yes Johnny, come in."

Ursula leaned forward and gave him a kiss. "Johnny, this is my Uncle Mike."

"Hello Sir," he said as he bowed.

"Hi Johnny, good to meet you. I've watched you wrestle. I applaud your success."

"Thank you sir, but Mr. White has done all of the work."

"We're a team Johnny," I added. "The four of us."

"Four?" Mike questioned.

"Yes, Jay Pan. He's Johnny's trainer and my business manager."

"Great wrestler in his time," Mike said. "I remember seeing him when I was in my teens. I saw that match in Oklahoma that ended his career. Where is he now?"

"He's next door in the other gym." I stated. Business has tripled since we started our road to stardom. I had bought the two businesses attached to the current gym, gutted them and made a second gym.

"So Mr. White, what do you have in mind after you nail down the Japanese title?" Mike asked.

"I myself would like to get back to the U.S. I'd like to take Johnny and do a run there."

"What about you kids?" Mike asked Ursula and Johnny.

"I like it here," Ursula piped up. "I love Japan and the money we're making is fantastic. I'd hate to see Johnny lose it."

"He wouldn't have to lose it if you kids are set on settling in Japan. All you have to do is make one U.S. tour."

"What do you mean sir?" Johnny asked.

"You fight every other weekend in Florida and every other weekend in Japan. I'll make you the champion in about five weeks, hold the title for a couple of months, and then return to Japan full-time. You can then decide how long you want to keep going here."

"I like the idea," I said. "There's only one change though, how about we do a three month stint all at once? You would save money on the travel."

"I'm okay with that," Ursula said.

"Okay, it's set," Mike said. "You fight Sunday for the Japanese championship."

"Yes Sir. Johnny is going to win." Ursula said.

"I'll head back to Florida, promote it and carry your fight in Japan on closed-circuit TV right before our title match. After he wins we need some anti-American hype, and then for the next three months you come to Florida."

"Okay but in November we have to do a rematch here. It's JWF policy."

"No problem. Fly out right after the fight, Johnny can win the FWF title."

"Wait a minute, you're moving too fast for me," Ursula said.

"Sunday, you win here, then fly out, and in the next four Saturday nights I'll move Johnny to the top. Comeback here for your rematch, hop on a flight and win the Florida title match the next night. Wrestle for the next two months in Florida, Johnny will lose the Christmas match and then you can come back here for good."

"What about the honeymoon?" Ursula asked.

"We can still have it, we'll just postpone it for a while," Johnny said.

"As for the wedding, can it be postponed until the rematch here in Japan? You can get married in the ring." I told them.

"Good idea. And for your wedding present, I'll give Johnny the Florida title," Mike said.

"I guess we could do that, how about it Johnny?" Ursula asked.

"It doesn't matter to me. You're the one in charge of the wedding plans. My family is all here in Japan. Yours are coming from the U.S.," he answered.

"Okay let's do it. I only have my parents, two brothers and a sister coming over. I'll call them and let them know."

"Well Darryl, it was a short but sweet stay and we got a lot accomplished. Good luck Sunday. I'll set up the two way video broadcast, you dream up some good old anti-American rhetoric. We'll see you on Monday."

They all left, leaving me standing in the office. I picked up the phone and called Lee. I hadn't seen her in awhile, we both had been too busy. As I drove over to her house, I only had wrestling on my mind. The set up for the murder had consumed me alive. I never really lost sight of why I was here, but the life I was leading now was really becoming interesting. Lee and Liam were outside as I drove up the laneway. Liam ran to the car as I opened the door.

"Hi, big guy," I said picking him up. He was a very friendly child, maybe a little too friendly.

"Hi, Darryl," Lee said.

"Hi, how are you?"

"Okay."

"You seem down."

"No everything's okay," she answered.

"Did Ursula call you yet?"

"No, why?"

"They've postponed the wedding."

"Nothing serious, I hope."

"Oh no, they're going to tie the knot in the ring during the wrestling match."

"On Sunday?"

"No, during the rematch in November. Afterwards we're off to the U.S. for awhile."

"Sounds interesting."

"It'll be interesting, that's for sure. How is it going here?"

"Good, a few changes coming up."

"Like what?" I asked.

"Nothing final yet, but Mr. Campbell is looking at a job change."

"What about you? Will you still be working for him?"

"I'm not sure, but I think so. Like I said, nothing is written in stone yet. I'll let you know when I find out."

I visited for about three hours. We took Liam to the park and afterwards we just sat around and talked on the porch.

"I've got to be going now. I've got some planning to do for the match," I said as I stood up and walked towards her. We embraced for a moment, exchanged kisses and I left. Liam was waving goodbye as I drove away.

It was finally Sunday morning. The day of the big fight. I headed to the stadium early. The producer assured me that everything was set with the videoconference. When it was time for our match we headed to the ring. We were introduced first. For now we were still the challengers. God Bless America started to play. The boos got louder as the All-American came down the aisle. He had been champion in Japan for over six months. He wore a red, white and blue-striped outfit and an American flag as a cape. Two blonde bombshells held open the ropes as he stepped through. The two girls removed his cape and folded it. The All-American grabbed the microphone. The ring announcer conducted the matches in Japanese, but when we spoke they put Japanese subtitles for the audience over the stadium and at home on the pay per view.

"Tonight is a special occasion for me," he started. "It's my birthday and to celebrate this match, it is being aired in my home state of Florida, isn't that right Mike?"

"Yes it is, we're showing it live here as it happens there, we've got fifty-thousand fans that want to sing happy birthday to you."

The crowd in Japan started booing again.

You could hear 'Happy Birthday' being sung through the speakers. Thomas, that was the All-American, handed me the microphone as they sang. He raised his hands in a pumping motion to entice the crowd in Japan to sing along. He was met with more booing. Even though Johnny and the All-American were both bad guys, it seemed Johnny was the favourite. The song ended and the two scantily clad assistants brought out a cake as I started to speak.

"Before you make a wish, can I make a suggestion?" I asked.

"What is it?"

"You'd better wish that you don't get caught with the Disease," I pointed at Johnny. "Because if you do, the doctor will have to deal with it." I held out the needle and squirted the green liquid in the air. "Now go ahead, make your wish."

He held his head back and closed his eyes for a few seconds. He leaned forward to blow out the candles. I pushed the cake right in his face. Ursula and Johnny each grabbed a handful and smeared it on the faces of his two assistants. The three of us scrambled out of the ring. The All-American cleared his eyes as his assistants left the ring and the bell sounded. Johnny climbed back into the ring and they started wrestling. The match lasted twenty-five minutes before Johnny put him in a Full Nelson. I climbed the apron and gave the shot of death. The All-American thrashed around and then collapsed in the centre of the ring. The bell sounded and Johnny was declared the winner. The announcer handed him the championship belt and Johnny put it on. I grabbed the microphone from the announcer as the fans cheered.

"Hey Florida, are you still watching?"

"Yes, Dr. Death, we're still here," Mike the Mouth answered back.

"What do you think of your All-American now?"

Mike focused the camera on the U.S. crowd for a minute.

The paramedics were now in the ring doing their part. What a contrast between the crowds. The crowd here was cheering and the TV screen audience in Florida was yelling names and throwing things at the cameras.

"Well Mike, look at your All-American now." The coroner had come in and shook his head, folding the All-Americans' arms on his chest and covered him in the American flag. His assistants were weeping and consoling each other in the corner. "Looks like another weak American has just bit the dust."

As the paramedics were loading him on the gurney, I grabbed the American flag; "Mike, one more thing."

"What's that?"

"If you have any other rednecks that you think can fight the Disease, just send them over."

"I'll do better than that Dr. Death. Why don't you bring your Disease to Florida, we'll show you how we in the South inoculate against diseases."

"But we're the champs here, why should we come to Florida? What's in it for us?"

"What's the matter, afraid to pick on people your own size?"

"We'll do it under one condition. For your big fall event, we want a title match. Winner takes both, the Japanese and the Florida title."

"You're on, but you have to beat four opponents over the next four weeks here in Florida, then you get a shot at The Bruiser."

"No problem, we'll leave on a flight tomorrow."

"We'll see you then."

The screen went black as the hearse drove away. Johnny raised his arm once more in victory and the crowd cheered. He had just become a national hero. We left the ring and went back to the dressing room.

My cell phone rang and I answered it.

"Great job, Darryl, you really stirred the pot."

"Thanks Mike, we fly into Miami tomorrow night at seven your time."

"Give my love to Ursula."

"Will do, bye." I turned to Jay, Johnny and Ursula. "We're a hit. Mike said the crowd went nuts."

The next morning the three of us grabbed a flight to Miami. Jay stayed back to run things at the gym. He was also going to show the matches on closed circuit at the stadium for free. That way the Japanese fans could follow Johnny.

The next four weeks went fast. We hopped from one end of Florida to the other. We were met with overwhelming hatred as we entered the ring. We spread anti-American propaganda at every match and interview we could. We won all four matches, defeating four of the best wrestlers Florida had to offer. Dave was there at all the matches. His character, The Playboy, had lost a lot of popularity while I was in Japan. He fought in the early matches every week. It looked like his career as a wrestler would soon be over. Since he was dubbed a bad guy he shared a dressing room with us every week. I pretended to befriend him. I added a lot of hype about the Japanese market and how maybe he should come to the East after Christmas. I had told him confidentially that I was going to retire once our reign in Florida was done and that Johnny would need a new manager. He bought it hook, line, and sinker. Of course that was strictly between us and if Johnny was to catch wind of it, there would be no deal. For the five weeks we were there, Dave watched our matches to get it down right.

We flew back to Japan for our rematch. The stadium was packed once again. This time we were the heroes. Ursula and Johnny received thousands of cards and gifts as people poured into the stadium. Johnny's dad announced us as we made our way to the ring. Ursula was dressed in a beautiful white wedding dress. We held the ceremony in the squared circle. The fans were cheering and throwing roses to the newly married couple. After their first kiss Mike the Mouth entered the ring and grabbed the microphone.

"Hello all you little people," he said. "Now that the festivities are over, we need to get down to business. Your champion was going to fight tomorrow night in the United States, against my champion the Bruiser."

The crowd booed.

"The winner of the fight will receive both championship belts, but that's not going to happen."

The crowd went silent.

"The reason it's not going to happen is because in the Disease's last fight here in Japan, he defeated the All-American."

The crowd cheered once more.

"But because of a foolish mistake by his manager, Dr. Death, the All-American was killed and sent on his way in a hearse. According to JWF Rules, any new champion must, and I repeat, must, give the fallen champ a rematch. Since the All-American is dead, this can't happen."

Johnny and Ursula looked at me in amazement. I had never really told them of this stipulation.

"I would like to introduce to you Mr. Takimotto, the President of the JWF to confirm what I have just told you."

A little gray haired man, dressed in a tuxedo made his way to the ring, Mike handed him the wireless microphone and stepped back.

"I'm afraid that Mr. Mouth is right. As President of the JWF, I must strip the Disease of his title." He handed the microphone back to The Mouth, went over to Johnny and removed the belt from his waist. The crowd was awestruck. You could have heard a pin drop.

"Now Dr. Death," Mike started again. "Since your man was to wrestle tomorrow night in Florida for both titles, and since he does not have a title to defend, I guess you have to forfeit and the Bruiser wins by default."

Ursula began to cry, "How could you do this, you bastard." she said to me. She took her bouquet and threw it to the canvas. Johnny was dumbfounded. "All those damn preparations, and for what?" she screamed at me. She grabbed Johnny by the arm and started to head out of the ring, slapping her Uncle Mike as she left. I reached out and grabbed the microphone out of The Mouth's hand.

"Now wait a minute," I said. Johnny and Ursula stopped. "I understand the rules of the JWF, but you're forgetting a little clause on page seven." I started reading the clause. "If at any time a former champion is unable to make the rematch under any circumstances, then any next of kin may take his or her spot in the ring," Mike and Mr. Takimotto were now leafing through the policy book. "Is that not right Mr. Takimotto?"

"Yes it is, it's right here," he said as he pointed to the manual.

"Well, I've got the All-American's brother in the change room and he is willing to fight."

God Bless America started to play as Thomas (the original All-American) made his way down the gangplank. Thomas had grown his hair, dyed it blonde and grew a beard for the occasion.

"I introduce The American Dream."

He entered the ring and grabbed the microphone.

"I am the brother of the All-American and I am here to regain his title."

I leaned forward and spoke into the microphone. "So Mr. Mouth, it looks like we've got a title match after all." I handed the microphone to Mr. Takimotto and pulled off my Velcro tuxedo. The three of us had got in our wrestling gear in the dressing room and had them on under our Velcro wedding clothes. The fans cheered once again. The bell sounded as the four of us left the ring leaving the two wrestlers in there. Johnny pulled off his tuxedo and began to fight.

"You're a bastard." Ursula yelled at me as she stripped off her wedding gown.

"I just wanted your wedding night to be something to remember," I said.

She looked at her Uncle Mike. He winked at her.

We ended the match in less than fifteen minutes. I had put us on the fight card in the first match so we could get back to the west for tomorrow night's match.

"Great job guys," I said as we all sat in the dressing room. I shook Mike's hand as he entered the room.

"We had you going for a minute, didn't we Ursula?" he said.

"I never even put any thought into it. It never ever dawned on me that we supposedly killed the former champion," Ursula said.

"You really are blonde," her uncle said.

She threw a towel at him. Johnny laughed and also caught a towel in the face.

"Okay guys, listen up. I've asked my friend John, you know the owner of the resort, if he could fly us to Miami. It would be very tight if we had to rely on a commercial flight. With all the security at the airport we might not make it. As soon as you're changed, throw your uniforms in the blue duffel bag. I'll hang them in the cargo bay of the jet so they'll dry. There should be a limo outside waiting. Ursula your family should already be on their way."

There was a knock at the door and it opened slowly.

"Lee, hi!" Ursula yelled as she ran and gave her a hug.

"Great show. You're driving them crazy out there."

"How are you doing?" I asked.

"Okay, I've got some news. Even though it's great news, I think all of you will be a little disappointed," she said.

"What is it?" Ursula asked.

"Mr. Campbell has taken another job. Just outside my hometown in Canada, it's for a Japanese automaker. I'm going to adopt Liam and move in with my parents. Mr. Campbell thinks it would be better if he had a full-time mom. He starts school in a couple years and Mr. Campbell says that he's not getting any younger either."

"That is great news," Ursula said.

"We're all going to miss you though," I said.

"You're busy enough, hopping back and forth from here to the U.S."

"But we can always make time to see you when we're here," I stated.

"Well, I know you've got a plane to catch. Good luck in Florida, if you ever get to Canada, look us up."

"When do you leave?" Ursula questioned.

"Mr. Campbell just has to sell his house, we're hoping by mid-December." She made the rounds, giving Ursula and Johnny a hug. I stood up as she approached me. I gave her a kiss on the lips and a very passionate hug and said goodbye. Lee left the dressing room.

"Okay guys, we have to go," I said as I wiped a tear away that was running down my cheek before anyone noticed.

I grabbed my suitcase and the blue duffel bag and we all made our way to the limo. We drove out to the airport where the jet was waiting.

"You guys go on board, I'll put the luggage in the storage compartment." I picked up all the bags except for the blue duffel bag and mine and put them on the airplane.

"How's everyone doing?" I said as I entered the jet.

"Nice airplane," Ursula's mother said.

"Thanks, but it's not mine. A friend of mine owed me a favour so I got to borrow it. Everyone, make yourself at home. Help yourself to whatever you need, there's pop and beer in the fridge and the pantry's full. I'm going to sit up with the pilot, that way you'll have some personal time for your families to get acquainted."

I had also invited Johnny's mother, father and sister to come along, a little wedding gift for the couple.

"Thanks Mr. White," Johnny said.

I made my way to the front of the jet. I entered the cockpit and closed the door. "Okay captain, is the flight plan all set?"

"Yes sir."

"Now remember, do not open the cockpit door to anyone, use the intercom, just rock the jet a bit and ask them to remain seated until you land. Once you get to Australia, hand them this envelope."

I opened the little access door in the cockpit and exited to the tarmac. I climbed in the back seat of the limo, which had pulled closer, and closed the door. The limo drove away and stopped behind the hanger. The jet pulled out and took off. Only Johnny and Ursula had seen inside my jet and they probably never even noticed that the jet they were on now wasn't the same one. It was a rental. With the jet now safely in the air, I called Jay from the limo. He was now back at the gym.

"Hi Jay, it's me Darryl."

"Hello Mr. White."

"Listen, I've got something very important to tell you. I'm not going to be coming back to Japan with Johnny. I've enjoyed all the fun we've had, but I'm moving on. When Johnny gets back, take care of him. You won't need me, he's the champion and the two of you can make it work."

"What does Mr. Sashi think of all this?" Jay asked.

"I haven't told him yet. I'll wait until Christmas, when he loses the U.S. belt, I'm sure he'll understand. I just got off the phone with Mr. Brown. Remember the deal I had with him? Well I bought the gym for a buck. I want you to run things. The royalty you are making off Johnny will last forever, but I did guarantee your salary for two years. It's in the top right-hand drawer of my desk."

"Okay."

"See the large brown envelope with your name on it?"

"Yes sir."

"After we hang up, I want you to open it, everything is explained in it. I will be in touch now and then to see how you're doing with the business. Any questions?"

"Not yet."

"Okay if anything comes up, give me a call, goodbye."

"Goodbye sir."

I shut off the phone, opened the limo door and put it on the ground and told the limousine agency driver to go ahead. The phone was smashed as we drove away. Jay was going to be pleasantly surprised when he opened the envelope. I had split the share I had in Johnny between the two of them. There was also a check for Jay's pay for the remaining two years of his salary. The most important part was that I turned the business I had bought as Mr. Brown back over to Jay, plus the adjacent gym that was opened. Jay would now have plenty of cash to last the rest of his life. If he were smart he would turn the gyms over now for profit.

I could see my jet had just finished fuelling as we drove up. As I sat there waiting, I wondered how Ursula and Johnny were going to take this. I knew Mike was going to be really pissed off because the FWF is holding it's biggest fight in its history tomorrow and he and Johnny were going to miss it. Yet, they will all come out okay. Johnny and Ursula could continue to wrestle and Johnny can find someone else to play Doctor Death, maybe even his dad. Their families will enjoy a five star holiday in Australia. I had booked them on several sightseeing tours and even a three-day adventure in the outback. Mike is just going to be pissed. I'm sure he'll make the best of it once he gets back. After all he is a wrestling promoter. There's an envelope of cash for all of them and flights back to the U.S. and Japan. I hope they have a good time. The limo stopped, I got out and picked up my suitcase and the blue duffel bag. I carried them on board the jet and checked with Kevin to make sure everything was okay. I grabbed a bottle of Coke from the fridge and sat down.

As I sat on the jet, I started to feel a real rush. The murder was really starting to turn me on. First of all, Dave the bastard will get what's coming to him. But the most exhilarating part is that I'm doing it in the same state where I revealed my plans to the world. There was only one variable of this plan that was uncertain but will probably not be too hard to solve: I need someone to play Nurse Nasty. I had thought about using Maria from the island, but Manny wouldn't let her come alone. Anyhow, there was no way he was going back to Florida. I finished my Coke, climbed on the bed and fell asleep as we took off.

CHAPTER 12

I called the Howard's two weeks ago to see how they were doing. I haven't been in much contact with them since I started my murders. Today was the day that Mr. Howard was to have a CAT scan at the Hospital in Tampa. I stopped by unannounced to pay a visit. I had three hours before the fight was to begin and it was only half an hour drive to the hospital. He had to be there two hours prior to check in and have some preliminary tests. They would be there a total of five hours.

"Hi Jack," Mrs. Howard said as she answered the door. "C'mon in. What brings you here?"

"I know today is the day that Mr. Howard has to go for his CAT scan, and I thought I would drive you. I'm not sure whether he'll be groggy afterwards and I know how you hate to drive after dark."

"You're such a sweet boy," she said as she gave me a big hug. "Robert, it's Jack. He's come to drive us to the hospital."

"How are you doing Jack?"

"Good, Mr. Howard."

"Sounds like things are okay."

"I still miss Lynn a lot, and my dad, but I still have Jimmy. I see him quite a bit. Who knows, one day maybe he'll get out."

"Laws change, you never know."

"I've got nothing to do today so I thought I'd drive you to your tests."

We drove to the hospital and I pulled into the underground parking. That way I had a record on videotape of my being there. We got out and went up to the waiting room. Mr. Howard checked in while Mrs. Howard and I sat and chatted. She was a sweet lady.

"Looks like we could be here for a while, they are little bit behind," Mr. Howard said as he returned.

"No problem. I've got nothing but time to kill." I laughed inside.

We sat there and waited awhile. There was one hour to go before the matches were to begin and Johnny wasn't scheduled to fight until forty-five minutes in, somewhere around 3:45. The fight was only going to be twelve minutes. That's when Johnny would win both titles.

"I'm feeling a bit fidgety. I'm going to take a walk. I'll be back in about half an hour," I said as I stood up.

"We'll be here waiting," she said.

I left the room and headed down the stairs and out to the street. I got in a rental car and quickly drove the eight blocks to the arena. I had preferred parking right inside the building. After the match, Dr. Death will get into his car and leave in a hurry, shown on the big screen. Once I get around the corner, I'd park the car and join the rest of the wrestlers in the dressing room. I got out of the car and headed to the office after I pulled in my parking spot.

"Where the hell have you been?" Ed Chalmers yelled. He was Mike's assistant. "I haven't seen any of your team yet. Mike hasn't shown up either, where are they?"

"I don't know," I said lying to him.

"What do you mean you don't know? Weren't you on the same flight?"

"No actually, I had stayed behind to take care of a problem at the stadium. They flew out two hours before me on a private jet."

"What are we going to do?" he asked.

"Have you tried his cell phone?"

"Yes, but they must be out of range, I keep getting a message that the caller is unavailable. I've even checked with the airport to see if any airplanes have crashed."

"Okay, let's not panic. Let's figure this out. Is the Bruiser here?"

"Yes."

"Okay I've got the Disease and Nurse Nasty's outfits. We'll just have someone fill in."

"But who? Who can we get?" Ed questioned all flustered.

"Well I know The Playboy has been around the last few matches, and I know he's not on the card tonight. We can use him. He's about the same size as Johnny."

"You're right, and the costume has a full mask." Ed replied somewhat relieved.

"Call down and have him come up. Tell him to bring one of his assistants, too. She can play Nurse Nasty."

We sat there waiting for a few minutes before Dave entered the room.

"Dave, we need you to fill in as The Disease, and you, Jenny, as the nurse." Ed directed.

"I know you're familiar with the routine, but here's the script. We've got about an hour and fifteen before were on. I'll meet you in the dressing room. I'm superstitious and I won't show up until ten minutes before we wrestle," I said.

"There's one more thing, Dave. This is a one-time shot. You cannot let anyone know it's you, and when Johnny shows up, he's back in. Understand? Any questions?"

"No, sir," he said as he and Jenny left the room.

"Okay, Ed, I'm going to give the script to the Bruiser and then I'm going to my dressing room to go through my rituals. I do not want to be disturbed. I have to get focused."

"I'll see you after the match," Ed yelled.

I left and went to the Bruiser's dressing room.

"I brought you the script. Mike and I revised it last night. There's been a death in Johnny's family and he couldn't make the trip. Dave, The Playboy, is filling in, so don't try to take off his mask. We're also going to have you win. Johnny will be out for a while. This way we keep the U.S. fans happy. We'll figure out a rematch after Johnny returns in a few weeks."

"Okay, I hate losing anyway."

"Dave's a little pissed off, so stay away from him until we're in the ring."

"Will do."

I ran out the back door, and drove back to the hospital.

"Well, did you get all the bugs out?" Mrs. Howard asked.

"What you mean?" I asked puzzled.

"The fidgety bugs. Are they gone from your legs?"

"Yes, ma'am."

Mr. Howard was called in the room.

"We'll, see you in about an hour, dear," he said as he kissed Mrs. Howard.

"I'm getting hungry, do you want anything?"

"I'm okay. I better wait here," she said.

I knew she wouldn't want to go, and I was counting on it.

"I'm going to go and get a bite to eat. I'll be back in about an hour or so."

"Here's some money. Grab Robert a muffin or something," she said as she tried to hand me a twenty.

"I've got it. I'll see you in a bit."

I left the room and ran to the lobby. Kevin was in Tampa that day. I had arranged to meet him for lunch. I explained to him that Mr. Howard was almost done and he would have to go for lunch himself. I bought a muffin using my debit card and then handed the card to Tim, hopped in the car and drove off. I pulled into the building and headed to my dressing room, I quickly got changed and went to Dave's room.

"Are you ready?" I asked.

"Bring it on," he replied.

We knocked on Jenny's' door and she opened it. She was more voluptuous then Ursula and she looked good in the nurses' outfit. Our theme music started playing and Jenny and I strolled down the gangplank. Dave followed dressed in the Disease outfit, he was a good choice to disguise as Johnny. The place was packed. The bell sounded and the match began. We got to the ten-minute mark and I gave the cue to Dave. He got the Bruiser in a Full Nelson. Nurse Nasty and I went through our routine and I climbed the apron of the ring. This time I had a real syringe. I had filled it with 200cc of regular insulin. Not being diabetic, this would surely kill him. I had to be quick when I pushed the plunger. Once Dave feels the needle in his arm, he is sure to resist. I winked at the Bruiser. This was his cue. He reversed the Full Nelson and put one on Dave. I could see Dave's eyes questioning. He didn't know he was suppose to lose.

I leaned in close to him so the Bruiser wouldn't hear. "This is for the Tiger fraternity initiation, courtesy of Pencil Dick," I whispered in his ear as I thrust the needle in his arm and pushed the plunger as hard as I could. I snapped the needle off right in his arm and hopped down to the cement floor. The crowd were on their feet screaming. I ran down the gangplank as Dave was thrashing about in the ring, and soon collapsed. I turned to the camera and laughed. I got in the car and drove out of the building. I didn't stop until I pulled up in from the hospital. I had already pulled the skullcap off and removed my doctor's coat when I left the arena and threw them in trashcan. I entered the hospital, stopped and grabbed a magazine from the gift shop. I paid for it with my MasterCard.

"I brought you a magazine. Is he out yet?" I asked Mrs. Howard.

"Not yet, thanks. How was your lunch?"

"I grabbed a quick meal at the restaurant down the street."

Mr. Howard appeared about twenty minutes later. He had a big brown envelope in his hand. "We're ready," he said.

We left the hospital and went down to the underground parking. Mr. Howard got in the front with me and Mrs. Howard sat in the back.

"Here honey," he said handing her the envelope. She put it on the seat beside her.

"What's this for?" she asked.

"Its a copy of my CAT scan. Dr. Chimo needs it when I go see him tomorrow."

"What time is that?" I asked. "Would you like me to stay and drive you over there in the morning?"

"Oh no Jack, you've done enough for me today, I owe you one," he said.

"Don't worry about it Mr. Howard. Just being here all day with you is payment enough."

"Jack, you're so sweet," Mrs. Howard said.

I jerked the car to a sudden stop as we pulled in the driveway. We all lunged forward. "Sorry about that." I said.

I dropped them off and drove back to Keycoast.

Mr. Howard called to inform me that Mrs. Howard forgot to grab the envelope in the car. It must have fallen under the front seat as I stopped suddenly. It was a four and a half hour trip back. Mr. Howard called the Dr. at home and got his fax number. I faxed over the results as soon as I had the number.

At six in the morning the guardhouse called and woke me up.

"Mr. Stevenson."

"Yes," I replied.

"It's Stan at the guardhouse. There's a couple of detectives down here, they want to talk to you."

"Send them up Stan. You come up with them and bring the log book please."

"Yes Mr. Stevenson."

I threw on a robe and answered the door when the bell rang.

"Come in gentlemen," I said. "Can I get you anything?"

"No sir, were here on business," the young pimply faced cop said. I recognized the other one from somewhere, probably the night of Lynn's accident.

"Sounds serious," I said.

"We're checking into a murder in Tampa and we wondering where you were yesterday," the older cop said.

"Yesterday, let's see," I said as I rubbed my chin. I thought I might have a little fun at their expense. "I arrived in St. Pete's' around 1:00 p.m. Drove to Tampa for awhile and arrived back here around 2:00 a.m."

"2:33 a.m." Stan said.

"What did you do while you were in Tampa sir?"

"Please call me Jack. I was going to take in the wrestling match, but I didn't."

They both looked at each other.

"Do you know a wrestler by the stage name of The Playboy?"

"No sir, is he good?"

"That doesn't matter," the young copy yelled.

"So you didn't go to the fight. Where did you go?" the pimply-faced cop asked.

"I went to see some old friends."

"What time was that?"

"I'm not sure about times."

"Can they confirm that you were there?"

"Oh sure, actually I have a parking stub from the medical centre. Here you go."

"So you spent the whole time at the Hospital?"

"All of it except for about an hour, you don't think I had anything to do with this, do you? The news conference was just a joke."

"Where have you been the last six months?" the young cop asked.

"Sometimes here, sometimes Fiji, actually the day before yesterday. I was in Japan."

"Japan?"

"Just to refuel. I've got the receipt if you want it."

"That we might need," he said.

"Speaking of Japan, isn't that Dr. Death a neat wrestling manager. Did you see the fight?" I said to egg them on.

The young cop was now frantically searching his notes. "I thought you didn't go?"

"I didn't, I saw it on TV at the restaurant."

The acne-faced cop looked disappointed. I'm sure he thought he had me.

"I left my friends, grabbed a muffin in the lobby. Then walked about two blocks to a restaurant. They had the fight on there. When I was done I stopped at the hospital gift shop, and then went back upstairs."

"Can you prove that?"

"Sure, check my debit receipts."

"I will need your card number."

I handed my cards to them and the young one wrote down the numbers. "Don't think I'm going to give you my PIN number though."

The older cop laughed.

"You asked me about The Playboy, what was his real name?"

"Dave Masterson."

"I knew a Dave Masterson, we went to school together. I got pissed one night because of him, what a night. Was that who was murdered?"

"Yes."

"Stan, find out when his funeral is."

You could tell the older cop was seasoned. He just sat listening. The younger one squirmed as he took notes. I'm sure in his mind he had me tried, convicted and sentenced to death.

"Should we take him into custody?" the young cop asked.

"We don't have anything on him. We've got to check out his alibis."

"He was in Japan and Tampa, he knew the victim," the younger cop exclaimed.

"I like the good cop, bad cop routine. Wear me down, break me down, I'll cry and confess?"

"Now wait a minute," the older one said. "All we need is the name and address of your friends, and we'll be on our way."

"Mr. and Mrs. Robert Howard. I'm not sure of the house number. Your Chief Milner will have it though. I think he and Chief Howard know each other."

"Chief Howard?" the young one asked.

"Yes Chief of Pinellas County and a good friend of mine. Gentlemen have a nice day. Stanley show them out."

The older cop grabbed the notebook from the young cop and pushed him towards the door. "We'll be in touch Mr. Stevenson," he said as he left. I could tell he was pissed off.

I broke into laughter as the door closed behind them. I got a call about two hours later from the young cop saying that they were sorry to bother me earlier. They had spoken with Chief Howard and everything checked out.

CHAPTER 13

I had already picked the third victim. I sat at my computer and got the information I needed.

The scenario happened when I was young. Mom was still alive, for half of it anyway. About a year and half after Ramona was born, Dad got promoted to detective. Mom had just been diagnosed with cancer. Dad's first undercover case was to play a junkie. He made a drug deal and arrested a two-bit dealer by the name of Dick Harris. Dad was proud of this bust, it being his first as a detective. I think the guy spent a couple of years in jail. It was a few months after Dick got out of jail that Dad was accused of rape and suspended from the force. Dick the dealer had turned and become an informant. He often called our house and would help turn in some of his suppliers. He had told Dad that he was grateful for being in jail and that he had straightened his life out and wanted to help. I think that Dad got two arrests thanks to Dick's help. After Moms' death, Dad filled me in about the whole thing, although I got most of my information at the time from the newspaper.

The day Dad was accused was the same day he had gone for his one-month vasectomy check up. The court case lasted four months. Mom had become very ill and didn't see the end of the case. She died not knowing the outcome. A couple of days later, the trial was over. We soon moved to Florida so Dad could escape the stigma of the case, even though the alleged victim dropped the charges. The prosecution had a good case. They recovered Dad's semen from a vaginal swab and his pubic hair from the scene. Mom was aware of these facts and hated him for it. Like I said, she never saw him get off the charges and she went to her grave hating Dad. Out of all of the murders I plotted, this one was my most passionate. Not only was I doing it for my dad. I was also doing it for my mom. In Dad's suicide note he asked me to clear his name once and for all. Even with the little knowledge I had, I wasn't sure that Dick was even responsible for it. All I had to go on was Dad's request. He said that Dick set him up. After I found Dick's last known address over the Internet, I drove to South Dakota. I found a motel and checked in, under my own name. I had telephoned Adam and Mark to meet me at the motel room. I wanted everything recorded.

"Hi guys, c'mon in," I said as I opened the door of my motel room. Even if they weren't my buddies from high school, I would have helped them out because they were damn good filmmakers. I was impressed with the bit they did on me buying Keycoast to help make my younger brother's stay more comfortable, and I knew they would do a great job with this one also.

"Does this have to do with the murders you said you were going to carry out?" Mark asked.

"No, that was just a fleeting comment. I was pissed off at the reporters because they kept shoving those damn cameras in my face. Besides the last murder the police suspected me in, I had an airtight alibi. I spent the day with the police chief. Are you familiar with my Dad's case of alleged rape?"

"Sure we are, but you never talk about it, so we never wanted to bring it up."

"We'll, we are going to do that now. Whether I find out that he was guilty or innocent, I need to do this. Set up whatever you need to." I booked them in the room beside mine. "Give me half an hour to unpack and we'll be on our way."

They left without asking any more questions. I unpacked my things and went to get them when I was ready.

"Okay guys, you can start your film whenever you want. First we're going to the Court House."

We drove the seven blocks to the Municipal Court House. Once inside, we found our way to the records department.

"Can I help you?" a stern lady behind the counter asked.

"Yes, my name is Jack Stevenson and I'd like to see the transcript of a court case from a few years back."

"A few years is a long time you know, what year are you looking for? What are of the cameras for? We don't allow cameras in the Court House, you'll have to shut them off."

Mark shut it off and dropped it to his side.

"The Detective Stevenson case, the cop accused of rape," I said.

"That one I know," she said. "Made big headlines here. I'll be right back."

She returned with a small roll of film.

"What is this?" I asked.

"It's what you asked for," she put the microfilm on the counter and then left.

Mark set up the machine and we browsed through the records until we found it.

"Here Jack, let me print it off for you," Adam said. He hit a button on the terminal and the printer started. It was a three hundred-page transcript and cost me ninety bucks to print it. I returned the roll of film to the counter and we left. Once back at the hotel room, Mark started filming. This time he put the camera on a tripod.

I started reading the transcript aloud.

"Does the prosecution have any witnesses?" the judge asked.

"Yes we do. The prosecution calls Dr. Drummond to the stand." The female prosecution lawyer said.

I can remember seeing her picture in the newspapers. She was a blonde lady about mid-forties at the time.

"Do you swear to tell the truth, the whole truth and nothing but the truth so help you God?" the bailiff asked as he swore in the doctor.

"I do," he replied.

"What is your job?" Roberta Newman asked him.

"I'm the Chief Forensic Officer of South Dakota," he answered.

"Can you please tell the court what you found in regards to evidence from the crime scene."

"During our investigation we found semen on the sheets of Miss Laura Melrose's bed. We also have five hairs that were found on the sheets."

"Were the samples tested?"

"Yes they were."

"Can you please tell the court the results of the testing?"

"I compared the semen and hair samples taken from the scene, to samples taken from the defendant, they were a perfect match."

"Objection," Dad's attorney Bartholmew Hibbs yelled.

"Sustained," the judge said.

"In your opinion Dr. Drummond, what is the probability that the samples recovered at the scene and the samples taken from the defendant came from the same source?"

"In my opinion, the results are ninety-nine percent certain that the samples came from the same person."

"DNA technology was just being introduced to the courts back then." I said into the camera.

"Were there any other samples taken from the scene?" Miss Newman asked.

"Yes. There was an empty glass that was recovered from the nightstand. There were fingerprints lifted, and a saliva sample taken. The saliva sample matched the DNA profile of all the other samples."

"So therefore they came from same person?"

"Yes ma'am."

"That's all the questions I have at the moment. I'd like the right to recall the witness with regards to further DNA testing."

"Granted, your witness council."

"No questions Your Honour."

"The prosecution then calls Dr. Brian Shaw to the stand."

The Bailiff swore him in and he was seated.

"Dr. Shaw, you are a medical doctor?"

"Yes I am."

"What hospital?"

"County General."

"You examined Miss Melrose after the alleged rape, did you not?"

"Yes I did, about two hours after."

"Had the victim showered or bathed before coming to the hospital?"

"Objection," Bart said. "How would he know?"

"Sustained."

"Did the victim appear to be freshly cleaned upon arrival of the hospital?"

"No she did not."

"What were the results of your examination?"

"I did a vaginal swab of the victim, removing some semen."

"Did she appear to have had intercourse recently?"

"Yes she did."

"How do you know?"

"There were signs of internal vaginal trauma, her cervix was slightly bruised."

"Any other signs of trauma?"

"Yes, there was extensive trauma and bruising of the labia majora and the pelvic region of the victim."

"From your experience does this trauma happen during normal intercourse?"

"No, we usually see this trauma in rape victims that have tried to fight off their attacker."

"Was there any other sign of trauma to the victim?"

"We also discovered some flesh under the nails of her right hand."

"Did you do any testing of either the flesh or the semen?"

"I examined the semen."

"Did you find anything unusual?"

"Not unusual, but the semen was sterile."

"Is this similar to that of a man who would have had a vasectomy?"

"Yes it would."

"Any other testing?"

"I sent the semen and fingernails scrapings to Dr. Drummond's office for a DNA mark-up."

"Was there any other trauma to the victim?"

"Yes, she had a bruise that was starting to appear on the right side of her face."

"Can you describe the bruise?"

"There were four distinct lines of bruising."

"I have a photograph here, do you recognize that?" the attorney asked.

"Yes, that's the picture I took of the victim's face during my examination."

"Please describe the bruise."

"There were four distinct markings."

"What do you think caused this mark?"

"The back of a hand."

"Was anything else in your findings?"

"Yes, the victim had six small red dots on the top of her head."

"Dots?"

"Yes there had been six follicles of hair removed from the victims scalp."

"From your experience doctor, what does this tell you?"

"They were all pulled out all at once."

"Why do you say that?"

"The police brought in three strands of hair found on the victim's pillow, the three follicles were attached to each other by a thin layer of skin. Indicating that they were all pulled out all at once."

"Now doctor. Did you examine anyone else that night?"

"Yes, that man."

"Let the record show that Dr. Shaw is pointing at the defendant. What did you find when you examined the defendant?"

"A fresh wound to the left side of the defendant's face."

"What kind of wound?"

"Scratches, two scratches, two and three quarter inches long running parallel in a downward motion."

"How do you know they were downward?"

"The way the skin was ripped indicated this."

"How many nails of the victim did you scrape for evidence on her right hand?"

"Five, but I only found flesh under two of them."

"What else did you examine on the defendant?"

"His right hand, actually the back of his right hand."

"What did you find?"

"His skin was slightly bruising and his knuckles showed signs of swelling."

"No further questions Your Honour, your witness."

"No questions." Mr. Hibbs said.

"The prosecution calls Detective Fulcher to the stand."

After his swearing in, Roberta asked, "Detective Fulcher, you were the leading investigator in this case were you not?"

"Yes I was."

"Where was the defendant when you found him?"

"He was in Sam's Diner having a coffee."

"Was he alone?"

"Yes he was."

"What time was that?"

"About 2:00 a.m."

"How far is Sam's from the victim's apartment?"

"About five miles."

"How did you know he was there?"

"I spotted his truck there on my way to the victim's to check into her complaint."

"What happened?"

"I arrived at the victim's with my partner. We entered the house and called for a female officer. When she arrived we headed for Sam's because Ms. Melrose stated that Detective Stevenson was her attacker."

"How long after you received the initial call did you meet up with the defendant?"

"About forty minutes."

"What was the defendant's mood?"

"He was visibly shaken, he had a fresh wound to the left side of his face, it look like a couple of scratches."

"Did you see his right hand?"

"No, he was drinking coffee using his left hand, I thought this was unusual."

"Why?"

"I was his partner for two years, I knew he was right handed."

"What happened next?"

"We escorted him outside. I asked him to lock his truck up and we put him in the back of our cruiser."

"Where did you take him?"

"To the hospital to have his wounds cleaned."

"Do you recognize this clothing?"

"Yes, it's the clothing we confiscated at the hospital. They belonged to Detective Stevenson."

"You mean the defendant?"

"Yes ma'am, they belong to the defendant."

"Did you recover any evidence from the clothing?"

"Yes, there were two strands of hair retrieved from around

the button on the right sleeve, and a spot of dry semen found inside the front of the underwear."

"No further questions, the prosecution would like to recall Dr. Drummond to the stand."

"May the court remind you that you are still under oath." The judge advised him as he took the witness stand.

"Dr. Drummond, did you do any DNA testing on the evidence that either Dr. Shaw or Detective Fulcher sent to your office?"

"I concluded the hair strands found at the scene and the three turned in by the police were that of the victim."

"I thought the police only found two around the button?"

"They turned in three."

"You tested six hairs all together, were they all the victims?"

"Yes."

"What were the findings of the nail scrapings found under the victim's nails?"

"The samples taken had the same DNA as the semen, pubic hair and saliva found at the scene."

"What about the sample found in the underwear of the defendant?"

"It matched the others."

"Thank you Dr. Drummond. Oh, one more question, did you find anything else when testing the pubic hair?"

"Yes we found traces of a lubricant on the hair."

"Isn't that odd?"

"Not really. Older couples sometimes use it to help aid the hormonal changes after menopause."

"Yes doctor, but the victim was only nineteen."

"It is also sometimes used on rape victims. Their unwillingness to participate doesn't allow natural lubrication."

"Thank you Doctor, that's all."

"Does the prosecution have any more witnesses?" the judge asked.

"No new witnesses, I would like to recall Detective Fulcher to the stand," Roberta said.

"You're still under oath Detective," the judge reminded him.

"Dr. Drummond testified that he tested three strands of hair you turned in. You said you only found two around the button."

"We did only find two around the button. The other one came from the cab of the defendant's truck."

"Where in the cab?"

"On the driver's side floor mat."

"Was there any indication that the victim was in the truck?"

"No, that's the only evidence that was found in the truck."

"Did you find any evidence outside of the truck?"

"Not belonging to the victim. We did lift a shoe print from the mud outside the victim's apartment."

"Who's shoe did it match?"

"The defendants. If you look here you can clearly see the diamond design, and the cut right here, it matches the right boot here, and there's the diamond design."

"So that proves he exited the truck?"

"Yes."

"Objection."

"Overruled," The judge replied.

"How did you know he exited the truck?"

"When people step out of a vehicle they put their left foot out and then step out with the right."

"We're there any left foot impressions in the mud?"

"Yes."

"Was there any mud on the boots?"

"Yes, we took samples off both boots and compared it to the sample taken at the apartment, they were consistent."

"Any other findings?"

"We took mud samples from the tires of the defendant's truck, they were also consistent with the other two samples. We also took tire track impressions at the scene and they matched the tires on the defendant's truck."

"Just one more question. The finger print recovered from the glass at the scene, whose was it?"

"The defendants."

"Your witness," Roberta told Bart.

"I just have two questions. Was there any mud found in the house?"

"No."

"Was there any of the defendants footprints leading from

the truck to the house?"

"No."

"No further questions."

"You may step down," the judge said. "Court adjourned until tomorrow at 9:00 a.m."

"What the hell was Dad's lawyer doing?" I asked Adam who was reading along with me in the motel.

"I don't know Jack. The evidence is pretty strong against him, there wasn't much to argue."

"It is hard to dispute the facts isn't it?" I said.

"Listen," Adam said. "Do you want us to stop taping and destroy the film we've already shot?"

"Are you saying he's guilty?"

"No, I'm just saying that it looks like it could get pretty emotional. Are you sure you want to do this?"

"Dad wants me to, so I am."

We continued reading.

"Please rise," the Bailiff stated. "I call to order this session of the State of South Dakota Supreme Court, The Honourable Stacey Sullivan presiding."

"Please be seated," she said. "Mr. Hibbs you may call your first witness."

"Your Honour, if it pleases the court, may I approach the bench?"

"Ms. Newman, would you come to the bar please?"

"What is it Bart?" The judge asked quietly.

"My client's wife is very ill, terminal cancer. Last night she was rushed to the hospital. Could we get a postponement for a few days, to see how she makes out?"

"What do you think Roberta?"

"I'm done with my witnesses, I've only got to cross examine any that Bart has."

"Bart, what are your plans?" Judge Sullivan asked.

"I just have the defendant, Your Honour. He's my only witness."

"If things go right, maybe we can get an early adjournment. Depending on his testimony, I don't have a lot of questions," Roberta replied.

"Why don't we start, if your client gets a call, we'll deal with it then."

"Thank you Your Honour," Bart replied.

"The defense would like to call Jerome Stevenson to the stand."

"Mr. Stevenson," Bart started. "The evidence against you is very strong. Why don't you recount the events of the day?"

"It started like any typical day, I headed to work around seven. I was undercover in a drug sting that day. Traveling to the east side of town."

"Did you work there all day?"

"No, actually I got a call from Mrs. O'Malley. She was our neighbour. She had said my wife wasn't feeling very well that day."

"Your wife has terminal cancer, is that right?"

"Objection, Your Honour," Roberta jumped in. "Council is just playing to the emotions of the jurors."

"Your Honour, I'm just trying to establish the mood of my client," Bart said.

"Overruled."

"Please answer the question," Bart said.

"Yes she does."

"So you went back home."

"Yes, I arrived around 11:00 a.m. and spent the day there, until around 4:15 in the afternoon."

"What did you do then?"

"I had an appointment at the urologists. I had a vasectomy a month earlier and I was going for a one month follow up exam."

"Did anything unusual happen there?"

"Not that I'm aware of. I had to provide a sample."

"Did you take it with you?"

"No, I um, gave it while I was there."

"What happened after that?"

"I was also having some problems with blockage. My testicles would swell up every now and then."

"What did the doctors say?"

"He wanted to do an ultrasound."

"Who performed the ultrasound?"

"He did it, with the aid of his nurse."

"What were their names?"

"Dr. Jensen, I believe, the nurse's name was Heidi."

"What was involved?"

"I had to strip and wear a gown. I went into a room with the nurse, the doctor came in a couple of minutes later. Then they preformed the ultrasound."

"Had you given your sample yet?"

"No, after the ultrasound the nurse wiped off the left over jelly stuff that they use to glide the ultrasound wand, and then she escorted me to a room. I had picked up my clothes and went into the room. She told me there were magazines, and a movie if I needed it. There were several jars on the counter. I must have looked tense."

"Why is that?"

"She told me to relax and to leave the sample on the counter when I was done. She said there were water and glasses by the sink if I needed a drink. She then left and closed the door.

I was nervous, not having had sex since the operation. I didn't know what to expect the first time. I sat there for about ten minutes with no luck. My forehead was sweating, my throat was dry and I wasn't getting aroused at all."

"So what did you do?"

"The nurse knocked on the door and asked if I was okay. She informed me that the office was closing soon and would I like to come back tomorrow. I told her I was okay I grabbed a drink of water and popped a movie into the VCR. After about ten more minutes I did what I had to do, and quickly got dressed. I left the sample on the counter without saying a word and I left."

"What did you do next?"

"I went home and made supper for the family. I played a few games with the kids and eventually by 10:00 p.m. I got them all settled."

"You have a child with Downs's syndrome, don't you?"

"Objection, irrelevant, playing with emotions again," Roberta piped up.

"Sustained."

"So after you put your three children to bed, what did you do next?"

"I got my wife ready, and put her to bed at around 11:00

p.m. I fell asleep in the chair in the living room."

"Did you sleep until the morning?"

"No sir, about 12:15 a.m. my phone rang, it was Dick Harris. I had arrested him once for possession and dealing."

"Why did he call?"

"Since his release, he had become an informant."

"For the department?"

"In a way, he got out of prison and he called me. He said he had found the Lord and wanted to help me take the scum off the streets. I hadn't told the force yet. I wanted to put a couple of feathers in my hat first. I was a rookie in the detective department."

"Was that the first time he had called you in the middle of the night?"

"No, twice in the two weeks prior he had called. Both times I got an arrest out of the deal."

"Didn't the force wonder why you were out in the middle of the night, off duty picking up dealers?"

"No, we often worked out of our houses under cover, working strange hours."

"So what happened on the night in question?"

"After hanging up the phone, I checked on my wife and left in my truck. I drove to the location he had given me."

"Was it his place?"

"I don't think so. I hadn't met him there before. I pulled my truck in the dirt laneway in front of the apartment. It was dark and no one was there. I sat there for a minute and double-checked the address. I started to step out of the truck when I saw Dick. We talked for a minute and then I was jumped."

"By whom?"

"I don't know. They wrestled me to the ground. One of them held my right arm to the ground and another one came down on my right hand, full force with his knee. I didn't know it at the time, but I also got scratched."

"Where?"

"The left cheek, we wrestled for a couple of minutes. They told me this was payback for putting Dick in jail. They threw me to the ground and took off in a car."

"Why didn't you call for back up, or use your gun?"

"My gun was in the glove compartment and I didn't have my radio. I didn't radio in. I got in my truck and left. I stopped at Sam's to have a coffee and wind down before I went home. Half an hour later Doug showed up."

"Is that Detective Fulcher?"

"Yes it is."

"At anytime while you were out, did you see the victim Laura Melrose?"

"No I did not."

"Your witness," Bart said to Roberta.

"How are you holding up Mr. Stevenson?" she started. "I understand your wife is gravely ill."

"Yes she is."

"So you mentioned that you went for your post vasectomy test, and that you had not ejaculated since the operation. So does that mean that you and your wife hadn't had sex since the operation?"

"No we hadn't. She was becoming quite ill with the chemotherapy."

"Is it true that you and your wife were having some marital problems?"

"We had the odd argument."

"Did she not accuse you of having an affair and that's why you were sneaking out in the middle of the night?"

"I was a devoted husband and father."

"When the police arrived, they only found Miss Melrose. There were no signs of your thugs, can you explain that?"

"I told the court: they took off in a car."

"How come the department dispatch had no record of an incoming call in regards to the alleged drug deal?"

"I told you, he called the house."

"The evidence against you is pretty strong. You did it, didn't you Mr. Stevenson?"

"No I did not."

"If you didn't see Ms. Melrose, how did she know exactly what you were wearing that night?"

"I don't know."

"No further questions Your Honour."

"The witness may be excused," the judge said. "Court

adjourned until tomorrow at 11:00 a.m."

"I remember that day." I told Adam and Mark. "That was the day that my mom died. When I arrived home from school Mrs. O'Malley was there. She said that they had taken Mom to the hospital and that my dad was already there. She said he would be home around 9:00 p.m. It was suppertime when he came in. I could tell he had been crying. He asked Mrs. O'Malley to watch Jimmy and Ramona. Dad took me right to the hospital."

"Jack, Mom is staying here at the hospital. They are taking her to where they can help her with her pain," Dad said tearfully.

"Will she come back?" I asked.

"No, she's going to help God. He needs another angel to watch over some people. You know how good she is at taking care of you."

I nodded.

"Well she's so good that God needs her help, but she told me to tell you one thing. She loves you. Let's go in and see her. She can't talk, she has a tube in her throat, but she can hear you. If you listen real close, look deep into her eyes, you'll be able to hear her," he said.

"Listen Jack," Mark said as he shut off the camera. "Why don't we go and get a bite to eat, we could all use a break."

"Good idea," I said as I wiped a tear away from my eye. "There's a great spot not too far from here."

We left the room and got into the Jeep.

"Where is the camera?" I asked Mark.

"I left it behind. I thought we were taking a break."

"We can mix business with pleasure, now go get it." I demanded.

We headed to the restaurant.

"So Jack," Adam said. "If your father was accused of rape, how come he was allowed out of jail?"

"Dad never spent any time in jail, he was suspended with pay and was able to post bond. The judge felt that because he was a cop he would have a hard time in prison. The police chief arranged to free up three guys to keep him under surveillance. The D.A's office agreed to that."

We ate lunch and sat around having a couple of beers.

"My mom died that day," I told them again.

"Jack," Adam said. "We don't have to cover that part, especially here."

"Actually I would rather talk about it here, that way maybe I could hold back some of the emotion."

Mark turned on the camera.

"Dad and I left the hospital and went back home, Mrs. O'Malley had already put the kids to bed by the time we got there. In the morning Dad tried to explain it to them but neither one of them comprehended it. Her funeral was small, mostly family and a few cops from the department. Dad had a tough time the next couple of days. I know now it was because of the impending verdict in this case. Mr. Hibbs had arranged through the courts to have a four day adjournment until the Monday after the funeral."

"Stop the tape Mark," Adam said. "We'll pick it back up with the court case, once we get back to the motel."

"Alright," I said. I ordered another round of beers. I enjoyed Adam and Mark's company, we had been best friends for a very long time. Nothing would separate us. I just wish I could tell them what I was really doing, but I did not want to get them implicated into my plan in any way. We had a couple more beers each and went back to the motel to read more of the trial transcript. Mark had the camera rolling as we did.

"All rise," I started to read the transcript.

"Please be seated," the judge said. "First of all I would like to extend my condolences to the defendant, whose wife passed away late last week. I would also like to remind the jury that this turn of events should in no way influence their judgment in the case. Council where is Ms. Melrose?"

"She called me this morning and said she was going to be late Your Honour. I would like to start with my closing arguments anyway."

"Do you have any objection Mr. Hibbs?"

"No Your Honour."

"Please proceed Ms. Newman."

"Ladies and gentlemen of the jury, you've heard all the evidence presented in this case. It is now time for you to decide whether the defendant is guilty or not. That is your job, your only job. If you find him not guilty he will be on his way, free and clear and you will have to live with that decision the rest of your life. The facts speak for themselves. He admitted he was there. The DNA proves almost one hundred percent that he did it. Do the right thing and find him guilty. It's true that he has never been in trouble with the law. In fact he is an officer of the law. But that gives him no right to hide behind that badge. No one is above the law. You may be sitting there today feeling compassion for the man. His wife died less than a week ago. We all feel for him this day. What about his three children? Your job is to look at the facts and do what is right. Thank you."

"Mr. Hibbs, your closing arguments," the judge said.

"It's hard to argue with the facts. It is your job to find him guilty or not guilty beyond a reasonable doubt. As you head back to make your decision, I just want you to think about one thing. Why did Ms. Newman not once call on Miss Melrose as a witness? Was it due to the fact that she's a confirmed junkie, who has been in trouble with the law? Is it a fact that she can't be trusted? Even her own lawyer didn't trust her enough to put her on the stand. Was she so stoned that night that she can't even remember the facts? Yes the DNA testing was ninety-nine percent a match, but what about that one percent. Let me give you an example. Let's say there are a hundred of us in this room. What if I walked around and handed each of you one of these little pills and asked you to take it. Ninety-nine of them contain sugar, but there is one that contains cyanide. They all look the same and you can't tell the difference. The person that has the cyanide pill will die. Would you take it? I think you'll find that there's a reasonable doubt that my client did not commit this crime. I thank you for your patience."

"Ms. Newman. I see your client has arrived," the judge said. "Miss Melrose are you ready to give your victim impact statement to the court?"

"Not really Your Honour," she replied. "I'd just like to say one thing. After seeing the funeral on the news, I'd like to withdraw the charges."

"Pardon me," the judge said surprised.

"I would like to drop all of the charges against the defendant," she repeated.

"I don't think that is possible," the judge said.

"Your Honour may we approach the bench?" Bart asked.

"What is it Bart?"

"I would like to move that we accept the statement by the plaintiff," Bart said.

"Of course you would, it would mean your client would walk away scot-free," Ms. Newman retorted.

"Your Honour, my client is innocent of the charge," Bart shouted.

"Mr. Hibbs, that is for the jury to decide," the judge said.

"I know Your Honour, but given the turn of events in his life and my closing arguments, I may have cast a shadow of doubt in their minds. I feel he will get off."

"What do you think Ms. Newman?" the judge asked.

"It could go either way Your Honour. We have all worked with the defendant in a professional manner one-way or another. He does have a lot on his plate right now, but I think that is for the jury to decide. I will leave it up to Your Honour's judgment."

"Your Honour, I'd just like to add one thing," Bart spoke up.

"Go ahead Bart," the judge said.

"We know it could go either way in the judicial system. My client's reputation has already been tarnished, win or lose. The people on the streets and for that matter everyone on the force will never look at him the same way. His life will never be the same, even if he is found not guilty. After all, even innocent people have been put away for years."

"But Bart, now with DNA testing, it's almost certain that we have the right person," the judge stated.

"I know that to be true, but even the experts agree, it's only ninety-nine percent accurate. You said it yourself, almost certain. If I asked you to take one of these pills would you do it? Even if I told you I was almost certain that it did not contain cyanide?"

"Point well taken Bart, both of you may return to your clients."

"Miss Melrose, will you please rise. You've put me in a tight squeeze here. We went to trial and spent hundreds of thousands of dollars on a court case. Several people including the jury had put their lives on hold. For me to accept your statement would make it all a waste. You have brought one thing to light though, that the South Dakota judicial system may have loopholes that certainly need to be reviewed. I'm not sure whether you're doing this to make a mockery of the court, or if you're doing this because the accused never did rape you, or whether as you say, it is simply compassion in light of his family situation. No matter what, I'm faced with a tough decision. If I were to declare this a mistrial, am I sending a rapist back to the streets? By sending it back to the jury to decide his fate, has your statement cast doubt in their minds? No matter what I do, the defendant will be scarred for life. His reputation will be tarnished. So I have decided to throw it back to you one more time. If you wish to rescind your statement you may, but if you do not and still wish to drop the charges, I will find you in contempt of court and you'll be charged. The maximum penalty of six months in jail will be imposed. What is your decision?"

"I would like to drop the charges Your Honour," she replied.

"I hereby call this case a mistrial, case dismissed. I hereby find you in contempt of court Miss Melrose, bailiff take her away. This court is adjourned."

I am not sure if I heard the pounding of the gavel as I read it or whether it was my heart beating so loud.

"Once this airs, your dad's story will be out and it will clear his name," Mark said.

"I wish that was enough to do it, but all it says is that he was found not guilty. It doesn't clear his name."

The three of us called it a night.

CHAPTER 14

In the morning we headed out to locate Dick Harris. I wanted to find him to see if I could get any information out of him. All I had was a name. I started at the police station.

"Can I help you?" the officer behind counter asked.

"Hi my name is Jack, we're doing a documentary, and part of the documentary has brought us here. I'm interested in finding out some information on a two-bit drug dealer by the name of Dick Harris."

"I'm not at liberty to give out personal information, but let me have a look in our database. May I also remind you that you cannot use any electronic recording devices in the precinct."

"Yes sir, the cameras are off. All I'm looking for is a current address."

"Okay, all I can let you know is that he spent time in and out of jail. He got out about six years ago. He must have gone clean, there's nothing in here since then. You could try the public records at the courthouse."

"Could he have moved out of State?" I asked.

"He could have but this is hooked up to the national records, if he was convicted in another state it would be in here."

"Okay, thanks for your help, Adam, I guess we go back to the courthouse, thank you officer."

"By the way, what's the documentary about?" the officer asked.

"I'm on a quest to clear my dad's name. He was accused of raping someone a few years back," I told him.

A gray-haired officer entered through the front door behind me, scanned his I.D. badge in the little box on the wall and pulled the door open as a clicked. He disappeared behind it as it shut and he reappeared behind the counter.

"Why is it so important for you to clear his name?" the first officer asked.

"The trial never finished, my mom passed away during it and the girl dropped the rape charges, she said she felt sorry for my dad."

"Well good luck in finding Mr. Harris," he said.

"This sounds awfully familiar to me," the gray-haired gentleman said. "What's your name son?"

"Jack Stevenson."

"Not little Jack Stevenson, from Division Street?"

"Yes sir."

"It's me, Doug Fulcher. I used to be your dad's partner, you always called me Uncle Doug."

"I'm sorry, I didn't recognize you," I said to him.

"That's okay, it's been a long time, c'mon into the office and bring your friends," he said.

Doug pressed a button behind the counter. I grabbed the handle of the door and pulled it open. He shook my hand as I walked through the entranceway, he then led us down the hall to a small office.

"These are my friends, Adam and Mark."

"How are you doing guys?" he asked. They all shook hands. "So what kind of information are you looking for?"

"I am trying to locate Dick Harris but he's been clean for a few years and seems to have dropped off your radar. I've got to go to the courthouse to see if I can find an old address on him. I doubt if he'll tell me anything, but I've got to try. I promised Dad I'd look into it."

"Sorry to hear about your dad, I am also sorry I never made it to his funeral, but after the trial we were sort of at odds with each other."

"You were only doing your job. I'm sure Dad understood. During your investigation did he ever say anything about that night?" I asked Doug.

"No he denied ever being inside the place."

"Can you help me with anything?"

"I've got Dick's last known address, it's about five-or-six years old, it's all I have."

"It's a start," I said.

"I also wrote Laura Melrose's last address, I have no information on her at all. If she is married it might be even tougher finding her," he said.

"Thanks for all your help," I said.

"No problem, sorry to hear about your dad," he said again.

"Thanks, he had a tough time after my sister died and even tougher when he retired. He didn't stay involved with anything and had too much time on his hands to sit and worry, and it eventually got the best of him."

"Did he seek any help at all?" Doug asked.

"He saw a shrink a couple of times, but you know how stubborn he was. It didn't seem to help. He became strange near the end."

"What you mean?" he asked.

"The night he died, he shaved his head bald and then shot himself full heroin."

"I didn't know he used drugs," Doug said surprised.

"Neither did I, the last month he spent a lot of nights just wandering the streets, he obviously got mixed up with the wrong crowd," I said.

"He was a good cop when he was here. That trial sure must've changed him."

"I think his retirement was the start of his downfall. Anyhow thanks for the information, we've got to go now," I said.

"Good luck Jack, good seeing you," he said.

The three of us left through the secured door. We left the police station and drove to a gas station. I ran in and bought a map of the area. I looked up the street name that Doug had written down and we headed over there. It was in a bad part of town. The buildings were run down and most of the windows and doors were boarded up, the streets were dirty. Mark had the camera rolling as I pulled up in front of a run down shack. I approached the door and knocked. A lady in her fifties answered. She had on torn clothes that obviously hadn't been washed in awhile. Her hair was in rollers, which were covered by a kerchief. I noticed as she smiled that she only had a few teeth.

"Can I help you?" she asked through the broken screen on the door.

"Yes, I'm looking for Dick Harris."

"You ain't gonna find him here," she replied.

"Do you know where I could?" I questioned her.

"What do you want him for?" she snapped.

"I just want to ask him some questions."

"You a cop?" she asked.

"No Ma'am."

"Must be a reporter then, with all those cameras," she said as she pointed to Mark.

"No, we're filming a documentary. I just wanted to interview him."

"Like I said, you ain't gonna find him here."

"Do you know where he is?" I asked again.

"Hell, probably," she answered emotionless.

"Pardon me?" I asked.

"He died over five years ago, in a car accident."

"I'm sorry to hear that," I said.

"Don't be sorry, for a son he was a no good son of a bitch."

"Do you know where I could find his ex-girlfriend Laura?" I asked.

"That good for nothing junky, I have no idea, I haven't seen her since that night," the lady explained to me.

"The night of the accident?" I asked quizzically.

"Yep, she got hurt in the crash, ain't seen her since."

"Okay, thanks for your time," I said as I walked away.

"Why don't we try the library?" Adam suggested. "We can look through the newspaper archives."

"Good idea."

I drove to the library and we went inside. We started looking through the microfilm at the obituaries. I started back seven years, Adam and Mark started three and six months after that. It took well over two hours, but eventually we did find something. There was only a small article about the crash, it didn't provide much information on Laura, other than saying she was a passenger in the car and that she was seriously injured in the accident. It didn't have any mention of the address, but it did list a Mr. Ben McLennan as her stepfather. It seemed he was a local politician.

We printed what information we needed and headed to City Hall. After asking at the front desk, we were directed the fifth floor, where we found a large cherrywood door with his name on it.

"May I help you?" a lady asked from behind a desk as we entered through the door.

"I'd like to see Mr. McLennan if I could."

"He's in a council meeting right now, but he should be out momentarily if you'd like to wait," she said pointing at a naugahide couch against the wall.

"That would be great," I said as I slumped in the soft leather sofa.

We sat around discussing the documentary. After starting with the footage of the trial transcript, there really hasn't been much else. Adam and Mark didn't seem to mind though.

"Most documentaries have their dry time, but you still capture it on film and edit it later," Mark said.

The door to the office opened. In walked a very short bald man. He was not what I would have expected for a city councilor.

"Mr. McLennan, these gentlemen would like to have a word with you."

"Sure, come into my office," he said as he held the door for us. "Have a seat."

"Thank you," I said.

"How can I help you gentleman?"

"We're doing a documentary and are interested in locating your stepdaughter," I said.

"Documentary. How come the camera isn't rolling?" he questioned.

"You don't mind?" Adam asked.

"Not at all. I wouldn't have become a city councilor if I was afraid of the camera now would I?" he asked with a chuckle.

Mark picked up the camera and started filming.

"We're looking for Laura Melrose, I'd like to talk to her about her involvement in a court case about six years ago."

"The cop case, I know it well," he said.

"That cop was my dad. The trial ended with your stepdaughter dropping the charges at the last minute. His guilt or innocence was never proven. My mom went to her grave not knowing. Dad said he was innocent. Before he died he asked me to clear his name, and that's what I'm trying to do."

"The evidence against your dad was pretty strong. I was hoping that the whole thing could have been settled outside the spotlight myself."

"Why's that?" I questioned.

"I had thrown my hat in the ring for city councilor at the time. The trial made big headlines. Not only would it destroy your father's reputation, my political career was sure to be damaged also."

"Did you convince her to drop the charges?"

"I tried to talk to her out of the charges in the beginning, but it was fruitless. She was an addict. Her boyfriend at the time had more control over her than her mother and I did."

"What do you think caused her to drop it?"

"I'm not sure. Her relationship with her boyfriend was very volatile, she was so stoned half of the time, it didn't matter what I said or did."

"Do you think my dad did it?" I asked him bluntly.

"I'm not sure, from all the evidence against him it sure looked like it."

"I'd like to talk to her about it," I said.

"I'm not sure whether she would talk or not, she's rehabilitated and has made a career for herself. She'd probably be afraid to talk," he said.

"I'm not looking for any repercussions. I just want answers."

"Well, all you can do is try, I'll get you the address," he said as he started flipping through a black book that he had on his desk.

"She doesn't live with you anymore?" I questioned.

"She's older now. She moved out once she sobered up and started training."

"Training, for what?" I questioned.

"The Olympics. She's on the U.S. team for the marathon," he said proudly.

"Where can I find her?"

"She lives with her mother and my son in Oslo," he said sadly.

"Norway?"

"Yes sir. Here's the address," he said as he handed me a piece of paper.

"Does she ever get back to the U.S.?" I asked.

"No, but I wish they would. Her mother and I have a son together. I haven't seen him in four years," he said as he reached behind him and grabbed a picture off his desk and handed it to me.

"Why don't you go there and visit him?" I asked puzzled.

"I simply can't afford it on my salary, and with the amount of child support I pay there's no way I could swing it."

"I'm sure it would be tough even getting the time off," I replied.

"No, I have enough time built up. City council doesn't even have meetings planned for a few weeks, but it would be too much of a financial burden for me to go," he said.

"Thanks for your help. Adam, I guess we're going to Norway," I said with a smile.

Mark shut off the camera and picked up his stuff. We left the office. I took out my cell phone and called Kevin. I told him to get fueled up and pick us up at the Airport. I then stopped at the Mayor's Office on the way out.

"I was wondering if I could see the mayor," I asked his secretary.

"Have a seat and I'll see if he's available," she said as she stood and walked towards his door. She knocked on it quietly and then entered. She closed the door behind her.

"Why do we need to see the Mayor?" Adam asked.

"I had a thought as we were walking out and I need to talk to him about something," I replied.

The door opened and the secretary emerged. Leaving the door open she said, "the Mayor will see you, but you have to leave the camera here."

"You guys can wait here, I'll only be a couple of minutes," I told Adam and Mark as I entered the Mayor's office.

"Good day," the Mayor said. "How can I help you?"

"Hi my name is Jack Stevenson. I'm interested in opening a business in town. I'm heading out in a couple of hours on a fact-finding mission," I told him.

"How can I help?"

"I know it's short notice but with your permission I'd like to take a city councilor with me to promote the city while I'm in Norway. I was wondering if Ben McLennan could come along."

"What type of business are you looking at?" he asked.

"I'd like to open a ski boot plant. I figure it will employ a thousand people once we're up and running."

"Sounds interesting. I've got no problem with him going for a couple of weeks. I'm not sure whether he has personal matters or if he can leave on such short notice," the Mayor stated.

"I'll check that out with him, thanks for the co-operation."

"No problem. I hope it can work out. I might have some explaining to do to the media and the taxpayers why we're sending a city official on their tax dollars, but I'm sure I can handle it," he said as he stood up and shook my hand.

"You won't have to, I'll cover his wages plus a $10,000 donation to build a community park or something," I said.

"Sounds good," he replied as he let go of my hand.

"Great, I will fill Ben in on the details."

I let myself out of his office and approached Adam and Mark. I asked them to wait in the lobby while I went back to Ben's office.

"Hi again," I said to his secretary. "I was wondering if I could see Mr. McLennan again for a minute."

"Sure, go on in," she said as she pointed the way.

"Hi Ben."

"Back so soon?"

"Yeah, I just wanted to let you know that I spoke to the Mayor. I'm heading to Oslo to try and see your stepdaughter and was wondering if you would like to come along?"

"I'd love to, but I can't afford it," he said.

"No problem, I'm picking up the tab. I told Mr. Chadsworth that I was thinking of opening up a business here and I'd like some city assistance. How about it?" I asked him.

"Are you really looking to do that?" he said with a strange look on his face.

"Hell no, but he docsn't have to know that. It's not going to cost the taxpayers a dime, and if you've got the time, I'd love to take you there."

"Why?" he questioned.

"You want to see your son, don't you?"

"Sure do, when do we leave?"

"In about an hour," I threw him a $50 bill. "Grab a taxi and meet me at the Capri Motel. We'll leave from there."

"Okay," he said puzzled.

I left his office and caught up to Adam and Mark.

"Ben's coming with us to Oslo. Let's get back to the motel and get ready, he'll meet us there."

"Why?" Adam asked.

"I don't know why, I like the guy. I don't think he can offer any help, but I'd like him to see his son," I said.

We drove back to the motel. I called Kevin to make sure everything was set. Ben arrived forty-five minutes later.

"I really appreciate this," he said.

"No problem. I think you should see your son. A father shouldn't go without seeing his son," I replied.

That was my real reason for taking him. I had no ulterior motives. He seemed like a nice guy, he wants to see his son and can't afford it. I've got enough money and wanted to do a good deed. I drove the car to the airport where Kevin was waiting with the jet. We boarded it and I settled in as it started to take off. I got to know Ben a bit. He really was a nice guy. I was glad I was doing this for him. Once we checked through customs. I went to the rental car agency and got two cars, one for Adam, Mark and myself, and one for Ben.

"I'm not sure what your plans are," I told Ben. "But I got you a car. We're staying for four days at the Hilton. If I don't see you again before Friday, be here at ten, do you need any cash?" I asked him.

"No, you've done enough already," he said as he gave me a hug.

"Okay then, have a great visit and we'll see you Friday." I handed him the keys and he left, constantly looking back at us, I'm sure in disbelief that this was actually happening.

It was now getting late. Adam drove us to the Hilton where we checked in and got settled in our rooms. I put Adam and Mark in one room and I had my own suite. I was catching my second wind so I headed to the hotel bar. Adam and Mark opted out. I pulled a stool up to the bar and had a couple of beers. I only had two, enough to catch a slight buzz, but not enough to cloud my mind. I wasn't sure where this journey would take me, but in the back of my mind, I knew why I was here. I went back to my suite and did some research on my laptop. I dug out Laura's address and searched for a phone number on the Internet. I called the number that I had found.

"Hello," a female voice said.

"Hi, my name is Jack Stevenson, is Laura there?" I asked.

"Speaking."

"Hi," I said again. "I'm not sure whether you recognize my name or not, but I would like to talk to you."

"Actually, I already spoke to Ben. Sorry to hear about your dad," she said.

"Thank you, the reason I'm calling is that I am the focus of a documentary. As part of that, I'm trying to find out what really happened. I would like to interview you for the documentary."

"I'm not sure whether I want to be a part of it and not," she said with her voice stammering.

"I'm not after anything other than the truth. I'm not looking to open up a can of worms. No charges can be laid and I'm willing to pay you for your story, but all I ask for is the truth. If he raped you I want to know it. If he didn't, I want to know that too," I said.

"How much are you willing to pay?" she asked.

"That I would like to discuss when we meet, I will make it worth your while though."

"Do you think your dad did it?" she asked me.

"I'm not sure what to think. I've read over the trial transcripts and I'm not sure. The evidence points to his guilt, but with you dropping the charges, I really don't know. All I know is my dad asked me to find Dick and get the truth, but that's not possible. I hope you can help," I said.

"I'm not sure I can do this. I'm in the middle of training."

"All I want is a couple hours of your time. I'm willing to pay you comfortably for the interview," I repeated.

"Tell me up front what you are willing to pay and I'll think about it," she demanded.

"How's fifty thousand dollars sound?"

"Give me your number, I'll think about it and get back to

you."

"Okay, but I'm only here for four days. Don't take too long," I told her.

"I'll call you back in the morning," she said.

"I'm staying at the Hilton, room 2012."

"I'll give you a shout in the morning," she repeated.

"Okay goodbye," I hung up the phone and called it a night.

The phone rang the next morning. It was Laura.

"Hi, Jack?"

"Yes."

"It's Laura, I'll take you up on your offer."

"Great, where is a good place where we could meet?"

"How about the bar in your hotel?" she asked.

"Okay, how's one o'clock?"

"I'll be there," she replied.

I hung up the phone only to pick it up again to tell Adam and Mark of the interview. I arranged to meet them for lunch at noon. We went down and scoured out the place looking for a good area to set up the camera. I left instructions with the hostess that we were going in the restaurant to grab a bite to eat and that we were expecting Miss Melrose. We then went and had lunch. We discussed some questions and the angles that we wanted to shoot them from. I was very nervous about the interview. My dad said that he didn't do it. I believe him but after reading the court transcripts, it cast a shadow of a doubt.

When we finished eating, we went back into the bar area. There was a lady already sitting in the booth that I had reserved.

"Hi, Miss Melrose?" I questioned.

"Yes, and you must be Jack," she said.

"I am, and this is Adam and Mark who are producing the documentary."

"Hi," she said.

Adam and Mark both responded with a hello.

"So, Miss Melrose?" I started.

"Call me Laura," she insisted.

"Like I told you on the phone, I'm the subject of a documentary and as part of that I am looking for some answers in regards to my dad's alleged rape charge. All I know is what I read in the court documents. My dad rarely discussed it. He said he didn't do it. He said to find Dick Harris to get the truth. But as we all know he's dead. I hope you can shed some light on it."

"I'll answer the questions the best I can, but there is the matter of the money," she said.

"I've got it right here," I told her as I pulled out an envelope containing five hundred $100 bills. "You can count it if you want," I told her.

"I'll have Harry do that," she said as she looked over to a man in the booth across from us and motioned to him. He came to the table.

"Gentlemen," she said. "This is Harry, he's my step father," I stood and shook his hand.

"Since I don't know you, Harry will count the money and take it to the bank. I'll start the interview in the meantime. If by chance the money is counterfeit, when Harry gets back, the interview is off."

"Sounds okay to me," I said.

She handed him the money and he left.

"Okay Jack were ready," Mark said.

"Roll tape," Adam uttered.

"What is your name?" I asked Laura.

"Laura Melrose."

"Hi Laura, I'm Jack Stevenson. You were involved in a trial a few years back involving my father. You accused him of a crime, can you tell me what that was?"

"Rape."

"Who else was involved in the allegation?"

"Dick Harris."

"Who is that?" I asked.

"He was my boyfriend at the time."

"What do you mean was?"

"He died in a car accident."

"What was his connection to my dad?"

"Your dad arrested him for trafficking. He was jailed for a while, but after he got out he became your dad's informant. He helped your dad take a couple of dealers off the streets."

"The night in question, was my dad at your place?"

"Yes, he drove his pickup there to meet up with Dick."

"That was the night you said that my dad raped you, is that

correct?" I asked her.

"Yes it was."

"Did he rape you?"

"I'm not saying any more until Harry gets back from the bank," she replied.

We sat there for a while and had a couple of drinks. The cameras were off. I took the time to size Laura up. Her hair was reddish brown, short, almost too short. I could see traces of her white scalp when she turned sideways. Her eyes were gray, maybe greenish, it was hard to tell in the light. Her face was more elongated than round. I could tell by the broadness of her shoulders that she was in shape. When she reached out to pick up her glass, her biceps and triceps tightened as she squeezed it. She raised it to her lips, which were pouty looking. I questioned to myself if they had maybe been injected with collagen. She was wearing a spandex top. I assumed that her lower body was as fit as her upper. I could only see her from the waist up, her bottom half was hidden by the table in the booth in which we sat.

"So Laura, how long have you been in Norway?"

"Only a couple of years. After Dick and I had the accident that killed him, I had spent enough time in the hospital to become clean. I signed myself into rehab once I was released and attended counseling sessions. They really helped. They got me thinking clean and they got me motivated. I put my past behind me and concentrated on the future."

"Ben was telling me that you're here training for the Olympics."

"Yes, I started training for the marathon once I learned to maneuver after the accident. They said I was a natural. It has taken a few years, but I'm going to race in three months for the gold. I've got a good chance of winning."

Harry arrived back at the restaurant and slid into the booth beside Laura. "Everything checked out Laura, the money is in the bank," he said.

"All I want is the truth. I'm not looking for trouble. I'm not going to sick the police on you. My dad said he didn't do it and if he didn't, I just want to clear its name."

"Go ahead and set up your cameras," Laura said. "I'll tell

you everything."

Adam adjusted the microphones and had Laura and I test them again. Mark grabbed a tripod and repositioned one of the cameras. I felt the lights warm up the booth as he turned them on. There were actually two cameras, one pointed at my face and one at Laura's, Adam was controlling the one pointed at me.

"Okay Laura," I said. "I asked you before the break if my father raped you."

She paused for a few seconds and then sheepishly uttered the word, "no." I dropped my head into my hands. Even though I didn't think he did it, I wasn't sure, the evidence was so strong. I didn't want it to be true. He loved my mom and I couldn't see him committing rape.

"But the evidence?" I stammered.

"It was his alright, the hair, the semen and even the skin under my nails," she reported.

"I can't believe he'd do that," I said.

"Do what, I told you he didn't rape me."

"No, I didn't think he'd ever have an affair on my mom. Did he dump you, is that why you turned on him?"

"No."

"Why did you drop the charge?" I asked. "You had the case won."

"Your mom had died and I had put him through enough. I felt sorry for him. During the trial, Dick was becoming a real idiot, abusing me more and more. I dropped it because I didn't want to see Dick win. It was all his idea. I was young, stupid and dependent on drugs. Dick was a very controlling and manipulating man. He even manipulated your dad into believing he was on his side, that he was an informant. It was all part of his master plot."

"Dick let you have an affair with my dad?" I asked.

"No, I never slept with your dad, I never even really met him. Your dad was framed."

"How?"

She paused and took a big drink of water. "Alright, I'll tell you all of it. I thought I was in love with Dick at the time. I would do anything he said, besides he controlled me and my mind with drugs. He made me do a lot of weird things. Otherwise he held back the drugs, it hurt too much not to have them. It was all Dick's idea," she repeated.

"I believe you, just tell me the truth."

"Dick spent some hard time in jail. Your dad had busted him for possession and trafficking. He blamed your dad. Nothing was ever Dick's fault, in his mind anyway. While imprisoned, Dick got beat up a couple of times, probably because of his mouth. He didn't care whom he mouthed off to. One night in jail he got jumped and raped by a couple of the other inmates and he blamed your dad. When he got out of jail he went right back to dealing and using. He swore to me he'd get your dad back no matter how long it took. He called your dad one night at home wanting to set up a meeting. Your dad was reluctant, but agreed. They met at the mall on your dad's day off. Your dad wanted a public meeting. I guess he didn't trust Dick either. Dick told him that he was clean and having served his time, wanted to turn his life around. He offered to help your dad out by setting up meetings with other dealers. He would help your dad as long as he kept it quiet from the other cops on the force. Dick said that if another cop found out or the word hit the streets he was afraid he'd be killed. It was all part of this plan to reel your dad in all the way.

At the meeting Dick supplied your dad with an address and the time of a major deal going down that night. Your dad showed up and made the arrest. This convinced your dad that Dick was for real. Over the next month your dad made a couple arrests with the aid of Dick. It even earned your dad a promotion on the force. While all this was going on, Dick was controlling my drugs more and more. He strung me along until I gave in to his demands and then he would give me a fix."

"What happened the night my dad was arrested?" I asked.

"Dick set up a meeting with a dealer. Before your dad got there we all went inside and got stoned on acid. Dick convinced the other dealer to get more stuff. He called your dad and asked him to come over to my place. It was late. The dealer had just arrived back and opened the trunk of the car for the exchange when your dad pulled up. Before your dad could get out of his truck, Dick told the other pusher that your dad was a cop. Your dad stepped out of his vehicle and that's when Dick and the other guy jumped him, wrestling him to the ground. They laid a beating on him and they both took off. Your dad took off too, but must have given up chasing them and went to the diner where the cops arrested him."

"If that's all that happened, how did you convince the cops you were raped, and how did they find all the evidence against him?"

"After your dad took off, Dick circled back to my place. We had sex, very rough sex and then planted the evidence. He then forced me to call the cops. If you read the court transcripts the rest is history."

"But where did Dick get the evidence?" I questioned.

"Dick was still dealing the whole time after he got out of jail. One of the junkies he dealt with was a girl named Heidi. She was the secretary at the doctor's office where your dad was going for a test, for his vasectomy follow up. Dick was in there the week before selling to her when your dad called on the phone to make an appointment. Dick overheard the conversation and made her tell him when it was. He showed up there that day at closing and waited until your dad and the doctor were gone. He gave Heidi a hit of acid in exchange for your dad's sperm sample. The bag also contained the tissue that was used after the ultrasound that contained his pubic hairs. Your dad was called that night to come to my apartment. That's how the cops got his tire tracks. He stepped out of the truck and put his foot on the ground, that's when he was jumped. I stood in the shadows and when they had your dad down on the ground, I took my hand and scratched his face. My hair was longer then. I pulled out a few strands of it and wrapped them around a button on the sleeve of your dads' jacket while he was on the ground, then I went inside. The whole thing only lasted a couple of minutes, and then your dad was gone. Dick returned a few minutes later. We got undressed and climbed in the bed. He laid me flat on my back and we started making out. At first it was passionate, then Dick got rough. He told me to try to fight him, to try and stop him from screwing me. He pumped hard. At one point he took the back of his hand and hit me on the side the face, hard. He wore a condom and said that none of his sperm could leak out anywhere, on me or on the sheets. Dick got up and got a small paper bag off the dresser. He opened it and took out one of those sample containers, you know the type they give you to pee in at the doctor's office. It contained some semen. He made me lie on my back, while he knelt at my crotch. He grabbed my legs and put them both over his head, spreading them and laying one on each of the shoulders. We've got to make you a bit swollen, he said as he slammed his fist hard into my crotch, three times. He then grabbed a clean syringe from the nightstand, removed the needle part and took the cap off of the bottle and inserted the syringe into it. He drew the liquid in it and then shot it on the sheets between my legs. He put the syringe back in the bottle tilting it, as he did he drew up as much of your dad's semen as he could. He took the syringe in his right hand. I couldn't see what he was doing, but I could feel it as he inserted it inside of me. He put it in as far as he could and expelled the ejaculate. He reached back in the bag and took out a couple of crumpled tissues, pulled off some pubic hairs and laid them on the sheets. We sat there for about five minutes. Dick then put the needle parts, the cup, lid, and the tissues back in the bag. He got dressed and told me what to do. He then left with the bag. I got dressed in the same clothes I had on earlier. I then started pulling off my T-shirt, tearing the seams as I did and I threw it on the ground. I grabbed my bra strap and yanked on it, breaking it at the shoulders. I laid back on the bed and ripped the button off that held my pants together. I grabbed the one side of the waistband and pulled, as I did the zipper broke. I pulled my pants off inside out and left them at my ankles. I then grabbed my thong underwear and pulled until one side gave way. I kept pulling until I had completely ripped them off. I threw them on the floor at the end of the bed. I then called the police and told them I was raped. They arrived ten minutes later, as I yelled to the door for them to come in I hit myself a couple more times in the crotch with my closed fist to maintain the swelling. I gave them my description of your dad and his license plate number. When the ambulance arrived, one of the cops took off. He said he saw your dad's pickup at the diner just down the road.

The ambulance attendants came in and took me to the

hospital. Once there, the doctors took some swabs that they pulled out of a rape kit. The police took my statement and I was released. Dick and I got stoned when we got back to my apartment. The rest was documented in the court case."

"I need to go to the washroom," I said calmly and headed to the bar. I stood there thinking about what Laura said until the bartender asked me what I wanted. I ordered a double scotch and threw it down my throat. I went to the washroom, opened the stall and sat there. I knew Dick was the mastermind behind this plot, but she was as much to blame. I wrestled with the thought. Was Dick's death justice enough? Or should I blame her for her actions? I opened my wallet and looked at the picture of my dad. He wanted his name cleared and now I had the footage to do that. I could rent some airtime on one of the networks and show the documentary. I could look for a different victim, after all Dick was holding her ransom with the drugs. I pondered the thought for a while.

"Are you okay Jack?" I heard Adam's voice say as the washroom door creaked open.

"Yes, I'll be out in a minute," I stood up and flushed the toilet even though I had never even attempted to go. I slid the lock handle sideways and exited the stall. I made my way to the sink and splashed water in my face.

"Well Jack, we got what we came for," Adam said.

"Yes we did," I said. "Go on back Adam, I'll catch up in a minute."

Adam left the bathroom and I made my way to the paper towel dispenser, I pulled about a foot of towel and walked back to the sink and stared in the mirror. I looked rough. I hadn't shaved in three days, and my eyes looked tired. I stared at my image in the mirror and asked myself a question out loud. "Well, do I or not?" the face in the mirror stared back, sizing me up. "You've come this far, she did cause turmoil in your parents' life and she does deserve it. Right?" the face in the mirror replied. I crumpled the paper towel and tossed it over my head towards the wastebasket. It hit the rim and dropped in. I left the washroom and again stopped at the bar. I ordered another double scotch and this time I downed it with vengeance, slamming the glass on the bar as I finished. I rejoined the others and took my spot in the booth. "Just one more question Miss Melrose. Why did you drop the charges?"

"Your mother had just died on the weekend, when I arrived in the courtroom I looked at your Dad. He looked haggard, sitting there motionless. I could see the pain in his face. I grew up without a dad so I knew what it was like. I knew the whole ordeal was a lie and even though I had carried it through to the end, I couldn't bear to be the one responsible for the fate of you, your brother and sister. You needed your dad. I knew Dick would be pissed. I'm very sorry for what I did, but I was too dependent on the drugs at the time, please forgive me," she said tearfully.

"I do forgive you," I said. Knowing in my mind she was going to be victim number three.

CHAPTER 15

The cameras kept rolling.

"Well Harry, I think it's time to go," Laura told him.

Harry got up out of his booth and disappeared behind it. He arrived back a minute later with a wheelchair and positioned it at the end of the table between the two benches.

"Slide over," he said to Laura.

She inched her way to the edge of the bench, Harry reached for her and snatched her from the booth. He lifted her and put her gently in the chair. She had no legs from about the middle of her thighs down. Adam, Mark and I must have been staring.

"What's the matter?" she asked. "Haven't you ever seen an amputee before?"

"I'm sorry," I said as I could feel the redness growing on my cheeks. "I didn't know."

"I can thank Dick for this," she said pointing at where her legs should be. "After the trial I spent six months in jail and then I went into rehab for eight months. Dick picked me up from the center that day. He had only visited me twice at rehab while I was there. I was surprised to see him. As soon as I got in the car he started to push the drugs on me again. I told him that I was clean and staying that way. He pulled over to the side of the road. He slapped me around a bit and tried to force the needle into my arm. I knocked it away, kicked him and took off running. He started his car and came after me. He chased me down and hit me with the car. I fell to the ground in the middle of the road. I must of broken my ankle, it was sore as hell and I couldn't get up. Dick sped by me and headed down the road about three hundred yards. I tried to drag myself to the side of the road as I heard his tires squeal. He turned his vehicle around and was headed right for me. I crawled as fast as I could to get out of the way but he ran over my legs anyway. I heard the bones crush as the tires rolled over them. I lay there writhing in pain as he headed down the road again. His tires squealed once more. I was now in the other lane, as I looked behind me I could see a semi barreling down on me. I sat up the best I could and waved frantically to get the driver's attention. He must have noticed me because he was blasting his air horn like a locomotive. He was a lot closer to me than Dick was. I couldn't move. I had no feeling in my legs. As I looked at them I could see blood, there were bones sticking through the skin on both my legs. I said a quick prayer and waited for the semi to hit me. I thought I was going to die. Dick backed up and made a run for me. I closed my eyes as the transport swerved around me and into Dicks' lane. I opened my eyes as the transport hit Dick head on. There wasn't much left of his car, the poor bastard died instantly. I must have passed out, The next thing I knew I awoke in the hospital, both of my legs were gone. I went through numerous surgeries and massive therapy. I became quite good at maneuvering my chair. I was clean and was going to stay that way. Even though I had been crippled I felt like I had a new lease on life. I worked hard at it and here I am today, ranked number one in the world thanks to Harry's help. That's how he and my mom met."

"That's an incredible story," Adam said. "Maybe we could do a documentary on you next?"

"If the money's right," she said as she wheeled herself out of the restaurant.

Mark shut off the camera.

Adam, Mark and I had one more beer each and then headed back to the hotel.

I awoke the next morning, bright eyed and bushy tailed. I pulled my wallet out of my pants that I had thrown on the floor. I opened it and pulled out a family picture of Lynn, Jimmy, myself and my dad. My decision came easily. I opened the door after hearing a knock. It was Adam.

"What's next boss?" he asked.

"I think I have everything I need here. I'll give Kevin a call and we'll head back to the States. Call your wives and tell them to pack. We'll all take a vacation to my island. We can edit the tape there. We'll spend a week or so on the island and then I'll air it."

We packed our bags and headed to the airport. I paid for a

private jet to fly Ben home when he was ready. I called Ben and informed him that we were heading home. Kevin flew Adam, Mark and myself to St. Pete's Airport. Their wives were waiting, Adam and Mark's anyway. Kevin's wife was still back home in Fiji. Once the jet was refueled we headed for Fiji. This was going to be a working vacation. There was Adam and his wife Amanda, Mark and his wife Stephanie, Kevin and I. It was a long flight. We stopped once for fuel and finally got there the next day. That was pretty well a write off as we all suffered from jet lag when we arrived.

The next day was the final rest day before we sat down to edit the tape. We all hung out around the pool and gorged on the food that I had made. I enjoyed this part of my money, being able to treat my friends to a vacation. I turned the island into a paradise retreat. There was everything you could possibly want on the island, a theater, go-cart track, arcade and endless amounts of food and booze. I had it made and treating my friends and seeing their faces beam was reward enough. There were plenty of hiking trails, ATV'S, catamarans and speedboats to keep them amused for hours.

As nighttime fell we all met back at the pool. I had Kevin take the helicopter in the afternoon and pick up the members of the band that I had hired for the evening. We danced all night and into the early morning hours. We watched the sun rise from the horizon. What a beautiful time. I'm going to miss those days I thought, remembering I was in jail.

I awoke around one o'clock in the afternoon. Adam and Mark were already up and had the equipment set up to edit the tape. Kevin was down in the shop somewhere doing tune-ups on some of the equipment. He spent a lot of time there. Maria, Manuel and Patrick had gone to the mainland for a holiday and would be back soon.

"Good morning guys."

"Good morning Jack," Adam replied. "Have a good sleep?"

"As a matter of fact I did, I usually do here, it's like a different world. I don't have to worry about anything while I'm here."

"It's quite the place," Mark said.

"Are your wives enjoying it?"

"I know mine is," Adam added. "I haven't had sex like that in a long time."

"It's amazing what a little relaxation can do," I said.

"The booze helps too," Mark commented.

"Okay boys let's get to business with this film. I want my dad to be proud."

"I'm sure he'll be smiling down on us when we're done. What angle do you want to take?" Adam asked.

"Of course I want my dad to be a hero, but I also want to portray Laura as an abused, pathetic junky. I want to lay all the blame where it's deserved, on Dick."

We worked hard viewing all the tape that we had filmed, marking what should be left in and what should hit the cutting room floor. We broke for the night after reviewing it all. The girls helped Maria prepare a huge feast when she arrived. The band was still there from the night before, so we partied once again. Tonight Maria joined us, so I had a dancing partner. The music started with a slow song and I asked her to dance. She was a little shy, but I convinced her to. I pulled her close, feeling the curves of her body against mine. It felt good holding her tight for the whole song. A second song started, we were still holding each other close. We danced all night.

The next day Adam, Mark and I got together to cut and piece the documentary together. I was proud of the way it came together. It was a poignant piece.

We spent a lot of time just relaxing around the pool. Finally when the week was over I was able to send Adam, Mark and their wives back to the U.S. I stayed back plotting my move for my next murder. Again I tossed around the idea of quitting my plan. Laura's role was secondary and Dick was already dead, the loss of her legs tugged at my heartstrings, but in the end I felt she deserved it. Sure I had the footage to exonerate my dad, but the turmoil she put my mother through in her last days on the earth bothered me more. My mom died thinking her husband was a cheat. I know in my heart that she knew Dad was incapable of the crime, but with all the medication she was on in her final days she had a hard time distinguishing between fact and fiction. Laura played a large part in hurting my parents and for this, no matter how disabling her life became, Laura had to die.

I summoned Kevin to take me to the airport. I took a commercial flight to Tampa, using my own name. Although I wasn't sure about how I was going to set up an alibi for this murder, I knew I would have to start to be seen in the U.S. now and then. I got a small motel room on the gulf and visited with the Howard's for a couple of days. I told them I was traveling down to Keycoast for a month to spend time Jimmy. I had been neglecting him lately and I felt it was my duty. I was also feeling guilty. I missed the little guy. There was about three weeks before I had to go back to Norway to get things ready there. I left Indian Rocks and headed down the coast. Jimmy stayed with me at the house for a week. We had an awesome time together. I forgot how much I really loved him.

I called Adam and had him come to Keycoast. We sat and reviewed the tape once more. I asked him to go and buy some airtime to play the tape. He was more than willing. This meant exposure of his talents. He and Mark had done several films, but could never get any to air. I handed him a MasterCard and told him to pay whatever it took to get my dads' story out. Adam had to go by himself. Marks' wife was expecting a baby any day.

I finalized all my details, packed my bags and left Keycoast. I drove my car to a hotel in Miami and checked in under the name of Brian Walkerton.

I slept very well that night. In the morning I put on a long blonde mullet wig and had a limo service pick me up and take me to the airport. I flew to Oslo International Airport. I had pre-booked a rental car and took it to the motel that I had booked a room at on the edge of town. All the hotels were booked for the Para-Olympics, but for enough cash I had the manager bump someone else out of a room. I unpacked and headed to the athletes' village to find Laura. I was posing as a fashion designer and I was going to convince her to wear my fashions. I had bought a few sets of clothes from an up-and-coming designer in Fiji.

I located Laura doing some warm-up laps on the track. I gained access to the compound by making a fake volunteer security pass. I took time out one day when Adam and Mark were in the hotel room and went to the Olympic headquarters and bought some souvenirs. Volunteers were popping in and out of the office wearing their security cards around their necks. I studied the design closely, with a little cut and paste on the computer I was able to duplicate one without any problem. All I had to do was flash the badge, show picture ID, and I was in, piece of cake.

It's funny how I pulled the wool over everyone's eyes. It wasn't until after this murder that Adam and Mark had any inkling that it could be me committing them. The first two alibis were airtight. They may have had a passing thought, but we were best friends and told each other everything. I kept this a secret and laughed it off whenever they even suggested it. They had no reason to doubt me. Even Kevin who worked for me was oblivious of the whole thing. I often gave him my card to use. He always had to pick up supplies. That way I had receipts to show the cops in case I needed to lie about where I was. The three of them knew that I had known the first two victims, but never put it together, hell even the police didn't clue in until I committed the fourth murder. I want to go on record saying that Adam, Mark and Kevin were in no way involved in any of the murders. I used them when I needed them, but that was their only involvement. They had no idea of what I was doing.

I could see on the monitor that Mark was starting the video feeds again on the prison monitor.

Laura had just finished a lap when I approached her.

"Hey man," I said in my best retro surfer dude voice. "You're radical."

"Thank you," she replied.

"How would you like to make some bones?"

"Pardon me," she said.

"I notice you don't have any sponsor logos on your bod."

"There's not a lot of support for my kind of sport," she said. "Besides, it's against the rules."

"Rules, schmules, the Walker lives on the edge, rules are for land lovers, when you're hanging ten, there ain't no rules."

"You're a surfer I take it?" she asked.

"Right on dude, you too?"

She pointed at her missing legs.

"Don't let that stop you, Boogi-boards; that's your answer."

"I could never," she started.

"Hey watch the language, never is a swear word." I jumped up in the air and landed in a surfer stance like I was riding a big wave, my arms out to each side to keep my balance.

"You're nuts," she said.

I looked at my crotch and pulled my flower shirt down. "They're not showing again are they?"

She laughed a little. "No, I mean your crazy. I should be going." She turned her wheelchair around and started to leave.

"Wait Laura," I yelled out in my normal voice. "I'm just putting on an act. The kids that buy my clothes expect me to be a surfer dude."

She stopped her chair and turned it towards me. "How do you know my name?" she asked.

I had to think quickly. "When you're the best, everyone knows your name. Besides, I really am looking to sponsor somebody."

"But I told you, it's not allowed."

"What's more important, a million dollars or some stupid rules?"

She wheeled her chair back to where I was standing. "I'm really listening now."

"Your the best Para-Olympic marathon athlete in the world. You should win the gold hands down. That's why I want you to work with me. We can pull this off."

"How?"

"There's a price to pay though."

"What's that?"

"Your medal, they will strip you of your gold when it's all over."

"But this is what I've worked for ever since the accident," she replied.

"What's after that, what do you do when you've won the race? Is there any future in it? I don't think so."

"There might be the odd TV commercial," she said.

"Right, how many disabled athletes do you know that have gone on to fame and fortune? Not too many. I'm offering a million dollars upfront even if you don't win."

"That is a lot of money."

"The fame alone of winning and then being stripped of your title will have you playing the talk-show circuit for a couple of years. You could even get a book or a movie contract out of it. If you turn me down and you win, you might get one-or-two interviews, something else will make sports history and you'll be thrown on the sidelines. I can make your name a national icon."

"I have to think about it. Can I call you?"

"I'll give you twenty-four hours. I'll meet you back here then."

"Okay, I'll be here tomorrow," she said.

"Later dude," I said as I flashed her the peace symbol.

I left as she still sat there pondering the thought. She didn't know it, but if I had to raise the stakes I would, money was no object. I left the athletic village and headed to the hotel. I knew I wouldn't be bothered because no one knew I was there. I was going to keep up the act at the hotel just in case. I don't think Laura clued into who I really was, she didn't flinch when I used my real voice. I went into the restaurant to eat dinner. The meal was good, not great. You would think for a five-star hotel it would've been better. After I ate I stopped by the bar and had a beer. I was in the mood to have more, but the place was empty. I asked the bartender to send a 12-pack to my room and headed upstairs. My room was on the sixth floor. I took the stairs.

For some reason I felt lonely today. I'm not sure what it was. As I approached the door to my floor I could see the bellhop knocking on it holding the 12-pack. I showed him the room key and he handed me the beer. I gave him 200 Kronos for his troubles. A huge smile lit up his face. He clenched it tightly in his fist and headed to the elevator. I went inside and threw the beer in the fridge. I went to the bathroom and stripped down to my boxers, grabbed a cigar from my suitcase, made my way back to the kitchen and grabbed a beer from the case. I passed by the little coffee table and picked up a book of matches the hotel had supplied. I stopped and looked at the cover. It had some advertising on it from a local nightclub. I pawed through the rest of them. They all had something different on them; some were advertising restaurants, taxi services and so on. The one that caught my eye was a pink one at the bottom of the dish. It was from the B.J. Escort services. I chuckled as the thought what the

B.J. stood for. It's funny, I thought Lee's picture would have popped in my head, but it didn't, Lynn's did. I wonder, if we were still married what she would think if I was away on a business trip and came home with these matches in my pocket. What would her reaction be? Would she question my motives, I never would know I guess. The short time we were together, we were always together. We never spent a night apart until her accident. I didn't even give a second thought to the advertising. I lit the cigar and threw the book back in the dish and went outside. I sat down in a plastic coated steel chair, opened my beer and took a drink. I sat there for a while and smoked half of the cigar before going in to get another beer. I again passed the dish of matchbooks and glanced at them pausing for a moment. I was very lonely, but I didn't want just anybody to spend some time with. I picked up the portable phone and went back outside. I sat there holding it for a while.

After finishing the 12-pack, I stood up and staggered towards the balcony and grabbed the railing. I stood there grasping it tightly, my knuckles turning white. My eye caught my wallet that had fallen off the chair. Although it was blurred from the beer, the date jumped out and hit me. It was Lynn's and my anniversary. It had totally gone unnoticed. Also staring at me was Lynn's picture on one of those cheesy photos from the booth at the mall. We went to a mall the day after we were married and paid two bucks for them. Since we eloped we didn't have a photographer for the wedding. The picture staring up at me was the only photo of us taken right after we were married. When we went to Atlantic City we never even took a camera. There she was, staring up at me in all her beauty, begging me not to jump. I pushed myself back from the railing and stumbled to the bedroom and passed out on the bed.

CHAPTER 16

I awoke the next morning with one of the biggest headaches I've ever had. I called down to room service and ordered up some aspirins. The bellhop from the night before must have spread the word about his tip, I barely hung up the phone and there was a knock at the door. Glancing in the mirror I realized that I had lost my wig somewhere. I opened the door slightly and extended my arm out through the opening. The bellhop set the little metal case of aspirins in the palm of my hand. I closed my hand around the little box, pulled my arm into the room and yelled "thank you" through the crack in the door and closed it. I peered through the peephole to see what he looked like. He looked like a deer in headlights, standing there momentarily. He shook his head as to say oh well and left. I felt sorry for him, I would catch up with him later and give him a tip, but right now I needed the aspirins. I took three of them. My mouth was dry but I managed to conjure up enough saliva to pull them down.

I still felt like shit, both physically from the hangover and mentally for forgetting our anniversary, I didn't even bother to shower. I threw on the same clothes I had on the day earlier. I found my wig tucked inside my crumpled T-shirt. I brushed my teeth and went to leave. I realized when I got to the door that I didn't have my wallet. I struggled for a moment trying to remember where it was and it dawned on me that I had it last on the balcony. As I headed across the room I felt even worse as I could see my open wallet lying on the cement, it was raining. Even though the picture was housed in a plastic sheath it still got damp. I took it out and examined it. The corners were wilted a bit but the picture was okay. I laid it on the coffee table along with a couple of other pieces of paper and left for the athletic compound. I rode the elevator downstairs to the lobby where I spotted the bellhop near the desk.

"Here's a tip for bringing the aspirins to my room this morning," I said handing him some cash.

"Thank you sir."

I went outside and had the Valet hail me a taxi. I had the driver drop me off as close as he could to the entrance, which wasn't really that close. Security reasons I guess. I made my way through the various checkpoints and out to the track. I could see Laura on the other side going full out. Harry was in front of me with a stopwatch.

"Dude," I said to Harry. "She's radical."

"Pardon me," he replied.

Laura was now rounding the bend coming towards the finish line.

"Hang ten baby, hang ten," I yelled to her as I stood in surfer style on my invisible surfboard, my arms pumping downwards as if I was spinning the tires of a wheelchair.

"Harry, this is the guy I was telling you about."

"Ryan Walkerton's the name, but my friends just call me The Walker."

"It's nice to meet you."

"You too dude," I said as I put my hand out to shake his. As he put his out I pulled mine back and raised it to the side of my head. "Gotta be quicker than that dude."

"Your right Laura," he said. "He is nuts."

"So how about it, you gonna slip some skin into The Walker's threads?"

"I'm considering it. Harry's my coach: he's a little reluctant."

"No worries man, the greenback's enough to cover the heartache."

"It's not the stripping of the medal I'm concerned about, it's the money," Harry said.

"Don't sweat about the clams man, they're genuine and the pearls are in the reef."

"What the hell are you talking about? Clams, reef?" he asked.

"For you mainlanders it means don't worry about the money. It's real, and it's in the bank."

"Before I decide, what's your game plan?" he questioned.

"No plan, Laura wears one of my shirts with a logo on it under her T-shirt that has a Velcro front. When she approaches the finish line, she pulls open her shirt exposing my logo, sitting high in the chair so the world sees my logo. That's it. Once all the controversy begins her face will be plastered in every newspaper around the world, she'll be requested for every talk show and news interview for days, and of course she'll be wearing my designs when she appears on them."

"And for that I get one million dollars," Laura piped up.

"Five million if you win the race. A little incentive for you."

"I know I can win," she said.

"It's up to you, you're on the board in the pipe, you decide whether the Big Kahuna is going to wipe you out or if you're hanging ten all the way to the shore," I said.

"Will you please speak English," Harry demanded.

"I said, she's got to decide if her morals are going to stop her from doing it or whether she's going to ride easy street all the way the bank."

"I'm in," she said.

"Cool. I'll catch you on the flip side of Monday. We'll have a few days to organize."

"But what about the money?" Harry asked.

"I'll have all the contracts for you to take to a lawyer. I'll present you with one of those big cardboard cheques after the race, on national television. I'll give you the real one the day before the race. I'll bring two cardboard ones, one for a million dollars, and in case you win, another one for four million. Of course you only get a million up front," I said.

"Okay, I'll see you on Tuesday," she said.

"Later, dude," I turned and walked away.

"How can I reach you?" Laura yelled.

"I'm out of town until Monday," I said as I flashed her the peace sign and left.

When I got to the main gate I grabbed the taxi at the head of the line and got in. I had the driver take me right to the airport. I was homesick and I just wanted to get back to Keycoast. I arrived at the airport and went straight to the ticket counter. I had not purchased a flight yet. I was planning to stay in Norway until the job was complete, but my loneliness was getting the best of me. I needed to be with people I knew. I had to wait seven hours before the next flight. I went to the airport

restaurant to get something to eat. I still had on my silly surfer
stuff that drew a lot of attention, especially from the guards. I
sat down to have lunch and called Kevin on my cell phone. He
was in Fiji picking up supplies. I told him that I wanted him to
pick me up at the Miami airport and to bring Maria and Manuel
with him. It had been a while since they had been back to
Florida and I wanted to have a party. I ate my lunch and then
headed for the gate. The lines would be long and I wanted to get
clear for boarding early to avoid any complications.

As I had expected, there was a long line up at security. The
security guards were thorough and it took over an hour for me
to reach the gate. I had to empty my pockets, which for me was
real easy. I didn't even have a carry-on bag. I put my wallet in
the little tray that sat on the conveyor belt along with my cell
phone. I could see there were two different line-ups past the
metal detector. The guards were pulling people aside that set it
off and were making them go to the right and through another
checkpoint. I walked through the security structure, not hearing
an alarm I preceded to the left. A security guard put her arm out
and stopped me. I must have aroused suspicion with my clothes
and the fact that I didn't have any checked or carry-on luggage.
I was pulled aside by two armed guards and taken to an area in
the middle of the floor. I had to remove my shoes and stand on
the two blue footprints located on the floor. They whisked my
shoes away and put them on the conveyor. I thought that was
funny since they were cheap foam flip-flops. One guard scanned
me with a wand as the other stood watch. Again I didn't beep.
I was then frisked and sent on my way to get my belongings that
had now made their journey through the X-ray machine. I put
my flip-flops on, grabbed my belongings and left the area. I
found a seat in the waiting area near the boarding door and sat
down. I watched the airplanes coming and going for a couple of
hours. I was a bit nervous about the flight. It wasn't the fear of
flying itself, I was concerned about all the hype about the
terrorists. It's funny how people get stereotyped, there were
only a couple of people with turbans on, but everyone kept
staring at them. There was another man travelling alone who
had black hair and olive skin. He sat down beside a lady and her
two toddlers. She quickly gathered them up and moved to

another seat two rows over. People can be so ignorant.

I noticed that the flight crew had made their way to the boarding counter. They showed their credentials and the ticket lady opened the door that led to the gangplank. I could now see the airplane that we were going to take. I didn't take notice of its arrival to the gate, but it was there now. My stomach was becoming increasingly unsteady as the take off time neared. I don't recall being this nervous when I came to Norway. They say that flying is safer than driving but that didn't ease my discomfort. What did ease my mind was that the captain was outside the airplane on the tarmac looking it over, examining it, walking around and under it, giving it the once over. He looked like a customer at a car dealership going over his dream car. He even raised his arm and used his sleeve to wipe off an apparent smudge. Kind of like you do when you bring that new car home as it sits in your driveway for the first time. Then he put my mind totally at ease. He kicked the tires. I sat back in my chair and relaxed.

It wasn't long until I heard the boarding call over the public address system. I was travelling coach. I had to wait until all the first class and preferred passengers loaded. I didn't want to draw attention to myself by buying an expensive seat. The flight was bumpy with a lot of turbulence. When it did arrive in Miami, security was even tighter. I had no problem though, because I had no luggage. I got through customs without a hitch. I ducked into the washroom and removed the wig. I stuck it in the barf bag I took from the pocket of the seat in front of me on the airplane. I had to make sure that Kevin didn't see me in my get up.

I rode the elevator up two flights to ground level and spotted my limo as I went through the door. Kevin pulled up as he spotted me. I climbed in the back. Maria was there, but Manuel wasn't. She said he didn't want to make the trip. She had her small nephew Patrick with her who was around three or four years old. He had come to live at the resort in Fiji shortly after I was there with Johnny and Ursula. Her sister was a single mom and had a tough time raising him on her own and asked Maria to watch him while she went back to school. I gave her permission as long as she kept up her duties at home. It wasn't a problem. He was a joy to have around. Whenever I had time at the resort I played with him. We were quite close. He had a slight hearing problem that delayed his speech and he wasn't able to enunciate a lot of words clearly. He called me pop as I wasn't often without a can of Coke. Whenever he saw me he'd point and say pop.

I was tired so it was a fairly quiet ride to Keycoast. The gates opened as we pulled up to them. Kevin rolled his window down and said hi to Stan, he never saw the three of us in the back. Kevin pulled up to the house and we all got out. This was Patrick's first time at Keycoast. It was dark but I'm sure in the morning he'd explore its beauty. Kevin led Maria into the house and got her settled. She and Patrick would be staying with me and Kevin had the apartment downstairs for the night. He dropped his wife off with family the night before he picked us up. She's coming over tomorrow afternoon. I was feeling restless so I took a walk down to the guardhouse. Whenever I arrived back from somewhere I liked to check in to see if anyone had come to the gates looking for me. This time no one had.

When I got back to the house Maria was putting Patrick down for the night. It had been a long trip for him too. I excused myself and went up to the lodge to see Jimmy, he was all smiles when I walked through the door. He stood up so fast that he tipped all the cards off the table; they were playing bingo. He ran over to me and just about flattened me like a pancake against the wall to give me a great big hug. I really should spend more time with him I thought. I took him for a walk around the grounds. We were gone for about an hour since it took that long to smoke most of my cigar. I always had a good supply of Cubans on board.

I took Jimmy back and helped him get ready for bed. This was always a chore as he liked to try to be independent and was reluctant to have anyone touch him. I tucked him in bed and read him a story. When I was finished I kissed him good night and went back to the house.

Maria was sipping a hot chocolate and there was some left so I poured myself one too. I flicked on the switch to the gas fireplace as I entered the room and put my hot chocolate down on the table. As I knelt on the bearskin rug in front of the fireplace, Maria stood up from the chair she was sitting in and joined me. The flames in the fireplace seemed to dance as they flickered between the fake logs. We sat and stared at the fire. Even though we had known each other for a while, we were both too tired from the airplane ride to engage in a deep conversation. I repositioned myself and leaned back against the sofa and stretched my legs out straight. Maria, who was yawning profusely stretched out and laid on the rug, her head next to my lap. It wasn't long before her breathing became rhythmic and I knew she was asleep. I sat there staring at the fire, now and then glancing at her as she slept. It wasn't long before I nodded off. I awoke a couple of hours later as a cramp had developed in my back from the pressure of the couch against my spine and my bum had gone numb from my position. I felt movement on my lap and looked down, Maria had squirmed her way up and now had her head on my legs. I struggled to get comfortable without disturbing her. She looked so peaceful. I put my arm over her back as she lay there and I fell asleep once more.

The warmth of the fire and the rays of the sun, which were now engulfing the room, woke me. Maria still had her head in my lap. I picked up my mug of hot chocolate, which had stayed lukewarm from the radiant heat of the fireplace, and I drank it.

Maria woke up as I leaned forward to put the mug on the table.

"Good morning," I said as she looked up at me.

She raised her head and brushed her hair out of her eyes, she had beautiful brown eyes.

She sat up abruptly as Kevin came into the room with Patrick.

"You two looked so comfortable I figured I'd get him up," he said.

"I'm sorry," she said as she called Patrick who came running to her.

"It's okay, Patrick likes his Uncle Kevin, don't you Patrick?"

Patrick nodded. With very little to do on the island we all became very close.

"What's the plan boss, what are we doing for the next little while?" Kevin asked.

"Nothing much, I'm just going to hang out here for a couple of days with Jimmy and then it's back to work."

"Where am I flying you next?"

"Nowhere for a while, I'm going to take a commercial flight to the mid-west. You can take the jet whenever your wife and Maria want to get back to Fiji, until then relax. Don't forget the party tonight."

"What would you like to eat Patrick?" Maria asked him as she walked him to the table. "What about you Jack, are you hungry?"

"I'm okay, I'm going to have a shower and go up to the lodge to have breakfast with Jimmy."

I went to my room and had my shower. I got dressed and strolled up to the lodge. The students, who were actually inmates, were already sitting around the tables. They sat with the group they lived with. There were six in each cabin. There was one staff member per cabin twenty-four hours per day. The lodge was plenty big enough to house them all at meal times. It had plenty of classrooms and a large gym area. It was more like a school than a prison. That's why when I bought it I had them use the word student instead of inmate.

The facility was not set up for vocational training. Sure they could learn life skills and earn some educational credits, but there was nothing available for them to learn the skills they would need to get a job in the real world if they were ever released. Keycoast just didn't have the room that was needed for that. I had thought of moving the facility to South Dakota, and that was my reason for going there. My roots were there and now that I had the money I wanted to give something back. I had a good childhood there and I had the opportunity to purchase two thousand acres overlooking Mt. Rushmore. The students would learn to farm and tend to animals. There would also be a small machine shop, automobile garage and a factory setting. The boys could learn a necessary skilled trade in a regimented setting to prepare them for the real world. I want to catch them before they wind up in a real prison setting. Most of them had either a low IQ or a psychological disorder that could be controlled with the proper medication, training and discipline and the combination would prepare them for a job.

The ranch wouldn't just be for those developmentally delayed boys that got in trouble. Anyone with a learning disorder could go. The government would pay for those who did break the law, the others could attend for free.

I wasn't thinking about staffing it at the time, I knew there would be enough cops that would have their time in but were too young to retire that would jump at the opportunity. Because my dad was on the force I knew a lot of cops from that area. For now I just wanted to secure the land.

Jimmy was halfway through his breakfast when I got there. They were having flapjacks. They were Jimmy's' favourite. I'm not sure if it was because he actually liked them or because he always called them fat-jacks. Using sign language when he referred to them he would make the letter J. and stick out his stomach indicating fat-jack. I sat down between Jimmy and his friend Billy. His counsellor Steven came over with a stack of pancakes. Jimmy stood up and signed Jack, fat Jack. Billy found it quite amusing, milk dribbling from his mouth as he laughed. I dug into my breakfast and when I was done I took Jimmy back to his cabin to wash up. His hands were sticky from the syrup.

I took Jimmy and Billy down to the pond at the end of the grounds. It was a freshwater pond stocked with bass and catfish. The pond was more for recreational fishing rather than for food, although once a month, usually the last Friday of the month, they would bring the students and let them keep one fish each. The boys would help clean them and the cook would prepare them for supper. We spent about three hours there. I sat and watched them fish. I hardly understood a word they said since they mostly spoke gibberish, but they seemed to understand each other. It was funny watching them pet and talk to the worms before they put them on the hook. Jimmy would wave goodbye as he lowered it into the water. They caught about eight fish in total. We released them all. I took the boys back to the lodge, let Steven know they were there and then I left. I wanted to get back to the house to see how Maria and Patrick were making out. This was sort of a holiday for them, but I wanted them to keep a low profile. If I was to fail at my plan and get caught, I wanted to make sure they didn't get implicated as accomplices. Patrick was obviously too young but I didn't want Maria to be involved. Like all the people I brought into the picture, she knew nothing about the murders.

I spent the afternoon playing with Patrick. Maria kept busy preparing food for the party that night. I invited Adam, Mark and their wives over. It was a long drive from Largo. It was going to be like a high school reunion.

I looked into the camera as the lights on the prison camera turned on. Adam sure had read the book, he knew exactly when to go live and turn the camera on me in the prison. At first I had reservations about hiring Adam and Mark for the live execution. I thought because we were such close friends their emotions might get the best of them. I didn't mind giving them first crack at history in the making, but doing it live was new for them and I was unsure if they were capable, but now I realize I made the right decision.

Back in high school the AV club consisted of Mark, Adam, Kevin, Amanda, Stephanie, Debbie, Teri and myself. Mark and Stephanie dated in high school and were the first to marry. Kevin and Amanda married just after that, followed by Adam and Debbie a year later. Teri and I were good friends but had no real romantic intentions. We used each other as stand in dates in case neither of us had one. She moved somewhere in South Florida around the same time Jimmy was sent to Keycoast.

My guests soon arrived and Maria put Patrick down for the night. I had hired the band that I took to my resort. We danced and talked all night. I offered them all a room for the night but they all declined. Even Kevin and Amanda didn't stay in the apartment.

I started to clean up while Maria checked on Patrick. I made a couple of hot chocolates and went into the living room. I turned on the fireplace and the television and sat back and relaxed. Maria came into the room. She was ready for bed, dressed in her bathrobe. She sat down on the couch beside me. I couldn't help but notice how pretty she was. She had developed a nice tan while on the island that highlighted her brown eyes. With her long flowing brown hair she looked a little Mexican. She wasn't though, you would think with a name like Maria and a father named Manuel they would be directly from Mexico, but they weren't. Apparently Manuel's father had owned a farm and often hired immigrants from Mexico. There was a large fire one day in the barn and Manuels father became trapped under some bales of hay that had collapsed. One of the farm hands pulled him out and saved his life. The worker's name was Manuel. Maria was named after her grandmother.

We sat and watched TV for a while, sitting very close to each other. Even though I had the fireplace on it was still a bit cool. Maria snuggled a bit closer. I reached behind her and grabbed a knitted afghan and laid it over her. I let my arm drape over her shoulder when I did, she put her hand in mine. That lasted about half an hour until we both fell asleep.

I woke up about an hour later and watched her sleep. I knew I had to leave in the morning for South Dakota and then off to Norway. I wouldn't be coming back to Keycoast for almost three weeks, not until the day of the race. Even then I would only be here a couple of weeks before I hunted down victim number four. I wasn't sure who it would be. I would return to Fiji again after I completed that murder.

I eased my arm from her grip and slid sideways, I removed her head from my shoulder. She moved a bit, but soon got comfortable on the couch. I went into my bedroom and stripped down. I threw on my robe and returned to the living room and shut off the fireplace. Maria was tossing and turning on the couch. I bent down and whisked her up in my arms. I carried her upstairs. Patrick was asleep in her room. I continued down the hall and laid her on my bed, as I did she woke up. Without a word being uttered she pulled me towards her and we kissed passionately. We made love for an hour and then fell asleep. As much as I knew it would come to this, I was apprehensive... not about making love to her but about clouding my mind with emotions. I had tried to put my life on hold until my plans were complete. Even Adam and Mark who spent a lot of time with me had noticed my withdrawn emotions.

I was now at the point where I just wanted to get the job done. There would be plenty of time for my life afterwards, or so I thought. Maria and I tried to connect before, but with Patrick around it was hard, and in the past year I only made it home a couple of times and I usually had company; whether it was Johnny and Ursula or the gang from the AV club. I could tell Maria was disturbed when I brought company, she was more reclusive when they were there.

I got up the morning and took a shower before she woke. I dried myself off, put the towel on a hook behind the bathroom door and lay in bed beside her.

"When are you coming back to the island?" she asked as she opened her eyes and looked at me.

"I'm not sure, I've still got a lot of work to do. It won't be long and I'll be back for good."

She rolled over and kissed me. We made love again. This time it was rushed as Patrick was now awake and had wandered down to the living room and was watching TV and calling her. Maria got up and went to see what he wanted. I got dressed and said my goodbyes as the taxi I called had arrived. I picked up my suitcase from the floor. It had Ryan's disguise in it. The taxi driver took me to the airport. I went to the boarding gate and took a flight to South Dakota. When I arrived in South Dakota I passed through the gate and looked for the person holding a placard with the name Jack Stevenson on it. The real estate company had arranged for a driver to pick me up.

I arrived at their office and entered into the meeting. Their lawyers were there with all the paperwork. It was a standard real-estate document for the purchase. I signed them and left. I had the limo driver take me over to the architect's office. The final plans for the youth farm would all have to be approved by City Hall. All I had to do was put a deposit in the developers' hand and the process would start. I left him in charge of the project. It was premature but he had invited a news crew there for a quick interview and unveiling of the details for the ranch. I gave them a small tidbit of information and made an appointment for a week from Thursday for them to have a full interview at the site. That day we would erect the sign for the future ranch. It would also be the day after Laura would be racing for the gold. I left his office and walked down the street to a restaurant. I ordered lunch and paid for it in advance. I left the change on the table as a tip. I went into the washroom and transformed into Ryan Walkerton 'surfer dude' and left before the meal arrived.

I hailed down a cab and took it back to the airport, boarded the airplane and flew to Oslo. I had reserved the same room I had before. When I checked in I picked up the parcel that was mailed to me from the designer. I laid the clothes out on the bed and picked out the outfit that would best display the logo on her chest. It was quite late with the time change and all, so I ran a nice hot bath and got undressed. I took the one million dollar certified cheque out of my wallet and put it in my fanny pack. The Walker had to look like a total geek. I sat in the tub for about an hour before I got out and went to bed.

CHAPTER 17

The first thing I did when I got up in the morning was to call Laura and arrange a meeting. I had to make sure she was still going to wear the shirt. The race was only a few days away. I picked up the fanny pack, snapped it on and left. It was about a mile to the athlete village. I was feeling spry so I made the journey on foot. I got halfway there when it started to rain. I ripped a poster off a wall and held it over my head, I wasn't sure how my wig would hold up in the rain. I went to the bathroom once I checked through security. I knew something was up, because the security people were laughing behind my back as I walked through the gate. I looked in the mirror and laughed myself. I had been wearing a little eyeliner and mascara and it had run down my face. It reminded me of the night with Ursula. I washed my face, took out my makeup and redid it. I only used a little bit to disguise myself. Even though Laura had only seen me once as Jack, I couldn't take any chances. I didn't feel the wig was enough to hide my appearance. I took off my shirt and held it under the electronic hand dryer.

She was alone this time, although I'm sure Harry was somewhere in the shadows.

"Hey dude," I said as I approached her from behind.

She turned her chair and faced me. "I like the purple shirt much better than the red you had on the other day," she said.

"Kind of gnarly, don't you think?"

"Whatever that means," she replied.

"So why don't we get out of this rain, before I melt," I said.

"But I've only done half of my training schedule," she replied.

"Hey Babe, if you're not good enough to win it by now you never will be, there's less than a week to the race."

"You're probably right, I'll call Harry to get me out of here."

"No need for that, I can help."

I grabbed the back of her wheelchair and wheeled her inside

the stadium. I grabbed two towels and threw one at her. We both dried ourselves off a bit.

"What the hell's going on?" Harry yelled as he came rushing over. "We've got training to do."

"Hey dude, have you been out there? It's raining," I said.

"It could also rain the day the race, that doesn't mean we stop."

"You're right," Laura said and started to wheel herself towards the door.

I reached down into the pouch I had around my waist and grabbed the cheque. "Maybe this will change your mind," I said as I held it up.

Harry reached for it. I pulled it back from his grasp. "Look, don't touch," I said. I held the cheque at either end and held it out for him to see. "Did I spell Melrose right?"

Laura wheeled her chair backwards towards us. I lowered the cheque to her level.

"There you go," I said. "One million dollars and it's certified, it's like money in the bank."

Harry reached for it again. I pulled my arm back. "We haven't got a deal yet. If you're in we have papers to sign and details to work out." I said.

"We're in," Laura stated. "We're in."

"Okay, I'm in room 52 at the Norse, be there at one so we can go over the contract."

"We'll be there," Harry said.

I put the cheque back in my pouch and left. It was still pouring out. I left the compound and removed my wig. I pulled my shirttails out of my pants and wiped off my face, you could hardly notice the makeup on my multicolor flowered shirt. I took a bus and got off a block away from my hotel. Harry was just lifting Laura into her chair as I approached. I damn near went up to them and talked, but I suddenly realized I didn't have the wig or the makeup on. I quickly threw on the wig and ducked inside unnoticed. I made it upstairs and into my suite before they made their way up the elevator. I feverishly slapped on some makeup and answered the door as they knocked.

"Welcome to my pad," I said.

I stepped out of the way so Laura could wheel her way into

the room.

"Can I get you anything to drink?"

"No were fine," Harry said. Answering for both of them.

I sat down in a wing chair next to Laura.

"So, we're all set, you're willing to do this?" I asked.

"I don't see a problem," Laura answered.

"You realize the consequences? They will strip you of your medal."

"I know, but with the one million dollars now, and a guaranteed four million royalty on the clothes when I win, I think I'll be set for the rest of my life."

"Not to mention the talk-show circuit, this will be big news," Harry added.

I got up and went over to the coffee table, opened the latch on my briefcase that was sitting there and took out the contracts, I handed them both a copy. "Okay all I need is a signature and we're set to go."

"Not so fast," Harry piped up. "We stand to lose a lot here, we need to have our lawyer take a look at them."

I had expected that, there was nothing the lawyer would find that should convince him otherwise. Although the business was a scam, the papers were legit. "That's fine, you still have a couple of days left. As long as I have them back the day before the race."

"Actually, you'll have them back within the hour. I took the liberty of inviting my lawyer up here. He should be here any minute," Harry said.

I was beginning not to like this guy. I know he didn't trust anyone, I got that impression from my first meeting with him when we filmed the documentary. "Oh," I said.

"Not that we don't trust you, but like I said we've got a lot to lose, Laura's future in racing will be over," Harry said.

I smirked inside. "You've got that right," I said. "She'll be dead in the water. I'll go grab the outfits." I stood up and made my way into the bedroom. I grabbed the three outfits from on top of the bed and carried them out to the main room. "Take your pick," I said as I laid them out for my guests to see.

Laura wheeled herself closer and went right for the pink one. "I like this one," she said as she held it up.

It was a simple outfit, plain pink spandex shorts and a small pink T-shirt with the word Hornet written on the front in baby blue letters.

"You can go into the bedroom and try them on if you wish," I told her.

She looked at the tags and said they'd fit.

There was a knock at the door, I got up and opened it.

"My Casa is your Casa," I said as I extended my arm back into the room.

A portly gentleman with a beard and glasses entered.

"Gregory?" Harry said as he rose to shake is hand. "Ryan Walkerton, Gregory Thompson the Third," Harry said as he pointed to both of us.

Gregory stuck out his hand for me to shake, I put both my arms out palms up. "Hang ten baby," I said.

He just looked at me confused.

"Give me some skin," I said as I held my hands there, he eventually slapped them.

"I told you he was off the wall," Harry said to Gregory.

Gregory walked over, picked up a contract and sat down in the recliner without saying a word. We all just sat there and watched him as he leafed through the papers.

"Looks good to me," he finally said. "Now where's the cheque?"

I reached down and undid the zipper of my fanny pack, I took it out and handed it to him. He held it up to the light, examining one side and then the other. He opened up his brown leather briefcase and put it inside.

I wasn't going to give it to him until the night before the race, but it looked like I had no choice.

"It's postdated until the day the race," I mentioned.

"I see that," Gregory replied.

"Is that a problem?" Laura asked.

"Oh no," Gregory stated. "It's certified. Sign the papers and I'm out of here," he said as he handed the contracts to Laura.

"Your all business, dude," I said.

"Time is money," he stated as he stood up.

Laura signed the two copies. He plucked one from her hand and headed towards the door. "Come by my office after the race," he said to Harry. "We'll deposit it and I'll take my fee."

He then left.

"Wow, man," I said. "I'd hate to face him in court."

"So what actually do I have to do?" Laura asked.

"All you have to do is wear the outfit and race. Once you're near the finish line, sit tall in your chair and show off my logo to the cameras."

"That's it?" she asked.

"You have to win if you want the royalties, come in second and all you get is the million dollars."

"Second isn't good enough," Harry added. "She'll win it, she's the best."

I grabbed the door and held it open. "I'll catch up with you somewhere after the race."

"Not at the finish line?" she questioned.

"I'll be tied up with interviews once you reveal the logo. I'll try, but I can't promise."

They both left and I closed the door behind them. I had a lot of work to do before the race. I spent the night reviewing my plans to make sure everything was in place. The race was three days away. I still had to pick up the supplies I ordered.

The next day I woke up early. I went to the local shopping mall and bought some gray coveralls, all the maintenance workers in the village wore them. I only needed them for a day. I ordered brunch once I got back to the motel. When it arrived I yelled from behind the door for the bellhop to leave it there, I didn't want him to see that I wasn't dressed as Ryan. I cracked open the door a bit to make sure the coast was clear and wheeled the white linen draped table into the room. I was feeling good about this murder I thought to myself as I ate the eggs Benedict and French toast. This one was for my dad, he deserved it. After all, that bitch put both my parents through hell. This one was a little trickier than the others, it was very complex, I had to make sure the mechanics of it were going to work. I was going to be back in the U.S. when the race began, and I hoped everything would go right.

I put on a brown curly wig once I was done breakfast and complemented it with a brown mustache and goatee. I grabbed the new ID tag from the briefcase and pinned it on my lapel. I snuck out of the hotel, taking the stairs to the underground parking garage. I was tired of taxi rides, but I didn't want to have to bother to rent a vehicle. I waited near the entrance door of the garage until I heard the rumble of the door as a car made its way down the ramp. I ducked under the door and hailed down a cab about a block away from the hotel. The cab took me to the machine shop where I had ordered the supplies I needed. I asked him to wait. After I had my supplies I had him take me to the maintenance area of the compound.

I had no problem getting past security at the maintenance compound. The badge I made looked authentic enough.

"Who are you?" the foreman asked.

"Scott Tufford," I said.

He pulled out a clipboard and scanned the pages attached to it.

"I don't have you on my list. Who sent you?" he asked.

"Norm."

"Norm Olstrom?"

"Yeah, he's my uncle, he said he wanted this banner hung."

"I don't know anything about it."

"Well, I can leave it here and tell him you didn't want me to put up."

"Oh no," he said as he looked at my name badge.

"Tufford, and Norm is your uncle?"

"My mom's brother, what do you want me to do with this stuff?" I asked. I knew he wouldn't give me a hard time. Norm was in charge of the whole maintenance department. This guy was about twenty rungs down the corporate ladder.

"If you know what to do then go ahead," he said.

"Great, thanks."

"What are you putting up?" he asked again.

"Just a banner, it's my grandpa's birthday. Uncle Norm thought he would like it. I'll need a couple of poles."

"Go ahead then, I'll get the poles."

I took the stuff over to the finish line and started to set up. I hadn't thought to bring any tools with me, so I just stood there for a minute surveying the area.

"Everything okay?" The foreman asked.

"I think so, by the way, what is your name?" I asked him.

"Olaf."

"Thanks Olaf, where can I get some tools?"

"Fred," he yelled to another gentleman who was standing with a coffee in his hand. "Come and give this guy a hand."

Fred took his last sip of coffee and threw the cup away, grabbed his toolbox and came over to us.

"Fred, give this guy a hand, something the boss wants done."

"Hi, I'm Fred," he said to me.

I glanced at my name badge, "I'm Scott." I stuck my hand out and shook his.

"So what are we doing?" asked Fred.

"I just have to hang this banner behind the one that's already there, and attach a mechanical pulley system and a light curtain and were done," I said.

"Sounds easy enough. What do you want me to do?" he asked.

"We've got to string this wire along the top of the banner through the grommets. Tape the bottom wire to the banner and tie in the light curtain to the poles. The top wire will stay stationary."

"Okay let's get it done," he said. Fred put the 1/4-inch steel cable through the top holes. I started duct taping the piano wire to the bottom of the banner. I measured the distance between the two poles that were already supporting the Olympic banner that faced the crowd at the finish line. Mine would be unfurled on the athletes' side as they made their way to the line. I never did let Olaf or Fred see the side the athletes would see.

"Will we be able to use the poles that are already here?" Fred asked.

"Yes and Olaf is bringing two poles for the light curtain," I told him.

"Sounds good," he replied.

"If the magnets are balanced, both sides should release together, gravity will do the rest. Grab a stopper, a bracket and a magnet, you're going to that pole," I said as I pointed to the one on the left.

We carried our supplies, to our respective poles. We both stood on a stepladder that we had placed against each pole.

"These are heavy magnets," Fred stated.

"I need them for the weight rather than their magnetic strength," I told him.

The stoppers were cast metal, half moons, one side of each had a hole, while the opposite side was female threaded to accept the shaft of the bolt. I put both sides around the pole, slid the bolt through the solid circle, lined them up with the female side and tightened them by hand. I took an Allen key and gave them a couple of turns, tight enough that they wouldn't slide to the bottom. They were only there for now so we had something to rest the magnets on. We each attached the magnets to the poles on top of the stoppers. There was about an eighth of an inch gap all the way around the pole. This would allow the magnets to slide down once the electricity was cut off to them. They were electromagnets, a wire would be attached to the leads, once the light curtain was broken so would the energy source. The magnets would then free-fall down to the stoppers. The bottom of the banner was attached to the magnets and as they fall the banner will be unfurled. We attached the leads for the magnets and ran the wires back to the light curtains ten feet from the poles that held the Olympics sign. We pushed the two poles Olaf brought into the ground so that we could attach the light curtains to them. Once we plugged them into the power supply that was already there we were able to line them up so they would work. For those of you that don't know what light curtains are or how they work, let me explain. They are two rectangular boxes about two inches square and five feet long. They have sensors on both sides that shoot an invisible light beam across to the other side. Once something passes through the two curtains, the signal is broken and the power supply they are feeding is cut, in this case the power to the magnets. While energized the magnets would hug the pole. When the power is cut, the magnets will lose their power and act like a weight dropping down and pulling the banner open until they hit the stoppers.

"Is that it?" Fred asked.

"That's all the help I need," I said.

Fred picked up his tools and left. All I had to do was to lower the stoppers to the point that the magnets would stop, unveiling the full banner. The banner was three feet high, so I moved the stoppers down to three feet from the top and tightened them as good as I could.

Olaf made his way over to me. "All set to go Scott?" he asked.

"I just have to test it out," I said.

"I'll give you a hand."

"It's better if you don't. Uncle Norm wants it to be a surprise and the mood he's in nowadays trying to get all the last minute touches down, he might get pissed. Have you ever seen him pissed?" I asked.

"No, but I know he fired a couple of guys yesterday."

"That's what I mean."

"Okay, let me know if you need anything."

"I sure will, I'll test it at lunch when everybody's gone. I don't want to put anybody in jeopardy."

"I'll see you after lunch then," he said and left.

"Thanks, can you bring me a large coffee, extra sugar?" I yelled at him as he walked away.

I went back to the light curtain and installed a push button to the back of one of the curtains. I crossed over the track and wired in a green light on the top of the banner pole, if for some reason the curtain is broken before a competitor crosses the finish line, the green light will go off and indicate that it needs to be reset by hitting the button. It was all set to test. Everyone had gone for lunch and I was the only one around. The green light was lit meaning everything was ready. I stood about a foot back from the invisible beam. I took a deep breath, crossed my fingers and walked forward, as I stepped into the curtain the green light went out, I simultaneously heard the click of the power de-energizing. I focused my sights on the banner as the magnets dropped pulling the bottom of the banner with it. The magnets were quite heavy and they made a thud as they reach the stoppers. It worked like a charm. I stepped back around to the grass that edged the track and reset the magnets with the button. I heard the click as the power put life back into them, they hugged the pole once again with force. I looked at the green light, it was on. I walked back through the curtain, the magnets pulled free from their captor. I rolled the banner up again, this time a little looser to allow for a better and easier time on its descent. I shoved a nail through each pole in the hole that Fred and I had pre drilled below the magnets. This would hold up the banner in place until I reset the magnets once more. Again the magnets clanged as they mated with poles. I pulled out a sticker from my pocket. It was bright red and waterproof. It read, "did you make sure to take the nails out after resetting the curtain?"

I had no way of controlling this. I was going to have to rely on someone else resetting it right before the race, and I didn't know whom would be assigned. I was going to be back at Keycoast when Laura crossed the finish line, hopefully first. My flight was leaving in an hour and I had to be on it, or should I say Ryan the Walker had to be on it.

I had invited the Howards down to Keycoast for the day. It was Jimmy's birthday and the Howards would be excellent alibis again for when I killed Laura.

Olaf had returned from lunch with the other guys, he had my large coffee in his hand.

"Scott, are you all done?"

"Yes I am, here's how works. The magnets are electro-magnetic and," I started.

"I know, once the light curtain is broken they drop towards the ground, landing on the stoppers, unfurling the banner. Fred explained it to me at lunch."

"I've set the curtains two feet off the ground, that way an animal won't trip it if they run by before the race. The green light over there indicates that it is all set to go. My Uncle Norm came by while you were at a lunch and reminded me to have a TV camera facing the finish line, one inside and one outside to capture both the front and back of the winner. As the winner approaches and breaks the curtain the banner will fall, the TV cameras will capture the moment and Uncle Norm is happy."

I reached around and broke the light curtain releasing the magnets, the nails held them up.

"Here's the button to reset it. The only thing that needs to be done after resetting it for the final time is to remember to pull the nails out so it works properly. My Uncle suggested you put one of your best guys here for the whole race to make sure it's reset in time. He doesn't want the curtain to get broken early, They also have to make sure the nails are removed just as the winner approaches. He suggested not doing it until the leaders are approaching the crest of the last hill. He said something about a bonus in it for you if all goes well."

"I'll do the job personally," he said.

"Great I just have a couple of adjustments to make and I'm out of here," I said.

"There's your uncle now," Olaf stated.

"Good, I'll tell him that everything is set, I'll be right back."

I grabbed the coffee and headed over to Norm, I knew quite a bit about him, his profile was on the official Web site of the Oslo Olympics. I've never met him personally but I had Olaf convinced that he was my uncle. Norm was a creature of habit according to the website. He was very superstitious and once he had a routine he stuck to it in fear of jinxing something. I had observed him a couple of times making his rounds throughout the complex. He came by the same place at the same time every day, checking his watch constantly. I also knew he liked his coffee with extra sugar. I pulled off my name badge and shoved it in my pocket. I exchanged it with another one I had made. One designed for the media. I stuck it on as I walked towards him.

"Mr. Olstrom," I said as I approached him and put out my hand for him to shake. "Jerry Burnett, Burnett films," I introduced myself to him. "I'm not sure whether you received the e-mail or not, but I've got everything set for the finish line. The network should have given you the information. They're having two live camera angles. I'm doing a documentary on Ms. Melrose, A rags to riches story. I just hope she wins. The cameras are controlled by a light curtain and will activate when tripped. The cameras are unmanned. I was told you don't like a lot of people near the finish line," I had also read that on the web site. He didn't like a lot of clutter around and considered people milling about as clutter.

"You've done your homework boy," he said.

"Thank you sir, I also have a coffee for you sir, extra sugar."

"You have done your homework, thank you," he said as he took it.

"Don't thank me sir, Olaf told me to give it to you."

Norm turned in Olaf's direction and raised the cup of coffee in the air. He then gave Olaf the thumbs up signal to thank him.

"Okay sir," I said. "You have a good day," I turned and walked away. Norm looked at his watch and sped off. I had put him four minutes behind schedule and he had to catch up. I knew that Norm and Olaf would never cross paths before the race. Norm had media interviews, a dignitary dinner tonight and would be in the VIP box for the race. I had done my homework very well. I exchanged name badges again as I walked towards Olaf.

"Well Olaf," I said. "I told him that you had everything set for the banner and he was quite pleased. I told him you would personally make sure it was all set for the race."

"There will be security here all night and I will be here myself to make sure things go right for the race," he said.

"Don't forget about the nails, my uncle's happiness is riding on it. And when my Uncle Norm is happy with a worker, he rewards them."

"I won't forget, I've got to run, I'll see you in the morning," he said.

"I wont be here, I'm sitting with my grandfather tomorrow, I'll be leaving soon, I just have to make sure the stoppers are set."

"Okay goodbye," he said as he shook my hand.

I made my way back to the banner as he left and made my final adjustments. All I had to do now was pray everything went okay. I was flying out shortly and I'd be back in Keycoast when the winner crossed the line. I sure hope it's Laura. I threw the coveralls in a trashcan and made my way out of the complex for the last time. I grabbed a taxi back to the hotel and changed into Ryan's' clothes, grabbed my stuff and hailed down a taxi which drove me to the airport. I had just over a two-hour wait at the boarding gate. I put my things on a chair and made my way to a pay phone. I called Laura.

"Hey dude, what's up?" I said as she answered.

"Hi Ryan."

"Are you all set for the Big Kahuna?"

"I hope so," she replied.

"You've got the cheque for the million dollars, you've got your outfit, all you have to do is win the race and there's another four million in sponsorship. Do what ever it takes and sit high in your chair for the cameras so they can see the logo as you cross the finish line."

"No problem, I'll do my best, Harry won't let me lose, it's not in his playbook."

"I left an envelope for you at the registration desk. Don't open it until after the race. Put it under your cushion for good luck."

"What is it," she asked.

"Just a good luck charm my grandmother gave me when I was young. Alright, I'll catch you after the race, good luck."

"Thanks."

I knew I had nothing to dread here. Laura was the best. Besides with four million dollars at stake, Harry would do everything in his power to make sure she won. I boarded the airplane and was soon in Miami. I walked through the airport just gazing around. I found a nice shop where I bought a pair of pants and a shirt. I kept them on and had the cashier remove the tags for me. I put my other clothes into the shopping bag. I threw them into a garbage can as I made my way to the taxi depot outside the arrivals door. I took a taxi to a little strip plaza that was about five miles from Keycoast. I picked up some beer and then called my guardhouse and had one of my guards come pick me up and take me home.

The Howard's arrived about an hour later. The guard brought them up to the house, Steven from the lodge brought Jimmy down. He seemed very happy that it was his birthday, he knew it meant presents and cake. Mrs. Howard had baked him his favourite, chocolate. We ate supper, just the four of us and then returned to the living room. Jimmy opened his presents. The Howards bought him a toy fire truck with lots of lights and sirens. It even had a hose that squirted water. I had just picked him up some markers and a couple of coloring books. There isn't much he likes to do and I never know what to get him. Jimmy went off to the spare room with his new truck and played. The Howard's and I sat around talking. I had flicked the TV on when I came into the room, I muted the volume and turned it to the sports channel on the satellite that was covering the race. We never really paid much attention to it. I'm not sure if the Howards even knew it was on; they were sitting on the couch with their backs to the TV. I had a pretty good view of it from were I was sitting, but focused more on the conversation than watching it. I needed them for an alibi, but I didn't want their attention to focus on the race. We sat and chatted for a couple of hours. The race was about two-thirds over when they decided to leave, they walked Jimmy back to the lodge when they did. I grabbed a beer and a cigar, turned up the volume and settled in to watch my plan unfold.

Laura was in the lead, by at least seven minutes. The crowd was large, screaming and cheering her on. The camera following her must have been in a vehicle as she made her way through the course. I had an uneasy feeling grip my stomach as I watched. What if the camera crew over-took her near the finish line and tripped the light curtain as they crossed. My plan would be ruined. The camera angle switched as they neared the finish line. I sighed with relief as I saw the camera truck veer off the track. I also caught a glimpse of the little green light that was lit on top of the pole. The stage was set. I only had to hope that Olaf had removed the nails that held the magnets in place. I could see Laura as she reached the crest of the last hill, from there it was only about a thousand meters downhill to the finish line. My heart skipped a beat as I realized she was in fact going to win. As she reached the top of the crest she looked back to check on her opponents. I could see her undoing her blouse, ready to expose the logo on the T-shirt she wore underneath. This was it. Payback time was almost here. My heart raced as she started down the hill towards the finish line. Her momentum picked up as she reached the point of no return on the hill. The camera that was positioned past the finish line zoomed in on her face and chest.

My heart stopped and I held my breath as she reached the imaginary line that crossed between the light curtains. I focused my eyes on the banner, but could not see the one I had strung up because of the camera angle. Laura pulled open her blouse and sat tall in her chair smiling at the camera, she had realized even though she had won the race, the five million dollars was worth losing it. I'm sure Harry and his lawyer were also grinning from ear to ear. There was only one problem though, the cheque I gave them was worthless.

I had gone into the bank and certified one payable to Laura. I left the bank with the cheque securely tucked under my overcoat. I picked that day because it was rainy. I took the cheque to the local stationary store that specialized in color scanning. I made a copy of it and went back outside and let the rainfall smear Laura's name on the original beyond recognition. I took it back to the bank. They had to cancel it because it was illegible. They issued another one and this time I made it payable to myself. Harry is going to be pissed when he finds out the copy I gave him had been cancelled.

Then it happened.

The magnets fell with great force and hit the stoppers unfurling the banner that read "this one's for my dad." I had loosened the stoppers just enough so that they stayed in position until the magnets hit them. The stoppers and the magnets continued on down another two feet, not stopping until they hit the spot of the pole that was an inch wider than the top. The piano wire came to rest about thirty-eight inches off the ground. Laura continued forward, still sitting high in her chair. As she crossed the finish line the wire severed her head. The blood from her juggler vein spurted upwards until the last beat of her heart. Her body slouched forward in her chair. Her head rolled for another eight feet on the cement before it came to rest on the stump of her neck that was still attached, her eyes were still open. The TV signal went snowy as soon as the director could scramble to hit the button, but I'm sure there'll be plenty of angles of the mishap from amateur videographers. I wonder how long before they find the envelope under her cushion with the #3 on it.

I finished my cigar, took a shower and went to bed.

CHAPTER 18

I awoke the next day feeling rejuvenated. That was my most gruesome murder, but it was the one that made me feel the best. Laura made my family suffer a lot. My mother went to her grave not knowing the truth, I owed it to her and my dad.

It wasn't long after I got up that the security guards were calling me from the guard shack. The police had arrived and wanted to question me. I had no concerns. The Howards could vouch for that. There was one flaw in my plan though, they were able to trace the copy of the cheque back to the bank, but it was my word against the tellers. I had obtained all copies of the original money order payable to Laura when I canceled it. I purposely got them all and explained that I'd feel better if I destroyed them myself. When you've got two hundred million in the bank, they don't question much. The signature, even though I wrote it, was a fake. The scribbled fake signature was nothing to go on.

The police left after talking to Chief Howard on the phone and he confirmed my alibi. They were suspicious though. It seemed everywhere I went they were watching me. I got several visits from them over the next two months. They were starting to make connections. Now there were three unsolved murders in which all the victims had some link to my past. I played it cool for a while and spent a lot of time at Keycoast. I spent a lot of time with Jimmy, rekindling our brotherly bond. He was starting to make progress in his life skills. I didn't travel to Fiji at all since Laura's murder. I still had two more victims I wanted to seek revenge on.

After a while though, I was going crazy. I had to get out. I was becoming a prisoner in my own home. I wasn't sure at this point who my fourth victim would be. The guard shack called up to the house.

"Hello," I said answering the phone.

"Mr. Stevenson, George here. Inspector Winthorpe is at the gate, he'd like to see you."

"Thanks George, send him up."

Jamie Winthorpe was an inspector with the police department, he'd only been on the force for a short while. He made it through the ranks very quickly. He was a security guard here when I bought Keycoast. He was the supervisor then. He was a tall man, about six-foot-six-inches, sandy blonde hair, not a bad looking guy. He had a bushy mustache at the time. He worked for me for about three months and then left to join the force. I had him as a personal bodyguard when I first came to Keycoast. He spent a lot of time at the house.

I hung up the phone and went to the door. I stood there waiting, peering through the tight-knit mesh of the screen on the wooden door. He pulled up the laneway in a neon green Barracuda. It was his personal car, he had it when he worked for me. I could see he was dressed in jeans and a T-shirt as he exited from the car.

"Hi Jamie, how are you doing?" I said as I pushed open the door with my right hand. The hinges squeaked. The sunlight entered gradually as the opening in the door became wider.

"Very good Jack," he answered. "How about yourself?"

"Can't complain I guess," I responded. "C'mon in, can I get you a drink?"

"A Coke is fine," he said. "I'm on duty."

"Make yourself at home."

"The place hasn't changed much," I heard him yell from the living room as I grabbed two cans of Coke from the fridge.

As I re-entered the room Jamie was sitting in the leather recliner, he had it outstretched, his feet extended past the end of the footrest, his hands folded behind is head. I reached out and attempted to hand him his Coke.

"The tables fine," he said still maintaining his relaxed position in the chair. He was cocky like that, he would grab his drink when he was ready.

"You said you were here on business?"

"We'll get to that, how's your brother doing?"

"As well as can be expected, I guess."

"Sorry to hear about Lynn, I would have come to the funeral but I was away at police academy at a time. Probably should have sent a card or something."

"It's okay it was quick."

"Yeah, gators or something wasn't it?"

"A car accident, down the road at Lovers Lagoon."

"So young and beautiful, what a waste," he said as he folded the chair back into its upright position and grabbed his Coke.

"So what kind of business brings you here?" I asked.

The phone rang again. It was George.

"Mr. Stevenson," he said.

"Yes George, what is it?"

"There are three police cruisers here at the gate, they say they're here to meet with the inspector, should I send them up?"

I covered the phone with my hand, "Jamie, there's three cruisers at the gate, they say they're looking for you."

"Send them up," he said. "I'll explain when they get here."

"It's okay George, send them up," I said into the telephone.

Jamie took a big drink from his Coke. I hung up the phone and sat on the couch. "What's up?" I asked.

"I've got a search warrant Jack, it's with regards to the death of Ms. Laura Melrose."

"I've already been through this. I was here the whole time. Chief Howard and his wife were with me."

"I don't know Jack, I'm only doing what the Sergeant told me."

"What are you looking for?"

"Anything out of the ordinary."

I heard the car doors shut out in the front yard and the sound of footsteps echoing as they walked up the wooden stairs of the porch.

"C'mon in boys," Jamie yelled to them.

I had recognized one of them as Phil. The cop that was there at Lovers Lagoon the night Lynn's car was found.

"Here you go Jack," Jamie said as he handed me the search warrant.

I set it down on the table beside me.

"I guess it's all legal," I said. "No need to read it."

"Your choice." Jamie stood up and directed the three officers to different rooms in the house. I turned on the TV, sat back and relaxed. I knew there was nothing here, nothing they would find anyway.

ᅟ

After an hour they all converged back in the living room.

"Well," I said. "How did you make out?"

"Didn't find a thing Jack."

"I told you," I replied.

The three officers exited through the screen door, down the creaky stairs and left in their cruisers.

"Well Jack, it's been nice seeing you again. Sorry about the circumstances."

"No problem Jamie, you're only doing your job."

He shook my hand.

I knew they wouldn't find anything here. Once I was done with any of my disguises I threw them out. The only thing I did at Keycoast was research, and printing what ever fake IDs I needed. The computer was so well hidden that they would have to tear down the house to find it. I sat around the rest of the day just watching TV.

I hung around Keycoast for a couple more days. Spent some quality time with Jimmy. On the Wednesday I took him out to the pond at the back of the property. We spent several hours fishing. We must have caught about forty fish in all, mostly catfish. I had the pond well stocked. The students from Keycoast used it a lot. Keycoast ran independently. I owned the place but really had nothing to do with the day-to-day operations. There was an excellent staff working with the students. The managers and the full-time assistants took care of the business end of things. The only real crazy day was Saturday. That was visitation day. This was the only part of the operation that was still monitored by the State of Florida. Keycoast was privatized just after Jimmy arrived, thanks to the Governor. I had started to pressure him soon after I won the money. There was a lot of red tape, but everything has its price. I wonder how the Governor liked his new yacht.

The only real contact I had with the lodge, was when I called up to get Jimmy, I didn't even check on the finances. I didn't care whether it made money or not. I went into the computer room behind the fake wall to try and figure out who my next victim would be.

I answered the phone as it rang.

"Hello," I said.

"Jack, it's Jamie Winthorpe."

"Yes sir what can I do for you?"

"I would like to meet with you if I could."

"What's up?" I asked. "I thought you were done questioning me?"

"It's a personal matter, I've got some information you might be interested in."

"Information about what?"

"I'll discuss it when we meet."

"Okay, how about meeting me at the Yellow Jacket?" I asked.

"Sure, how's seven tonight?"

"I'll be there," I said.

I closed up the computer room and grabbed a shower, I was going to wait until I got to the club to eat. They had the best French onion soup and shrimp cocktail I've ever had. The shrimp were as big as rats.

I drove to the bar and pulled up to the valet parking. I had only been here a couple of times before and never really saw the purpose of the club. This one was very exclusive. It was mostly high paid executives who brought business associates there to schmooze, much like the golf course, I'm sure there were a lot of business deals struck in this place. I went inside, signed myself in and waited at the bar. Jamie hadn't arrived yet. I glanced at my watch as I lit up a big stogie. It was 6:40 p.m. I never recognized anyone in the place. I basically joined for the same reason the other members did. I used it for the odd business meeting and the tax write-off. The maitre d' came and got me when Jamie arrived. I signed him in at the front door, he slipped on his green jacket and followed me back into the bar.

"What will it be?" the bartender asked.

"I'll have a Heineken," Jamie replied.

"So what's up?" I asked Jamie.

"I'll explain later," he said. "Let's have a couple of beers first."

We grabbed our drinks from the bar and made our way to a table.

"Would you like menus?" the waitress asked.

"I'll have the baked French onion soup and the shrimp cocktail please," I said.

"I guess I'll have an order of escargot," Jamie said. "Can you also bring me another Heineken when you come?"

He invited me out, but the way he was ordering I guess he figured I was paying.

"So what did you want to see me about?" I asked again.

"Lots of time for that, let's eat first."

I was getting a little annoyed with the situation. He kept dragging out the evening. He ordered a huge lobster dinner, I was surprised he ate the whole thing.

"Alright Jamie, I need to know what's going on." I demanded.

"Well Jack, concerning the Melrose murder."

"I thought you said this was personal?"

"It is, we're going to talk off the record."

"So what about the murder, I told you before I was with the Howards when she was killed."

"What about the three weeks prior to the murder?"

"What about them?"

"Where were you?"

"I was in and out of the country on business. I've answered all these questions before."

"Hey, I'm just letting you in on some of the stuff that was found during our investigation."

"What stuff?"

"They found a pair coveralls in a garbage can near the racetrack in Norway."

I could feel myself starting to sweat. "What about the coveralls?"

"Like I said, they found them and a name badge. Olaf the maintenance foreman said that the name was the same name that the guy used who installed the banner at the finish line of the race. The same banner in which the bottom wired decapitated Ms. Melrose."

"What does that have to do with me?"

"Nothing yet, but they did find an envelope stuffed under her seat, with a number three on a card that was similar to the other two unsolved murders. One in Florida, and the other one in Arizona. You've been linked to knowing all three of the victims."

"That doesn't mean that I killed them."

"No it doesn't. But right now it's evidence, circumstantial as it may be."

"Who's in charge of this investigation?" I asked.

"I am at this end, that's why I'm coming to you, and right now I'm the only one with all the details. The coveralls have been sent for DNA testing along with the envelope the killer may have licked, I'm sure they'll find something to do a DNA markup."

Now I was starting to fidget, my legs were getting twitchy. I didn't think that I would have been linked to any of the murders. I knew they would figure out that I knew all the victims, but I thought I covered my tracks pretty good. I pulled myself together as best as I could. I couldn't let Jamie see that I was uncomfortable. My alibis were airtight, my disguises were great, as long as I stuck to my story it shouldn't be a problem.

"Why are you telling me all this, and especially off the record as you say?"

"Jack, I used to work for you, I have some loyalty to you."

"But you're a cop."

"A cop, yeah, do you know what we make?"

I started to figure it out. He was going to blackmail me for money. He had a link to the evidence. He could have it destroyed whenever he wanted, before any other authorities found out.

"Is this about money?" I asked.

"What do you take me for?" he shouted. "I'm just trying to tell an old friend to watch what he does, to let him know that he is being watched."

"I don't know Jamie, I can't figure it out, why? Cracking a case like this would promote you through the ranks so quick. These coveralls, when will the test results be in?" I asked.

"They're running them now. I asked them to send the results to me as soon as they have them."

"I don't know, Jamie."

"Know about what?"

"It sure sounds like this is about money."

"If you think this is about blackmail, you're wrong. Yes it's about payback, when I worked for you I just got married, you gave Sarah and I a very generous loan at zero percent to get us started. Even though I paid it back, I owe you."

"But it's your job to find killers."

"Jack listen," he leaned towards me. "Evidence goes missing all the time, and I'm in control of that evidence."

"So what are you saying?"

"Well, what I'm saying is, I owe you one."

I sat back and looked at him for a moment trying to figure him out.

"That's a hell of a risk you'd be taking."

"Yes, I know. I can alter or contaminate the evidence without anyone knowing. There is one drawback though. They may have enough to put you on trial, but with a good lawyer pleading to the judge about the inept professionalism of the department in gathering the evidence, you would get off. I will probably be reprimanded and demoted, if not fired, but I'll get a decent buyout. It won't be enough to live on, especially with my wife dying."

"Sarah? What's wrong with her?"

"Cancer, brain cancer. I need the time now to be with her."

"Then why take this on, why try to free me?"

"I owe you one."

We finished our meal, I paid the bill and we went outside. The valet brought my Jeep up and I left. I was confused. I felt so sorry for Jamie and his situation, but I also racked my brain trying to figure out where else I screwed up. Should I follow his plan to let him hide the evidence? Or should I pack up now and get to my island? As long as I never travel to the United States, the authorities couldn't touch me. I was leaning towards the latter. I honked at the guardhouse as I drove by. I parked and walked into the emptiness that filled the house. I wandered upstairs to the bedroom and flopped on the bed. I had decided that my plan was not worth continuing. In the morning I would pack up my things, grab Jimmy from the lodge and take off. To hell with everything, I kicked off my shoes and fell asleep. The phone woke me up abruptly, I scrambled out of the bed to answer it.

"Jack, it's Jamie."

"What's up?"

"I need to meet with you."

"I just left you a less than two hours ago, can't it wait until the morning?"

"It can, but I'm not sure you would want it to."

"Why?"

"I've got some information you might want, what they found in the coveralls."

"Where can I meet you?"

"The coffee shop on Paradise Lane, I'll be there in twenty minutes."

"I'll see you there."

As I approached the coffee shop I could see the red glare of his taillights illuminating through the fog. The lights in the diner were dim through the haze. I noticed four other cars parked in the parking lot as I pulled in the driveway. Jamie exited his vehicle as I parked beside him.

"Let's go in and grab a coffee," Jamie said as I opened my door.

I followed him up the stairs. A bell rang on the inside of the door as Jamie opened it. A gentleman sitting on a bar stool at the counter raised his head and glanced our way. Once we were inside he buried his head back into the newspaper he was reading. A head popped out between the swinging doors that led from the kitchen as we made our way to a booth.

"Two coffees," Jamie yelled to the lady who had emerged from the kitchen.

"Coming right up Jamie," she yelled back.

"Actually, I'll have a Coke," I informed Jamie.

"Mabel, make it just one and a Coke for my friend."

Mabel clinked the coffee pot on the mug as she poured his cup. The bottom of the pot sizzled as she set it back on the burner. The soda dispenser gurgled and spewed out a stream of water and syrup into the oversized red Coke glass she was holding.

"So what were the results of the test?" I asked.

"In a minute Jack. Wait until the waitress leaves."

She had made her way halfway across the room to our table. She put my Coke down in front of me. The plastic straw floating in the liquid was still partially covered by a paper sheath. The mug clanked the table as she put it in front of Jamie, the coffee tossing and turning inside. Two little creamer containers plopped on the table as she released them from her fist.

"Anything else boys?" she asked.

"Not at the moment Mabel," Jamie answered. She spun around and turned towards the kitchen and disappeared behind the swinging doors.

"Alright Jamie, the suspense is killing me."

"I got the results back on the coveralls. The DNA markup matches yours."

"What you mean it matches mine?"

"I compared the DNA against the cigar butt that was taken from your place."

"What cigar butt? The day you did the search with the warrant you left empty-handed."

"You're right we did, but I came back when you were out and went through some stuff."

"That's against the law, it won't stand up in court."

"I don't expect it to go to court."

"How the hell did you get past the gate? Security wouldn't have let you up to the house if I wasn't aware of it."

"I didn't use security I came in the back way."

"What back way?"

"Well Jack," he said as he leaned in closer. "I know from working your security that the cameras on the building catch about ninety five percent of the grounds, there's a blind spot in the northeast corner. As the camera scans the property, the steeple on the church blocks the view from the camera. Besides your security doesn't sit glued to the monitors."

"But there's razor wire around the compound."

"Bolt cutters can take care that."

"I simply cut a section of the wire," he continued. "I pulled it down and hopped over the wall. When I was done I set the piece back in its position. Your groundskeeper would never even notice it."

"You bastard," I yelled.

The man at the counter raised his head and looked at us again.

"Keep it down," Jamie said. "I'm trying to do you a favour."

"What kind of fucking favour is breaking into my house?"

"I wanted to be sure whether or not you were the killer. If you were I wanted to keep the evidence secret until I could talk to you."

"Sure the DNA was mine but it was obtained illegally and I can buy the best team of lawyers in the world. The charge will never stick."

"Well Jack, it's like this. Like I told you yesterday, Sarah is very sick. I need cash. I could take all the evidence and turn you in. I could have done this according to Hoyle and you'd be on your way to the chair. But I came up with a win-win situation."

"Why the hell should I help you out?"

"Not just me, you'd be helping yourself too."

"With the money I've got I could ruin your career if you turn me in. Your evidence sucks. I could create an alibi so strong that even the president would believe me."

"I've got more."

"Like what?"

"I've got copies of all the fake IDs and the files that you kept on all your victims."

I knew this was a bluff. The computer I used to gather my info and to print the IDs was well hidden.

"You're full of shit."

"You think so?" Jamie said as he reached in his pocket and pulled out some papers. "Here," he said as he threw them on the table.

I unraveled them and almost fell to the floor. There were some black-and-white copies of the IDs from Norway and info on Cheryl and Dave. There was also a list of contacts and rental receipts from the apartment in Japan.

"How the fuck did you get this?"

"I emailed them to myself."

"Emailed?"

"From your computer, the day I broke in."

The email address at the top was mine. I was stunned.

"But how," I started to say.

"Easy," he answered. "Jack, I was one of your security guards. I had access to your house whenever I wanted it, I even had keys, even though I didn't need one."

"So you had access to my place but the computer I used to

was not accessible to anyone."

"So you admit it. You killed Miss Melrose."

"Obviously, you asshole, you've got the evidence. But I still don't know how you found it."

"Good police work and a good memory. I was around when you first bought the place. I remember when you had the remodeling done. Your big mistake was trying to keep what you were doing quiet . It made me suspicious. At the time I spied on all the activities and found out about the fake wall you had installed. You spent a lot of time away from here, so I had a lot of time to get in and snoop. You've got quite the little hideout behind the bookshelf."

"You son of a bitch," I shouted.

"I was just curious at the time I never dreamt that the knowledge would be beneficial to me."

"What the hell do you want?"

"I need $10 million. I could take Sara to Europe. There's a specialist over there who can help."

"I thought we were friends. You could have asked me for help."

"I've been away from here too long for that. We lost touch with each other over time. Now that I have this info, blackmail is my only option."

Right then and there I knew Jamie was going to be my next victim, but how was I going to do it? I had witnesses here and nothing to kill him with. Not even a butter knife.

"And why the hell should I pay you? I'd be able to fight the charge. Or I could just kill you."

"Do you honestly think that I'm that stupid? I've got a copy of everything on CD in a safety deposit box. My lawyer has a key and instructions to open it if I was to die suddenly."

"I could run you off the road tonight, make it look like an accident and nobody would be the wiser."

"My lawyer would still have the evidence and besides there are witnesses to this meeting."

"Who? a waitress and a bum at the counter?"

"Ted," he yelled. The guy at the counter looked up.

"Yes Jamie?" he answered.

"You can go start up the truck Garret and Aaron just pulled

in."

I looked out the window and saw the silhouette of a cruiser as it shut off its lights.

The guy at the counter stood up and made his way over to us. His jacket fell open as he bent to pick up the keys off the table exposing his gun and a badge pinned to his shirt. He grabbed the keys and left.

"Listen Jack," Jamie said as he stood up. For now, no one on the force knows about the evidence. I'll be in touch," he turned and walked away.

I sat stunned staring out the window, watching until they left. Jamie's bombshell blurred my mind totally. I didn't even remember driving back to Keycoast.

I was pissed off, partially because Jamie was trying to blackmail me but mostly at myself for screwing up. I didn't know what to do. If I killed him I would get caught. If I paid him the blackmail money I might still get caught. There were too many loose ends I'd leave untied if I hopped on an airplane and took off. I didn't have much to hold me back, except for Jimmy. There was a lot of red tape to take him off the property, even for a day. Keycoast was still somewhat regulated by the State. I decided grabbing him and sneaking out of the country was my best bet, but I'd have to do it fast. The problem was that Jamie wasn't that stupid, my jet was probably under surveillance. I opened a bottle of Crown Royal, sat there and got drunk as I thought about my next move.

I got up the next day feeling like shit. I got dressed and headed down to the guard shack. I asked for the video surveillance tapes for last three weeks. I figured if I could catch Jamie on the tape breaking in it would help my case if I got arrested. As I walked down the path I noticed a white van sitting across the road. There were two people inside. I figured it was a police stakeout, they weren't even trying to conceal themselves. I picked up the tapes and headed back to the house. The phone was ringing when I stepped inside.

"Hello," I said as I put the phone to my ear.

"Jack, Jamie. What's it going to be?"

"I'm interested in your offer but how can I be assured that I won't be turned in after I give you the money."

"I'll give you the CD and all the keys to the safety deposit box. I've already deleted the files and email from my computer I couldn't take the chance that someone here would find them."

"How do I know you haven't made other copies?"

"You have to trust me."

"Trust a crooked cop?"

"It's your choice. It's either that or the chair. The CD has enough on it to convict you. All I have to do is put it in as evidence collected during the search warrant at your house. You do remember we did have a legal search warrant."

"You've thought of everything, haven't you?"

"Pretty much."

"Obviously I missed something," I said.

"The choice is yours, what are you going to do?"

"I'll pay the money but I need a couple of days to get it. I assume you want cash," I knew it was the only way. At least I would have a couple of days to think. "I also want the hounds pulled off. I'm taking Jimmy as soon as I make the drop and I'm leaving the country."

"I'll call you tomorrow with the details."

He hung up the phone before I could respond. I hate being cornered. I hung up the phone, grabbed my coat and headed to the bank. Most of my money was tied up in investments. I did have a cash account with $20 million though. I told them I wanted half of the money transferred to my bank in Fiji and the other $10 million in cash. Of course I was informed that there wasn't that much on hand and I agreed the next day would be fine. The bank manager strongly suggested I take a cashier's check but I told him that I was giving the cash away to the needy, stopping on the streets and giving it to the homeless.

"It's bizarre," said the bank manager. "But generous."

I went back to Keycoast and told the councilor on duty at the lodge that Jimmy was going to spend a few days at the house and to have him ready for the morning. I had no idea when Jamie would call, but I wanted Jimmy available. I called Kevin and had him rent a jet and fly it to the Miami airport and wait. He'd arrive in the morning. I grabbed a couple of briefcases to transport the money in and put them in the Jeep.

I ate some lunch before I got into the Jeep and left the

compound. I went to the bus terminal to get a locker. There was no way I was going to personally hand Jamie the cash. I would leave him a key and be halfway to Fiji by the time he got to the bus terminal. I drove back to the house to wait. I gathered everything I wanted to take with me. I knew once I left I wouldn't be coming back. I was sure one day the police would piece it all together, even without Jamie's help. Maybe not planning on getting caught was my real mistake. The one mistake that threw a wrench into my whole plan was licking that envelope.

Jamie didn't call for two days, when he did it was three in the morning. He was in Miami at the Sea Breeze Motel. I woke Jimmy and got him dressed. He was quite groggy, so it was difficult to get him into the Jeep. I had already loaded all of the things I wanted. I went back in the house and grabbed the money. I put it in the back seat and closed the door. As I climbed in the front seat I could feel my eyes well a bit. I was going to miss this place I thought to myself. I wasn't sure what would happen to it once I left. All I knew is that once I left the U.S. I could never come back. I was about to become a fugitive for the rest my life. I started the Jeep and drove it down the laneway to the guardhouse. The gate opened as I approached. I drove to the bus terminal, shut off the Jeep and grabbed a briefcase from the back. I lifted the briefcase and put it in the locker. I dropped two quarters in the slot, closed the door and pulled the key out slipping it into my pocket as I walked to the Jeep. Jimmy was sleeping with his face against the window. He didn't even stir as I unlocked the door and climbed in. It was a somber drive to the motel. The moon was full but the fog in front of us muted the glow. The Sea Breeze was a small seedy looking one-story motel on the outskirts of town. There were only two vehicles in the dimly lit parking lot, Jamie's truck and a beat up old Chevy van that sat in the corner. The van leaned to the left side because of two flat tires.

I pulled up slowly and parked in front of a room that had a dented screen door. The number eight was screwed to the inside door. I could see that the room was empty as my headlights shone through the dusty window. Jamie was in the next room to the right. It was the last unit of the motel. A slit in the curtains appeared as I shut off my jeep. A dim light cracked the night as it reflected off the fog that hung in the night air.

I reached over and snapped Jimmy's seat belt loose and then undid mine. I got out of the Jeep and went to Jimmy's side, opened the door and nudged him softly. Strings of drool stretched from his chest as he pulled his head back and opened his eyes. The saliva disappeared as he wiped it with his sleeve. He scrambled out of the Jeep.

We made our way to the door. The paint was cracked and the iron number nine hung upside down by the screw at the bottom that was loose but had not fallen out yet. Putting my hand threw the ripped screen I knocked on the door. The creaking hinges shattered the silence.

"C'mon in Jack," Jamie said. "Hi Jimmy," he added.

Jimmy gave him a hug.

I made my way past him into the room. It smelled like mothballs. I pushed open the door to the bathroom, cocked my head around the corner, no one was there. I turned back and faced them. Jimmy had made himself comfortable on the bed. The springs squeaked as he moved about. The headboard rattled off the wall, a result of the constant abuse the bed must have taken during its stay in the motel. I was sure this dive was rented by the hour.

"Jimmy don't touch anything," I told him more out of concern he would catch something, rather than him breaking something.

"So Jack, let's get down to business. Do you have the money?"

"Ten million dollars is a lot to get your hands on."

"Not for you, do you have it?"

"It's available."

"What does that mean?"

"You didn't think I'd carry $10 million in cash over here did you? You're smarter than that."

"Where is it?"

"In a locker. When Jimmy and I are safely on our way you'll be able to get it."

"So Jack, why'd you do it? Why did you make that statement about killing people and then actually be stupid enough to carry out?"

"Fuck you. I'm a lot smarter than you," I yelled becoming increasingly angry. "Nobody calls me stupid."

"Face it Jack, it wasn't a smart thing. So why'd you do it?"

"Because I could. I had a few people who pissed me off. When my baby sister died it hit me hard and I kept a lot of pent-up frustration for years. Once I had the money and my family was gone, what else was left?"

"So how many did you kill?"

"What the hell is this? Why are you giving me the third degree?"

"I'm just interested Jack. I guess it's the detective in me. Besides in a couple of hours you'll be halfway around the world. As long as you don't come back to the U.S. you'll be free."

"Three, I've killed three."

"I know Ms. Melrose was one. Who were the other two?"

"You've got the computer files, you tell me what you know."

"All I've got is names, no proof. I could dig deeper and find it but I've got Sarah to think about. I really could care less."

"There was Cheryl Hopkins. She fuckin' embarrassed the hell out of me in high school. Then there was her dumb boyfriend."

"The wrestler?"

"Yeah, the big lug really pissed me off. He not only hurt me mentally and emotionally, but he got physical. I enjoyed that one."

"Sounds like you planned them well. Who were going to be your next two victims?"

"I hadn't really thought that far yet. For my fourth though, I do have someone in mind."

"Anyone I know?"

"Yes, it's you," I said with a smirk.

"Me, why me?"

"Look what the hell you're doing to me, but I guess my freedom means more." I handed him the key to the locker.

"What's this for?"

"A locker at the bus station, your money's inside. Spend it wisely and always look over your shoulder. You never know, maybe one day I'll be back. C'mon Jimmy let's go."

Jimmy stood up and walked towards the door.

"Well Jack, have a good life."

I opened the door for Jimmy. We stepped through the rundown doorway and onto the broken cement outside the door.

Jamie followed. "The money better be there or I'll come looking for you."

"Don't worry, you'll get what's yours," I said as I walked over to open the Jeep door for Jimmy. He climbed in and sat down. "Give my love to Sarah, I hope she gets what she needs."

"She already got what she deserved. I divorced her a year ago."

"But what is the money for?"

"The money was for nothing. Sarah's not sick. It was only a ploy. I didn't think I had enough to get a murder charge. You cover your tracks very well, even using Chief Howard as an alibi. You were good."

I sensed something was up. I quickly made my way to the driver's side of the Jeep.

From where I was standing I could see in room number eight, the light was still off and the room looked empty. The parking lot looked the same. Jamie's truck was beside me and the Chevy van was still in the corner. I didn't hear any unusual sounds.

"It's my word against yours. Enjoy the money." I pulled on the door handle of the Jeep, the unlatching sound broke the still night air. "My lawyers would have a heyday with you. Have a good life." I bent down and sat in the Jeep.

Jamie walked in front of it and came to the driver's side, grabbed the door and pushed it shut.

"You have a good life yourself," he paused, still with his hand of the door. "One more thing Jack."

"What's that?"

"Take this, you'll need it," he said as he held out his clenched fist.

"What is it?" I asked.

He opened his fist to reveal a quarter resting in the palm of his hand.

"What's this for?"

"To call a good lawyer," he said as he stepped back and

pulled opened his shirt with a tug sending the buttons flying. Strapped to his chest was little black box.

"A wire, you're wearing a fucking wire?"

I heard the silence of the night crack and turned towards the sound. I saw the van doors fly open. I could only see shadows of people as they ran towards me. Beady red lights were dancing in the air as they did. As they got closer I could see the silhouettes of the rifles that the laser sights were attached to.

"Don't hurt Jimmy," I screamed as I reached for his door and opened it. I looked at Jamie. "You bastard! You fucking bastard!"

Jimmy started to yell as they forced him from the vehicle.

"It's okay Jimmy, these men are going to take you home."

Within seconds the parking lot was full of screaming police cruisers, their flashing lights illuminating the misty sky. I exited the vehicle staring down the barrels of three rifles, all of which I'm sure had their sights set on the middle of my forehead.

"Get Jimmy out of here first, he doesn't need to see this."

Jamie looked at one of the cops and motioned for him to take Jimmy away.

"I'll be home later Jimmy," I yelled as they drove off. Jimmy was now in the front seat of a cruiser.

The ride to the station seemed to take an eternity, the sun on the horizon seemed motionless, deciding whether or not it would make its appearance. The fog that filled the sky earlier was parting for the sun. The thin wisps of haze danced like ghosts as they flew towards the cruiser. It was haunting. The eerie clusters took on life-like features as they came towards the car, staring at me. As they passed by the window to my right, the flickering cruiser light added an evil aura to them, making them look like the devil himself, taunting me with their passing. For the first time since I started my plan I was scared, really scared.

As we approached downtown, the sun was in full bloom. I could see the police station as we drove closer. Three more stoplights and we were there. The officer driving the cruiser pulled to the curb a block away. Jamie got out of the car.

"I'll walk to the station Lou once I get the money," he told the driver.

"Are you sure?" Lou asked.

"I can use the exercise," Jamie replied.

I wanted the cruiser to go. As much as I didn't want to get to the station I knew I didn't want to stay in front of the bus terminal. The car started rolling towards the station. I looked back and watched Jamie enter the terminal. The cruiser pulled behind the station and stopped. Lou got out and opened the back door for me.

BANG

The windows of the station shattered as the blast from the bus terminal found its way through the alley.

"What the hell was that?" Lou yelled.

About half a dozen police poured out of the station.

"It came from over there," Lou said as he pointed towards the bus terminal.

I was whisked inside and thrown in a cell. Lou went tearing outside with the others. I knew what had happened. Jamie had opened the locker at the terminal. Within seconds shrill sirens littered the air. Lou came running back in, his clothes covered with dust.

"You son of a bitch," he yelled at me as he reached my cell.

"I guess Jamie found the right locker," I laughed.

"You're going to fry for this one," he said.

I had boobie-trapped the briefcase inside the locker with explosives. I didn't count on ever getting caught. I figured I would be in my jet and on my way with Jimmy by now. I didn't think Jamie had it in him to double cross me. I guess I read him wrong.

Three more cops had arrived. I could see the anger in their faces. The cell door bolt clanged as Lou inserted the key. The rusty hinges squeaked as he opened my cell door. The four of them stepped inside. I knew I was in for a shit-kicking. Cops don't like it when you kill other cops. Two of them slowly withdrew their nightsticks from their sheaths. Unable to protect myself, my hands still in cuffs, I turned to the side as I saw one of the cops raise his baton to strike me.

"Hold on boys," a voice from behind them yelled. It was Chief Milner. "As much as he deserves it, we have to let the courts decide his fate. He'll get what's coming to him."

The cops slowly lowered their batons and nestled them back in the leather holsters that hung off their belts.

"Follow protocol boys. We don't want anything screwing this up. He'll have a team of lawyers that will put us under if we don't follow the rules."

For the next two hours I was photographed and fingerprinted. My Miranda rights were read to me and I was thrown back in the cell. Chief Milner kept a watchful eye on everything they did. I knew my lawyers could get me out of the other murders, but this one wasn't going to be as easy.

I wasn't concerned about my fate. I had Jimmy on my mind. I wondered if he made it back to Keycoast.

"When do I get my phone call?" I asked the guard sitting in a chair at the end of the hall.

"When we say you can," he snapped back.

"I know my rights. I want my phone call and I want it now."

"I told you when we're ready."

I sat there for another hour before I saw Chief Milner again.

"Chief," I yelled when I saw him talking to the guard. "I want my phone call now."

The Chief whispered something to the guard who picked up the phone on the desk and made a call. Two more cops arrived a few minutes later. One of them was carrying a shotgun, the other had leg and wrist irons in his hand. They made their way to my cell. The one with a shotgun leaned against the wall outside of my cell and pumped the gun, then pointed it at me. Lou put the key in the lock.

"Turn around," he said. "Put your hands on your head."

I turned and faced the drab grey wall, raised my arms and interlocked my fingers and put my hands on my head. Lou turned the key in the lock. The door squeaked again as he opened it. The chains that one of the cops was holding began to rattle as he sorted them out. Someone grabbed my right arm and bent it behind my back. I felt the cold steel of a handcuff as it encircled my wrist, clicking tight, locking on to me. My left arm was then pulled down to my other one and the second half of the cuff clicked around my wrist.

"Spread your legs," Lou yelled.

I took a step sideways with my right foot. I heard the chains fall to the ground. The burly cop placed one of the shackles around my left ankle. I almost lost my balance when he grabbed my pant leg and pulled my right foot closer and shackled it. I could feel him breathing as he reached around me and pulled a chain from around my waist and fastened it behind me. The two chains that hung down on either side were fastened to the shackles on each of my lower legs. My arms were pulled away from my back. I felt the tension ease as Lou released the cuffs. Holding my left arm securely he forced it forward and placed a steel shackled around it. Once it was secured the cop holding my right arm put it into position at my side and slapped on the last shackle. I had very little freedom of movement from the chains that entombed me. Lou grabbed my arm and spun me around, forcing me to look at the open cell door. The cop outside had the shotgun raised, still pointing it at my head. I was pushed forward, my feet shuffling as I tried to keep my balance. I was escorted down the hallway and pushed through the doorway of interrogation room one. The sign on the door told me where I was.

The room was small, there was a table with one chair on either side of it. A phone and a tape recorder sat on the sturdy wooden table. The walls were pale blue and there were no windows. One large mirror hung on the fourth wall. I knew it was a two-way mirror; I've seen the movies. I was guided over to a chair where I was spun around and shoved in the chest, forcing me to sit as I stumbled into it.

"You get one call, three minutes," Lou said.

I knew my lawyer would hear about my arrest in due time. My concern lay with my brother. "Call my brother, the number is 555-1204."

Lou pushed a button on the tape recorder, the humming of the sprocket wheels told me it was working. Then he pressed the orange button on the phone. The dial tone echoed through the room as the speakerphone spit out it sounds. The phone burped a harmonic tune as he pressed each button of the phone number. The phone rang three times before it was answered.

"Keycoast, Julie speaking, may I help you?" the voice said through the little speaker on the phone.

"Hi Julie, it's Jack, is Jimmy around?"

"He's in his room."

"Is he asleep?"

"I'm not sure, would you like me to check?"

"No, it's okay I just wanted to make sure he got back okay"

"The police brought him here few hours ago, are you okay?"

"Yeah, yeah, I'm fine. Listen, can you do me a favour? Let him know I called, tell him I'm okay. I'll see him in a few days. Also could you call my lawyer Mr. Hibbs, Stan has the number at the guardhouse."

"Actually Stan came up when Jimmy arrived. The police filled him in. I believe he has already called Mr. Hibbs."

"Okay thanks a lot, give Jimmy my love, goodbye."

"Goodbye."

Lou reached over and pushed the orange button, silencing the call. The two officers escorted me back to my cell. I nodded off before I knew it.

I'm not sure how long I was out, but I awoke with a kink in my neck as the door opened.

"Hi Jack," Bartholomew Hibbs said as he entered the room.

I struggled to sit properly. "Hi Bart, how are you?"

"I'm okay, but it looks like you're in quite a mess."

"Looks that way."

"So what is going on, Jack?"

"They brought me in on a charge of murder, but it won't stick"

"I don't think they're too concerned about those ones right now. It looks like you may be responsible for the death of one of their own."

"He died did he?"

"So you know what they're talking about."

"Was anyone else hurt?"

"No, it seems that the terminal was empty. The lone clerk behind the desk was out having a smoke when the blast occurred."

"Now listen, I don't care what it costs you've got to get me off of this."

"I'll do my best. I'm not sure what evidence they've got."

"Very little, I've got alibis for everything."

"Are you saying you committed the murders?"

"Lets put it this way. I am a man of my word."

"Jack, you know you can tell me, I'm your lawyer. I need to know the facts. What we say between us stays between us. Even if you're guilty it's my job to defend you."

"They've got a pretty good case against me for the murder of Laura Melrose. There were two before that they suspect me in and this one."

"Did you commit all four?"

"Yes."

He stood up and made his way to the door. I sat in that cell for two days, never leaving it once. Mr. Hibbs never contacted me or visited me. I never felt so alone. It was early one morning. I'm not even sure what day it was when the door outside the cellblock opened and Mr. Hibbs walked in with Chief Milner. They stopped at the desk and spoke to the guard. The guard grabbed keys off his desk and walked towards my cell. Mr. Hibbs and the Chief followed him.

"I thought you took my money and ran," I said with a chuckle. "It's about time you got me out of here."

The guard put the key in the lock, turned it until it clanked and then pulled the door open. I stepped forward.

"Not so fast Jack," Mr. Hibbs said. "I need to talk to you."

I stopped where I was and Mr. Hibbs entered the cell, the guard closed the door and locked it behind him.

"What's up Bart?" I asked.

"The judge wouldn't grant you bail. I'm actually here because they want to charge you with the murder of Detective Jamie Winthorpe. We've got a court appearance in half an hour."

"What do they have?"

"I don't know, the evidence will come out in the disclosure hearing."

"What do we do?"

"We see what they have."

Now I was getting worried. I hadn't planned on getting caught, which was really stupid because I'm sure that all murderers never plan on getting caught. I started thinking about Jimmy. What does this mean for him? If they find me guilty will he survive? I guess I should have been thinking more of myself, but I just couldn't. I didn't talk much, I wasn't sure if this place was bugged or not. Bart assured me that anything said between us was confidential and if they were eavesdropping here or in the other room the other night and it came out at the trial, we could get the case dismissed. I almost wish they did.

The guard came to the cell door.

"Mr. Hibbs you'll have to step out," the guard said.

Two other guards came in and shackled me again. Hibbs followed as they escorted me out of the cell. They placed me in a cruiser and drove me to the Court House five blocks away. Hibbs followed in his car. We pulled into the underground parking garage. Once inside, the cruiser stopped and I was helped out. They took me to a small room on the third floor. Hibbs and I were left alone inside. Two guards stood outside the door. We were only in there a couple minutes before we went to the courtroom. I shuffled my way there. The judge entered and sat down. The prosecution lawyer stood up and addressed the bench.

"Your Honour, we would like to present evidence about the murder of Detective Jamie Winthorpe. I'm sure you have reviewed the evidence."

"Yes I have."

The back doors of the courtroom opened and Anthony Milner, the Chief, entered. He walked down the aisle and stood in front of me.

"Mr. Stevenson," he started. "You have the right to remain silent anything you say can and will be used against you in a court of law." He continued until I had heard all of my Miranda rights and I answered that I understood them. He then left the courtroom.

"Continue Mr. Connell," the judge commanded.

"Your Honour, we're going to present evidence that will prove a motive for the defendant to want to kill Detective Winthorpe. We'll present evidence placing the defendant at the scene of the crime prior to the bomb blast."

Mr. Hibbs stood up again. "Your Honour, in light of an the new charges I would like to call a recess so my client and I can confer."

"I object Your Honour," Mr. Connell yelled. "They are trying to stall the inevitable."

"Mr. Hibbs you have a point," the judge said. "Your client has been charged and that was the point of this hearing. Court is adjourned to allow the defendant time to review the evidence in the case." The smack of her gavel silenced the District Attorney as he rose again with his arm out and his finger pointed. He stood there with his mouth gaping as the bailiff told everyone to rise while the judge made her way to her chambers.

CHAPTER 19

Two guards came over and escorted me back to my cell.

The next few weeks flew by pretty fast as we pondered the evidence. The police had turned a lot over to the District Attorney. They had tape recordings of every meeting Jamie and I had and they had videotapes from the surveillance cameras at the bus terminal. They even had fibers from my living room rug that were found in the briefcase. The briefcase I used was empty. It was sitting around the house for a while and somehow fibers from the rug found their way into it.

The day before the trial Hibbs came to the station.

"Jack," Hibbs said. "We go back to court tomorrow. I will do my best but I don't know whether or not I can win. I suggest we plead guilty to manslaughter. You'll probably get ten to fifteen, out in eight for good behavior."

"It doesn't look good, does it?" I replied.

"Afraid not. If we don't cop a plea you could be looking at the death penalty."

"Let me think about it overnight, I'll let you know in the morning."

Hibbs called the guard to let him out. I crawled up on my thin mattress and went to sleep.

The trial was to start right away. Normally a killer would sit in jail for a couple of years before he went to trial. I guess because I killed a cop they wanted to expedite the situation. I also wanted it done right away.

It was 6:00 a.m. when the guard woke me for my breakfast. A bowl of corn flakes, two pieces of toast and a small glass of orange juice. I was getting sick of these meals. I ate what I could and slid the half empty tray through the bars as the guard walked by. Mr. Hibbs showed up about ten minutes later. He was carrying my freshly pressed suit. The guards opened my cell and let him in.

"Okay Jack, have you decided what you're going to do?"

"What else can I do, let's go for manslaughter."

"Okay that's what we'll do then," he handed me my suit and I proceeded to change.

We were moved from the cell to the Court House and put in a secure room with a guard both inside and outside the door. Both had shotguns. About half an hour later we were led into the courtroom and took our seats at the table assigned to us. The judge entered the courtroom and took her spot.

"Mr. Stevenson," she said. "Please stand and face the court. You have been charged with the murder of Detective Jamie Winthorpe. How do you plead?"

Before I could give an answer to her, Hibbs who was standing beside me spoke up. "Your Honour," he started. "May I approached the bench?"

The judge waved both him and the D.A. to the side of her bench. The three of them conversed for a few minutes and then he returned. He leaned over to me. "Jack, I'm afraid the judge won't accept the plea bargain."

"I knew it was a long shot, I killed a cop."

"Mr. Stevenson, I ask you again, how do you plead? Guilty or not guilty?"

I looked at Bart, he turned and faced the judge. "Guilty Your Honour," I said. "I plead guilty to the charge."

"Yes," Mr. Connell yelled quietly.

"Mr. Stevenson, please rise."

I looked at Hibbs. He looked shocked.

Without hesitation the judge spoke. "Mr. Stevenson, I find you guilty of first degree murder in the death of Detective Jamie Winthorpe and I sentence you to death by electrocution or lethal injection." She slammed her gavel down hard. "Court is adjourned," she stood up and left. The courtroom was silent. It all happened so fast. I thought it would be a while before I was sentenced. The guards quickly came over and escorted me out of the courtroom. As I walked past the D.A.s table they were all congratulating each other. The courtroom was now buzzing with excitement. The next few days were a blur. I don't remember what I did. I sat on Death Row for eleven months until today.

"Cut," said Adam. "Great job guys," he said as he and Mark stood up and applauded. Emily wiped a tear away from her cheek.

"I'm glad that part is over with," I said. "How much time do we have Adam?" I yelled through the microphone.

Adam leaned forward. "About half an hour, then we go live again."

"Good, I've got to go to the washroom."

Warden Howard stood up to the microphone and placed his hand-held synthesizer against his throat. "Seth, take Jack back to his cell. When he's ready bring him to the cafeteria. Wes make sure it's cleared out. Everyone should be gone by now, but just make sure. I don't need any problems. Jack you're allowed one inmate to join you, who would you like?"

"It's okay Bob, just the guards, yourself and the media crew is fine. Oh yeah, and Jimmy too."

Jimmy's ears perked up, he started waving at me, I waved back. Seth undid my chains from the pins and fastened them to my waist. He helped me up as the bolt on the door slid open. Rocco stepped inside and took his position behind me. He and Seth escorted me back to my cell. They undid my chains and left. Locking the cell door behind them as they did.

"So Jack," a voice from across the hall yelled. "Only a couple of hours left." The voice was that of Jason Jones. He was on Death Row for the brutal rape and murder of a nun.

"Yeah," I said. "I don't know whether I'm the lucky one or not."

"Anything beats this place, feeling like a caged rat all day."

He wasn't a bad guy to talk to. He seemed very intelligent, but he had a temper that you wouldn't believe. One minute he'd be fine, the next he would destroy everything in his cell. He spent a lot of time in the box. That was where they sent you for solitary confinement. A grey metal room that was no bigger than the cardboard box that a refrigerator would be shipped in. There wasn't even enough room to stretch out and grab a nap.

I never had to go there, I kept pretty quiet. This novel that I was writing consumed most of my time. I was also trying to finalize the plans for my ranch. I had enough money to fund it up front, but the more I thought about it, the larger the cash flow became. That's when I came up with the idea for the live execution over the Internet. I knew I could generate almost a billion dollars. With pay per view and the commercial advertisements I figured with some wise investments, the money would long out-live the ranch. It was a long shot that I would be able to pull the right strings, but I did. Warden Howard bent the rules a bit and allowed me to have Internet access on a computer in my cell. The administrator closely monitored my activities. A splitter was put on my cable and an extra monitor was put at the guard desk that mirrored everything I did. If I was to try to accomplish anything they didn't agree with, they would pull the plug on my network and my computer would lose its Internet connection. Warden Howard was a big help. He was very influential when it came to getting permission for the live execution. I don't think any of this would have worked without him.

"I'm ready," I yelled to Seth who was waiting down the hall.

"We'll Jason," I said to him as he lay on his cold grey cot in his cell. "I'll see you on the other side."

"Take it like a man," he replied.

Seth and Rocco entered my cell and reattached my leg irons. We made our way down to the cafeteria. Adam, Mark and Emily were already there.

"There are four cameras set up Jack, one in each corner of the room. Mark will control the feed to the Internet Service Provider. We'll be joining you for your last supper," Adam stated.

Emily walked over to one of the cameras and spoke into her wireless microphone. "Welcome back to *Death Row Diaries*. You have now heard the whole story of Jack Stevenson. You be the judge; Is he a cold-blooded murderer or simply a man pushed over the edge? Is what he did justified, or is revenge an illness that consumed him. Is his live execution just a stage for his own ego, or is it a platform to simply raise money for a dream of helping troubled youth so they never have to face the wrath of the very walls that surround the inner hell disguised as this fortress. One question will never be answered. Who is the lucky person that would have been his fifth victim? He admitted to the world he wanted to kill five people that have ruined him or his family's lives. By some twist of fate has he himself become the fifth victim? Has he betrayed himself in life? When that final lever is pulled at the bewitching hour, his plan will be complete.

For the next little while, the netcast will be unscripted. The cameras will be rolling throughout Jacks last meal. You'll be watching Jack and the guards banter about. When supper is finished Jack will be led to the Chapel for his final confession. The cameras will go off to respect the private conversation between Jack, his conscience, and his God. Following confession Jack will be led to the electric chair. He will not be speaking to the camera once inside the chapel. Just before his confession he will be administered a dose of Halidol to ease his mind of the scenario that faces him. I will be narrating the final moments from a jet that is bound for the Vatican. Father Joe is being appointed Cardinal and I am covering that story next. The execution itself may be gruesome. There will be a camera mounted inside the execution chamber to capture the sights and sounds as they happen. The screen will be split, half showing the electrocution, the other will have commentary from Jack's two friends Adam and Mark who have made everything you have seen today a reality, and by Warden Howard who will be with Jack's brother Jimmy, soon to be one of the richest men in the world. Jimmy is also going to Italy to live with Jack's late wife's family.

Sit back and join us as we sit with Jack around the dinner table."

"Nicely done Emily," I said as she sat down in her chair. "Very poignant, I hope I can eat with this lump in my throat."

As I sat there the reality of the day was finally sinking in. Up until now the retelling of my life had taken away all thoughts of what lay ahead.

They had a rule at the Florida State Prison. The "Fryers" meal had to be cooked by one of the other inmates on Death Row and he was only allowed $20.00 for the meal. Normally the prisoner would be eating by himself, but that's where Warden Howard bent the rules again. I was allowed to have Jimmy, the Priest and the TV crew eat with me. Warden Howard also allowed the three guards from my shift. This too was their last shift. Once the execution was carried out Wes, Rocco and Seth were quitting. They were off to start the ranch. I feel very proud for what I've done. Not the murders, but setting up the ranch so others would never wind up in my position. Warden

Howard was retiring in a month. He and Mrs. Howard would be moving to Keycoast with her family. Over the last two months, all the students had been moved to other facilities. The Howards are going to live at Keycoast and enjoy a nice retirement.

I had chosen Charlie, the guy from a couple of cells down from mine to cook the chicken wings. He would be using the same sauce from my favourite restaurant in Buffalo. I was allowed to import two bottles of their special chicken wing sauce. They don't normally do this, but I offered a thousand dollars per jug. They also liked the idea of the exposure they would receive. We had one hour for supper. I was starving. It was already after ten and I hadn't really eaten anything since lunch. I guess it wouldn't really matter if I ate or not, in just over two hours I would be dead. I wouldn't even have time to digest it.

The others had all joined us now. We were all in a relaxed mood. I just wanted to sit back and enjoy my meal and the company to share it with. As we started to converse we were oblivious to the cameras, all except Mark who was concerned about the cameras staying online. Jimmy came over and gave me a big hug. I'm still not sure if he knows what's going on. I highly doubt it. He wasn't fond of the prison setting. I hugged him back the best I could, I still had the waist irons on.

"Jack," Seth said as he approached me. "The Warden says I can undo your right arm, you're going to need it to eat with. I know you are not going to try anything but I have to warn you not to."

"There's not much I can do, my legs are still chained and besides, you've got the three stooges over there," I pointed to the three extra guards sitting in the corner behind me. All of them had shotguns. Seth undid my arm. I rubbed it a bit, the chains had dug in slightly.

I shuffled over to the rows of tables that had been pushed together and took my spot at the head. Jimmy sat to my left and beside him was Father Joe. Emily sat to my right, across from Jimmy. Seth pulled up next to Emily's right. Wes and Rocco grabbed a chair across from each other. Adam and Mark grabbed the last one in each row and Warden Howard sat at the end facing me.

As we sat and chatted, the cameras rolled in the distance. Mark had four monitors set up to his left between him and the warden. He had a box with switches sitting on the table that he used to control the cameras. Charlie came in carrying two jugs filled with Coke. His date was next, in almost a month. It was usually customary to pick the guy who was going to face the chair next to serve the last meal for his predecessor. They say it helps with the process, it didn't do a lot for me three weeks earlier except to remind me that I was next on the list. He put the jugs on the table and headed back to the kitchen. The jugs were soon emptied as they were passed. Charlie had two more in his hands as he made his way back to the table. He set one beside Jimmy who had already finished the glass I poured him. The other one he set in front of Wes.

"If supper is ready you may as well bring it out Charlie," Warden Howard told him.

Charlie nodded and went back into the kitchen. He soon emerged carrying a huge tray of steaming chicken wings glistening in sauce. Seth and Rocco both leaned away from each other so Charlie could set the tray down on the table. Seth grabbed some wings and passed the plate to Emily who set it in front of me. Jimmy snatched one before she even had a chance to let go of it. I made him put it down. Once everyone had some Father Joe stood up.

"Dear Lord," he started. "Bless this food we are about to receive. Thank you for this time together with Jack and may the company he enjoys tonight make his transition into your kingdom an easy one. Guide him on his journey and let him know there is nothing to fear, Amen."

Jimmy grabbed a wing and started eating. The rest of us did the same. There wasn't much conversation as we ate. We had about an hour or so to eat before confession and Emily had told us she wanted to have one last interview with me before I headed of to the chapel. We went through five trays of wings, six pitchers of coke, two bottles of blue cheese and a bowl of celery stalks. That's the only way to enjoy wings, lots of blue cheese to dip them in and celery to take off the edge of the hot sauce. It took us about forty-five minutes to eat.

"Hi, welcome back to *Death Row Diaries*," Emily said as she looked at the camera behind me. "So Jack, the time has come for you to say goodbye. Any last thoughts or comments you want to share?"

"I am not sure how the public sees me now. You can understand my frustrations in life, you have all seen the reenactments, you be the judge. Do I deserve to get what is coming to me or am I justified in committing the murders I did. I have held nothing back, I have not bent the truth. I have nothing left in life except for Jimmy and my money. Jimmy, although I love him dearly, will never fill the void of losing Lynn. My money could have given me a very easy life, but with no one to share it with, it would be pointless. I have been hurt badly by the people I have killed. I have no regrets and I am sorry to say no remorse. I am sure there are a lot of you out there watching, that if given the money to do with what you want, you would have also considered getting even with certain people in your life. I am not going to say I am sorry, but only say that I have had a lot of time to think, and given the chance to relive my life, I would probably have done it the same."

"That is very cold, Jack," Emily said.

"I know. But life is what it is and you don't get a second chance. You just play the cards you're dealt and do the best you can. Before I head down to the chapel I would like to thank everyone for their part in this journey. I hope that I have opened the doorway for others to tell their stories. I hope that Adam and Mark will keep the series alive and enjoy the island in Fiji. I hope that Seth, Wes and Rocco enjoy the rest of their working careers at the ranch and that they truly can make a difference in the lives of the misguided youth out there. Father Joe, I congratulate you on becoming a Cardinal, Warden Howard, you and I have been through a lot together, I have known you the longest here and I thank you for making this day possible. I hope that when this is all over you will appreciate the fact that you had a lot to do with all of this and the satisfaction that today was special. I hope that Mrs. Howard will appreciate Keycoast and that she will be happy there for a long time. I hope her family will help her in the transition to retirement an easy one. I owe her everything. She did a great job raising Ramona,

Jimmy and myself. I hope when this is all over she will forgive me for what I did. I know she will. She can see the good in people and why they do the things they do.

Jimmy, come here you big lug. I love you very much and I know that some day I will see you again. You see the good in all and embrace every little thing in your life with the utmost pride. You don't let the outside stimulants of life sway you in any way. I wish we all could have been born like you, the world would be a better place. Okay I am done with the mushy part, lets get on with the things at hand."

I wiped the tears away from my eyes, as did Emily. Although I couldn't see his as he stood behind me, I felt a tear hit my shoulder as it fell off of Seth's chin. We were all caught up in the moment, a moment that never should have been.

"In a few minutes," Emily continued. "Jack will be led down the hall to the chapel for his final confession. Once we enter through the hallowed doors of the place of worship, the cameras will stop rolling until we reappear. This is to give Jack some privacy. I will be attending along with Father Joe and Warden Howard. While he is in there, Warden Howard will administer a small dose of Halidol into Jack's arm. This will ease him in his transportation to the electric chair. The drug will render him speechless for the duration of his journey into the beyond. I will be narrating from the time he leaves the chapel until his final breath. Jack has written an autobiography that up until now he has been retelling. For the last chapter in the book Jack has speculated through conversations with the guards and prisoners, their thoughts, feelings and eyewitness accounts of live executions."

Seth finished wiping his eyes, he reached for his key that was on a big ring attached to a belt loop on his neatly pressed pants. He depressed the little flipper, turned the ring a bit and released it from the belt loop. He bent over and inserted the key into the lock that housed the chain that bound my arm to the table. The room was silent, the lock snapping open as Seth turned the key was the only sound in the room.

I rubbed my wrist.

Seth reached down and helped me up. You could tell by his grip that he wanted to give me a hug, but his professionalism wouldn't let him do it. The cold steel bolt scratched its way open as Wes slid it back, opening the cafeteria door.

Mark killed the lights in the room, sending a shiver down my spine. Seth guided me out the doorway and into the hall.

Rocco eased my arms to my sides, and then pulled them behind me. The handcuffs rattled as he tightened them on my wrists behind my back. The warden reached his hand out and Rocco deposited the key into it.

Mark walked backwards holding the camera as the warden led the entourage down the hall. We all walked behind him three abreast. I was flanked by Wes and Rocco, both of them holding on to one of my elbows. Seth, Father Joe and Emily brought up the rear.

I paused as I reached the door of the makeshift control room where Adam and Jimmy were now sitting. Jimmy hopped up when he saw me and ran towards me. Seth stepped forward to intervene him.

"It's okay Seth," Warden Howard commented. "Let him have one last moment."

Seth retreated as Jimmy barged by him and threw his arms around me. Wes and Rocco were almost hugged in Jimmy's effort.

"Jack come, Jimmy go, no more bad place," Jimmy said.

My lips began to quiver. "It's okay Jimmy, Jack's going to be okay"

Jimmy grabbed Rocco's arm and forced it towards mine. Placing his hand on the handcuffs. "No more bad place," he shouted at Rocco.

"Jimmy, stop it!" I yelled.

Jimmy released Rocco's arm.

"Jimmy, Jack is going to be okay do you remember where Moany is?" I asked him.

Jimmy clenched his fist and put it on his chest over his heart.

"Where are Mommy and Daddy?"

Jimmy again hit his chest.

"Jack's going to be with Moany and Mommy and Daddy, Jack's going to be okay."

Jimmy hit his chest and said, "Jack." A smile came over his

face. I leaned towards him and gave him a kiss on his forehead.

Adam leaned forward and gave me a hug. "Jack, thanks for all the good times, you take care."

He stepped back and wiped his eyes. Warden Howard started to move forward, we all followed. We continued down the hall until we reached the chapel. Warden Howard stopped when he reached the table that was positioned outside the doorway. He reached in his pocket and took out a small black box, it looked like a pint-sized eyeglass case. He pulled it opened, it made a soft squeaking sound as he forced the spring-loaded hinges apart. He reached in and removed a key. He closed the case with a snap and put it on the table.

He took the key and inserted it into the slot of the red box that was on the table and turned it a quarter turn clockwise. Pulling on the key, he opened the door of the box. Inside the box sat a stainless steel syringe encased in a grey-black molded bed of foam. The label affixed to the shelf it was resting on read *Halidol*. He reached in and grabbed the needle, leaving the key in the lock and the door to the box open. He made his way to the far side of the chapel door. Rocco and Wes escorted me through the door releasing my arms once I got inside. Seth took his position outside the doorway opposite the warden. Father Joe entered and stood beside me. Mark stood in the hallway pointing the camera at me. Emily entered next.

"I'll need my hands free to pray," I told the warden.

"Jack, come back out here," the warden called.

I went to the doorway. The warden turned me towards Seth. The warden handed Seth the key to the cuffs. "Take off the irons. He's among friends, let's make this as comfortable as possible."

Seth undid the cuffs, releasing my arms. He then put the key and the cuffs on the table beside the red box.

"I think the boys want to say goodbye," the warden said.

Rocco was first to extend his hand out for me to shake. We shook firmly. Wes was next, his eyes beginning to well up. I turned and faced Seth. He stuck out his right arm. I clasped it firmly and pulled him towards me giving him a hug. Seth hugged me back, pulling me tighter. I patted him on the back.

"You guys take good care of yourselves," I said. "Make a

difference in the world so those youths at the camp never have to wind up here."

"Thanks for all your help Jack." Seth replied.

"I know it's going to sound odd but, I wish we had never met," I said to Seth.

"Me too," Seth replied. "Me too."

I was glad we did, but another time, another place would have been better.

"I'll take it from here boys," the warden said as he held his microphone to his throat, there was a little squeal as the warden reached down and adjusted the volume on the box that was clipped to his belt.

I stepped back a couple of paces into the room. The warden then entered.

The light of the camera narrowed as Seth pulled the door shut. The warden locked it from the inside.

"Hello, and welcome back to *Death Row Diaries*. For the last few hours we have sat and listened to Jack Stevenson, a convicted killer, recall his life and give us the gory details of the four murders he has committed. While in prison he wrote his autobiography which he has narrated today while you watched video re-enactments. You also viewed the murders that Jack videotaped. I will now open the sealed envelope that Jack has supplied me with and read you the rest of the story interjecting personal comments and conversation with the others once we board the jet for Italy.

Jack has predetermined the rest of his plight and in his words will describe what will be his last hour on Earth.

We pick up where we last left off. Jack and Warden Howard in the chapel at Jack's last confession. The cameras will be live from here on in. I will be boarding Jack's private jet with Father Joe, Warden Howard and Jack's brother Jimmy. Father Joe and I will be heading to the Vatican where he will be ordained as a Cardinal. Warden Howard will be taking Jimmy to live with Jack's in-laws. With the de-certification of the criminal facility know as Keycoast, Jimmy's sentence has been dismissed and will now live a free man.

As you can see on the split screen Jack and the warden have just emerged from the chapel. I'll now narrate the rest of the story Jack has written."

Hi folks, this is Jack. The following is my rendition of my final hour. I have watched several men before me make this journey into the afterlife. I hope I can do it justice. As is common practice I have made my way down this hall before. It is customary for inmates awaiting their death to have a trial run. I have been strapped in the electric chair so the guards can practice their role for my final minutes. I've experienced the impersonal coldness of the chair, my arms and legs shackled. I've seen the darkness of death as the hood has been pulled over my face and the guards placed the halo around my head.

As I am walking out of the chapel I can hear the silence that fills these halls, my pupils fixated and dilated from the Halidol that was administered in the chapel. They say it's to give me inner peace, but I think it's given for the comfort of the guards. Too many men before me have fought their way kicking and screaming down these corridors. Now the guards have a peaceful walk as they escort me the one hundred and thirty four steps to the platform where the chair sits. I can hear the pounding of my heart as the two guards wrap their arms around mine. I use them as a crutch as my feet seem a mile away from me. I think back on my life as I make this journey. Do I deserve this? Was I justified in committing the murders I did? In my own mind I am.

I can smell death, the pungent stench seeping from these walls, the cold concrete embracing my body, chilling me to the bone. It is overcome by a warmth that unveils me as the warden gives me a hug, his lips touching my forehead sends a spike of heat down my spine to the core of my inner body. I glance in his eyes, I try to speak but cannot. I know he understands; we have been friends for a long time. He knows how my hatred has consumed me. How the love for my family had stirred up the rage in my blood. How Moany's death was the catapult for the vengeance I sought. As I look in his eyes I know he understands.

I know by the blemish on the wall I am at step sixty. Seventy-four more before I will take my last. The warden stands there as I take step sixty-one and pass by him. Jimmy stepped through the doorway at step sixty-five. He paused as if he didn't know me, my eyes blank, my body struggling for the next step.

He ran to the warden for comfort. This is where Emily and Father Joe will have their last look at me. I walk past them. The four of them will now make their way to the rooftop where the helicopter awaits. It's only a five-minute flight before they would board my jet and make their way out of the country. Step eighty-five, this is where I will sit. It is almost midnight. I now have ten minutes to reflect on my life.

CHAPTER 20

"This is Emily Dickson bringing you the conclusion of *Death Row Diaries*. We're enroute to Italy awaiting Jack Stevenson's final steps to the death chamber.

I am now on the jet with Father Joe, Jimmy and Warden Howard. Your monitor will be split, you will be able to see Jack's last twenty minutes of life, while at the same time witnessing our interaction aboard the jet. One question that haunts us still is who would have been his fifth victim. I have asked him several times but he never would tell me. The answer is inside this sealed envelope, here on the jet. As Jack takes his final steps I will read it to you now."

You are all probably wondering who victim number five was going to be. I had someone in mind, but with my capture I had plenty of time to re-think it. I guess the real victim could be myself. Like I stated in my interview over four years ago, I wanted to hunt down and kill five people that fucked my family and me. I guess now, I would be that fifth victim. I fucked up. It was because of the love for my family that I started committing the murders in the first place. But in doing so I fucked my own family. It was because of me that Lynn died. If I had let justice take its course Jimmy would have lived his life out in a halfway house. I could have let it be, but no. In doing so I brought him into my life with Lynn. It was because I did, that Lynn and I had the fight the night that caused her death.

I fucked my father by convincing him he needed to be closer to Jimmy. Now I have also fucked myself. I could have left well enough alone, but I felt compelled to carry out my plan. I had such a rush from the first one that it consumed me. I wanted to get to number five and leave with all my millions. Look at me now. I'm sitting in a chair waiting for the guard behind the controls to seal my fate. I guess I am victim number five.

"Now back to the live action. As you see Jack is sitting in the chair, his body arching not to let it capture him. He is struggling as Seth holds his right arm down. Rocco scrambling to entomb it in the leather strap that will secure it. His hand flinching upwards as Rocco tugs on the strap to tighten it. Rocco is now moving across in front of Jack and grabs the strap for his left arm as Wes holds it steady. Now that his arms are secure the guards move to his legs, first securing his left one followed by his right. Jack again flinches, all that's left to do is secure his head. A strap is fastened around his neck with enough room so he doesn't choke. Jack has chosen electrocution over lethal injection. Florida gives inmates the option. He figured the electric chair would offer more excitement for the viewers. After all, they paid money to see a show."

The camera spanned the airplane, Father Joe was sitting reading a magazine. He seemed disinterested, being a Priest he had witnessed this before. Jimmy was oblivious to the whole situation, he just sat looking out the oval shaped window watching the lights flicker in the distance. The camera in the chamber zoomed in on the motionless body in the chair and focused on Jack's eyes. They were staring back, almost screaming. This was the first time they looked scared. It was as if they were reaching out to grab you, begging to be heard, trying to communicate what his mouth, now quivering, was trying to say. Sweat was beginning to bead on his brow.

Seth moved in from behind grasping a black hood that he pulled over Jack's head. He wiggled it down over Jack's face, pulling open the tube-like top, exposing the crown of his freshly shaven head. He pulled it far enough down Jack's forehead so Wes could put the wet sponge on the top of his head. A metal dome was then placed over Jack's head. Wes struggled with it a bit as it was a tight fit. He and Rocco turned the screws on it ever so gently into Jack's forehead tightening them just enough to make contact and then gave them one last quarter turn. The three guards all patted him on the back simultaneously, saying their final farewell and then moved out of the cameras' view. From here on in Jack's fate rested with the unknown guard hidden behind a wooden partition. You couldn't see them because of the camera angle, but there are three levers that had to be pulled within seconds of each other. The first one will be supplying a jolt to numb the victim. The second one would supply enough juice to interrupt the regular heartbeat and the third and final one would deliver enough voltage feeding the five electrodes, two on his legs, two on his wrists and finally the metal halo around his forehead. As the audience sat motionless the camera in the airplane fixated on the warden. His image was on the left of the split screen, and the view of the chair on the right.

"I'll take it from here Emily," the warden said as he placed his handheld microphone to his neck. The twangy sound echoed through the speakers. "I have witnessed a few of these executions and will explain the process as we go. There's a microphone in the chamber to heighten your awareness of the sound of the electricity as it invades Jack's body. I know it sounds gruesome, but given the violence of his murders and that the viewers deserve what they paid for, this is his wish. Being the first of its kind, there are no FCC regulations. Jack captured most of his murders live on tape and wanted his to be no exception. The whole process takes about two minutes, his body will twitch and convulse as the different levers are pulled on my command. Once the third lever is pulled it will only be about a minute and a half until the thrusting will stop and his body sits limp in the chair. There are monitors present in the gallery as well as one in the chamber. It's five minutes to midnight as I speak. If there is any hope of a stay of execution, The Governor would have to call the direct line in the chamber within the next five minutes.

I have known Jack for what seems to be his whole life. His father came to work for me when I was Chief of Police in Pinellas County. They lived next to Mrs. Howard and me. The kids grew up right under my nose. Jimmy was always a happy child. He and I would spend countless hours together while his dad worked. I would have never suspected him in Ramona's death. If it weren't for his father bringing the evidence forward I don't know if we ever would have put it together. Ramona was a beautiful girl, the daughter I never had. She would sit for hours in my lap while I read her stories. She had a special place in my heart."

You could hear the clock in the chamber as the two hands intertwined at the top of the hour.

"I guess the Governor isn't calling, I didn't expect it, especially after he killed a cop. I almost forgot one of Jack's last wishes. Seth can you pull the hood back down? Jack wanted to watch his execution on the monitor."

Seth looked at him stunned and proceeded to comply.

"Thank you Seth. Well Jack, we wish you well. Pull lever one."

You could hear the clang of the lever as it mated with the contacts of the power box. Emily jumped as she watched Jack's body lurch forward.

"Jack loved his sister," the warden continued. "I think if she was still alive Jack wouldn't be in this predicament. Pull lever two."

Jacks body now tensed with force.

"I know this is unbearable for some of you, but this is what Jack wanted. He wanted you to witness all five of his murders, he wanted all five caught on tape, but this one's going to have to wait. Kill the power, shut off the chair. Give him three seconds of lever one."

"What the hell are you doing?" yelled Father Joe.

"Jack wanted it done this way, he said to give the viewers at home their money's worth. He said to cut the power before the final blast of electricity and play this tape."

The warden pressed the button on a tape recorder.

"Hi folks, as you hear this part of the story I have been zapped with a jolt of electricity, not enough to kill me, just enough to make it feel uncomfortable. The second did probably stop my heart momentarily, but the short blast of lever one should act as a defibullater and kickstart it again. I hoped it worked or I'm already dead, and I so much wanted to hear this part. The warden will be in a whack of shit for not following procedure, but he's retiring and I gave him $5 million to do it this way. I know it may be a little sadistic, but I'm sure you'll understand at the end. I wanted to take this time to thank some people. First the guards, Seth, Rocco and Wes you guys have been so kind and inspirational to me. The ranch will be totally paid for by the time it opens. There is also a $3 million cheque for each of you in my cell. Spend it for yourselves, but please run the ranch. I know we all believe in it.

Adam, Mark and Kevin, you and your wives enjoy your part of the island. I'll be right there with you. It'll be like we said. Friends forever. I know all along I said that my friends were never involved, that is true. I did however have two accomplices throughout my whole plan. The first was a male. He played Donald MacDonald, the Hollywood agent who helped me lure Lily in so I could take her part in the play. He was aware of what I was doing the whole time. He also played Mr. Campbell, in this role he was there to help take care of Liam so his real mother could help me with my murder of Dave, the Playboy. His third role was that of Manuel. In this role he basically stayed on the island and kept things running there. His role in all of this was to help out where I needed him. I also had a female accomplice that helped me out with the murders. She played the cosmetician that help set up Cheryl for her murder, She also was Maria, again basically staying on the island and keeping things running. Her biggest role was that of Lee. I needed her to infiltrate into Ursula's life so that we could make sure that we had an in on Ursula's Uncle Mike. I needed to get to Dave and this was the best way.

The two of them were there from the start and I want to thank them for their help. After Dave's murder, I didn't need them anymore and those were the only two murders they helped out with. I am sure after today that both will need to hide from the law. You are probably wondering who they are. First let me tell you that my plan was not mine alone. It was a collaborated effort by all three of us. We were all tired of being fucked around and wanted to get even. The four victims that I killed in our minds all deserved it.

Who were they, you ask? Let me tell you. Remember my Father, how he became more and more depressed once I won the money and he moved near Keycoast? How he shaved his head that one night and shot himself full of heroine and died. The coroner and police chief both examined his body and pronounced him dead. That was him, lying in that bed, at least while the coroner and the chief were there. They left the room and called the funeral home to bag the body. He had shaved his head but he never overdosed. His pulse points were covered with a layer of latex so that the coroner couldn't feel his pulse, as soon as they left the room he got up out of bed. The coroner and the chief left when the guys from the funeral home arrived. They were actually just a couple of guys I hired to play the roll. The funeral was a fake and the casket was empty. It was my father that played the roles I needed to commit the murders. I'm surprised Adam that you guys didn't recognize him on the island as Manuel, especially Kevin who spent a lot of time there.

Now as far as the female goes, it took a little more convincing as she had none of the victims piss her off directly. I remember so well the nights I made love to Maria and especially Lee. But let me go on record as saying that Lynn was my one and only sexual partner. Yes you guessed it. Lynn never did die in that car accident at Lovers Lagoon. The fight about Jimmy and the accident were all staged. The pieces of clothing and even the partial plate were all planted. With the gators being so prevalent, I knew they would not search long for a body. Again I thought for sure that my friends would have recognized her as Maria on the island. I know they only saw her a few times after we were married, but they should have recognized her from our days in the audio-visual club. Terri who moved south after high school made her way to Keycoast and got a job, we did have feelings for each other in high school and that is why Dad convinced the judge to send Jimmy to Keycoast so that I could catch up to Terri-Lynn. I knew that I wanted to marry her, but I never dreamed we would win the lottery.

You're probably asking yourself where they are today. Adam if you can go back to the split screen I will show you. Emily if you can just turn the camera on the airplane a bit and point it at yourself and Father Joe that would be great. Now the both of you can remove your wigs and show the world that there is no Emily or Father Joe that you are really my wife and my Father, that you have been in plain site all day. The next question would be if Terri-Lynn never died what about the child she was carrying at the time of her so-called death. Terri-Lynn, go ahead and call him out of the cockpit. The little boy she was carrying is alive and well and was with his mom the whole time. He was Liam and Patrick.

So who really was going to be my fifth victim? You may never know. Warden Howard go ahead and instruct the guard to carry out his duty, pull that third lever, I'm ready."

"Pull lever three," the warden said.

"As you folks see," the tape continued. "I'm almost at my last moment on Earth. I just wanted to put a couple more things in perspective and let you know who my fifth victim was suppose to be. I'll continue once the action in the chair is complete. Warden you may shut off the tape for now."

The gallery squirmed as the lights flickered throughout the room. The sound in the chamber was eerie. It seemed like hours for that minute ending Jack's life to be over. The guard behind the partition killed the power once the body went limp. Seth walked over and felt for a pulse, not feeling one he cued the Warden.

"Well folks, it looks like justice has been served. Seth, you may remove the body and place it on the gurney," the Warden's twangy voice said as he pressed the button on the tape recorder to start it again.

"Hi it's Jack again, now that I'm gone I want to clear up a couple of issues so you understand why I did what I did.

I know I lied about the death of my father and Lynn but Moany did die. That was her body in the sandbox. Jimmy's semen was there too, but he didn't kill her. The day of Moany's murder, Jimmy was sexually assaulted. The real killer then placed Jimmy's semen in the sandbox. That's why Jimmy was so reluctant to have anyone touch him.

Secondly, on the day I murdered Dave, even though it needed to be done, it was secondary in my mind. I needed to be with the Howards. I needed to get my hands on a copy of the Warden's CAT scan. I purposely made them fall under the seat when I stopped. I knew the images would provide the measurements I needed for the computer latex conversation program I developed. Today would not have been possible without it. Warden you take it from here."

The Warden's twangy microphone started to hum. "I guess I don't need this silly microphone thing anymore." I removed it from my neck. "You see," I said in my normal voice. "It all came to light the day that Lynn and I stopped at the Howards to set up his new computer. I found images of Moany and the Warden engaged in explicit sexual acts. My fifth victim was really the one that started this murderous rampage. The others were just for fun. I hoped that I would get caught. I was counting on it. I knew killing a cop would land me in this prison facing the electric chair with Warden Howard at the switch. Jamie's ex-wife contacted me the day after they divorced. As soon as Jamie said it was about the money for Sarah, I knew there would be a sting that night and I saw that as the key to trapping my final victim."

Seth sensing something was wrong pulled open the orange coveralls of the body to administer CPR. Adam zoomed the camera in closer on the big number five that was now visible on the hairy chest of the black body on the gurney.

I gave a smile as I pulled the camera plug in the airplane.

THE END

Chris (Toper) Thorne was born in Kitchener Ontario. He was educated at Niagara and Conestoga Colleges. An entrepreneur at heart, Toper developed the board game *CA$H for TRASH* which is now housed in the Museum and Archives of Games for being the first of its kind.

Toper received the Dale Carnegie award for the highest achievement in his class for Effective Speaking and Human Relations.

His sense of helping his community has led him as a twenty year minor hockey referee, a member of Grand River Collegiate parent council and President of The Optimist Club of Stanley Park for the last two years.

Working with a variety of people including developmentally delayed teenagers and adults, acquired brain injury patients and in a strong unionized automotive plant as a certified safety representative has given Toper a chance to study human behavior.

Being a self employed realtor has allowed Toper the time to complete the first of his books in the *Death Row Diaries* series.

After completing his novel *Death Row Diaries: Criminal Justice* and his thirst to learn more, at the age of 49 Toper became a Correctional Officer in the Ontario Ministry of Community Safety and Correctional Services and now works the front line in a maximum security jail.